CITIES
AND SERVICES

CITIES AND SERVICES

The geography of collective consumption

Steven Pinch

Department of Geography
University of Southampton

Routledge & Kegan Paul
London, Boston, Melbourne and Henley

First published in 1985
by Routledge & Kegan Paul plc

14 Leicester Square, London WC2H 7PH, England

9 Park Street, Boston, Mass. 02108, USA

464 St Kilda Road, Melbourne,
Victoria 3004, Australia and

Broadway House, Newtown Road,
Henley on Thames, Oxon RG9 1EN, England

Set in Century Schoolbook 9pt
by Columns of Reading
and printed in Great Britain
by T.J. Press (Padstow) Ltd,
Padstow, Cornwall
© Steven Pinch 1985

Library of Congress Cataloging in Publication Data

Pinch, Steven.

Cities and services.
Bibliography: p.
Includes index.
1. Municipal services.   2. Public utilities—
Location.   3. Public welfare.   4. Externalities
(Economics)   5. Urban economics.   6. Space in
economics.   I. Title.
HD4431.P56   1985   363.6   84–26214

British Library CIP Data also available

ISBN 0-7102-0054 4 (cloth)
ISBN 0-7102-0493 0 (paper)

Contents

Figures

Tables

Acknowledgments

This book, like most others, reflects the influence of many individuals too numerous to mention but it is a pleasure to be able to thank those more closely related with this work. My thinking about public service provision was greatly stimulated at the series of ESRC sponsored conferences held between 1982 and 1983 at the Universities of Southampton and Reading, together with the Virginia Polytechnic Institute and State University. I am grateful to all the participants at these conferences and to my co-organisers Andrew Kirby and Paul Knox for their enthusiasm and hard work.

Neil Wrigley of Bristol University first suggested that I write this book, and at Southampton University my colleague Colin Mason provided the necessary encouragement and example of hard work I needed to complete the manuscript. Alan Burn and his cartographic staff maintained their usual high standard of maps and diagrams.

Elizabeth Fidlon and the team at Routledge and Kegan Paul were always encouraging, efficient and patient: I am grateful.

Most male authors seem to end their acknowledgments with some eulogy to the self-sacrifice and dedication of their wives. Here I find myself in a quandary for Lyn's academic career has leapt far in advance of my own! Those who manage to combine a two-career, two (old) car, two-child family will know the debt we owe each other.

* * * *

The author and publishers are grateful to the following for permission to reprint or modify material from copyright: The Macmillan Press, London and Basingstoke (Figure 1.1, from P. Dunleavy, *Urban Political Analysis*, 1980); George Allen and Unwin (Publishers) Ltd. (Figure 1.2, from W.A. Robson and D.E. Regan (eds) *Great Cities of the World Vol. 1* (Third Edition) 1972); Penguin Books Ltd. (Figure 1.3, from T. Byrne, *Local Government in Britain*, 1983); Basil Blackwell Ltd. (Figure 1.4, from J. Stanyer, *Understanding Local Government*, 1976); John Wiley and Sons Ltd. (Figures 2.1 and 2.4, from D.T. Herbert and R.J. Johnston (eds) *Geography and the Urban Environment Vol. 3*, Copyright © 1980 John Wiley & Sons Ltd., reprinted by permission of John Wiley and Sons Ltd; Oxford University Press (Figures 2.2 and 2.3, from D.T.

Herbert and D.M. Smith (eds) *Social Problems and the City: Geographical Perspectives*, 1979); The Institute of British Geographers (Figure 2.5, from *Transactions (New Series) Vol. 3*, No. 1, 1978); Pergamon Press Ltd. (Figures 3.1 and 3.7, from *Geoforum* Vol. 14, 1984); Methuen and Co. Ltd. (Figure 3.3, from R.J. Bennett, *The Geography of Public Finance*, 1980); Croom Helm Ltd. (Figure 3.5, from A. Kirby, P. Knox and S. Pinch (eds) *Public Service Provision and Urban Development*, 1984); Koninkligk Nederlands Aardrijkskundig Genootschap (Figure 3.8, from *Tijdschrift voor Economische en Sociale Geografie, Vol. 67*, 1976).

Introduction

This book was written to fill a gap in the literature which became apparent to me during the course of my efforts to teach university undergraduates something about the geography of public service provision. The study of collectivised public services has been one of the major growth areas in urban geography in recent years but it is a field which both students and established researchers often find difficult and impenetrable. In part, much of the confusion stems from the enormous diversity of services which can be grouped under the term 'collective consumption': these range from public housing, hospitals, dental surgeries, old people's homes, day nurseries and schools, to parks, roads, sewage disposal, refuse collection, street lighting, public transport, planning systems, fire protection, police patrols and many, many others. The scale and complexity of these services often defy classification, but in my experience a far bigger stumbling block to the understanding of collective consumption is the diversity of theoretical perspectives that are available for studying these services. Thus, the same service may be studied from a variety of perspectives – some approaches providing different answers to different questions, and some providing different answers to the same questions!

In an attempt to throw some light on these issues I have therefore organised the book around theoretical orientations rather than service types. The book considers three basic geographical or 'spatial' approaches to the study of collective consumption – jurisdictional partitioning, distance-decay effects, and externality theory; together with three basic types of social theory – pluralism, neo-Weberian approaches, and neo-Marxist perspectives. The bulk of existing texts tend to be orientated towards either one or more of the spatial perspectives, or else are concerned predominantly with various types of social theory, often divorced from any particular geographical setting. Researchers are therefore forced to grapple with two somewhat distinct and complex sets of literature : one dealing with accessibility models, distance-decay effects and estimation procedures, the other with theories of the local state, the links between production and consumption, and the relations between politics and the economic base.

This book is an attempt to bridge the gap between these 'spatial' and 'social' perspectives. The need for such a book seems all the more pressing in the light of recent attempts by Dunleavy (1980) and Saunders (1981) to argue that space is relatively unimportant in understanding the politics of local service provision. The argument presented in this book is that what is needed is both a spatially and socially aware analysis of collective consumption. This argument is based, not on disciplinary chauvinism or the desire to carve out a little niche for geographers, but the belief that spatial issues cannot be isolated from any rigorous study of society. Fortunately, this is a view which many researchers, including political scientists and sociologists, have recently come to accept. Just how this task should be accomplished is of course a complex and controversial issue, as is demonstrated below.

The book is therefore designed both for the student of geography and for other social scientists who may be curious, and possibly sceptical, about the value of a geographical perspective on collective consumption. I have been guided towards this end by a number of principles. First, and most important, has been the desire to avoid some 'bland overview'. Each chapter seeks to examine specific and important issues and to develop particular arguments. Although the chapters are self-contained, they are designed to develop certain themes building upon the comments and points made in earlier chapters.

In the first chapter, for example, I have tried to describe some of the basic features of collective services, and the local government systems responsible for their allocation. This also explains why I have begun with the pure theory of public goods; for, although it is riddled with limitations, this theory does provide a relatively simple starting point and comparative yardstick against which to judge other perspectives. Another problem I have discovered amongst students is a basic lack of knowledge about local government, and this I have also attempted to remedy in the first chapter; for it is of little use plunging in with the complexities of the state derivation debate, or the merits of the 'capital logic' approach, if there is little understanding of what is meant by district councils, or the doctrine of *ultra vires*! There are, of course, some excellent general texts about local government available, but they do not usually emphasise the issues which are most important for a theoretical understanding of collective consumption. Another problem in this context is the difficulty of juggling between both the British and American local government systems. The nature of the literature is such that neither one of these local government systems can be ignored; indeed, for theoretical reasons it is desirable that both be compared. I have therefore tried to emphasise the main differences and some of the similarities between the British and American local government systems insofar as they have a bearing upon the distribution of public services, in the first chapter. I have made a few comparisons between nations in Europe, but it would appear that there is insufficient evidence to make detailed generalisations of the type which are possible in British and American cities. Further cross-cultural comparisons are clearly an important task for future research.

Another basic aim of the book has been to impose some order upon what at times seems like a chaotic field. For this reason I have taken some effort to classify particular types of work – such as the vast 'outputs' literature examined in Chapter 2. This has inevitably led to a great deal of generalisation and simplification. I am aware that many of the studies cannot be simply 'pigeonholed' (this is perhaps best revealed in the enormously complex set of writings dealing with the nature of the state); and some of the minor debates I have had to ignore. However, in my opinion, detailed consideration of anomalous findings, or of some debates which are not central to the main arguments can be counter-productive. Once the basics are grasped these issues can be pursued, and I have included a guide to further reading at the end of the book, together with a list of some of the important issues for further analysis.

Another important objective has been to give prominence to some of the empirical studies including the 'outputs' literature, accessibility models and 'decision-rules' work, all of which have been somewhat neglected in recent years amidst the proliferation of theoretical dialogue. These studies seem to me to contain important insights into the impacts and determinants of social policies.

On the theoretical side, I have emphasised some of the major differences between various neo-Weberian and neo-Marxist perspectives on collective consumption, since these are amongst the most important divisions in the literature. As revealed by the final chapter, however, some of the divisions between these 'camps' are beginning to break down. There is a growing theoretical diversity in urban studies which is beginning to undermine some of the conventional labels. There appears to be a growing recognition of some of the limitations of the functionalist-like reasoning of some of the earlier structuralist writings, and a widespread appreciation of the need to take account of the historical evolution of struggles between various complex groups. As is stressed in the final chapter, a crucial issue for further research is how to evaluate the relative importance of local political struggles in the context of economic or structural constraints imposed by the dominant mode of production. Ultimately, this would seem to be an issue for empirical study, rather than something which can be resolved by theoretical discourse.

Isolating collective consumption for separate study is a strategy which is, of course, resisted in certain quarters, especially by those who argue that the phenomena observed in cities should be related

to the underlying conflict between capital and labour within the
sphere of production. I would agree that there is a need to examine
in more detail the links between conflicts within the sphere of
production and those within the sphere of consumption; but much of
the existing literature which attempts to relate conflicts over
collective services to the dominant mode of production seems to
consist of broad generalisations and unsupportable assertions. A
central tenet of this book is that struggles over public services
cannot be reduced in any simple manner to struggles at the place of
work. Struggles over collective consumption have real and important
effects (both material and psychological) which cannot be dismissed
as epiphenomena.

The geography of collective consumption 1

A book entitled *Cities and Services: The Geography of Collective Consumption* must at the outset address two important questions: first, just what is meant by the term 'collective consumption', and second, why is it appropriate to consider this phenomenon from a geographical perspective? After considering these issues, this chapter will lay the foundation for the rest of the book by outlining the history of geographical approaches to the study of collective consumption, and then considering the basic features of British and American local governments – the main bodies responsible for the administration of collective services. Allied to this is a discussion of why the book concentrates on cities and what is meant by the term 'urban' in the context of collective consumption. Finally, there is a brief outline of the major theoretical perspectives currently available for explaining the distribution of collective consumption within cities.

The meaning of collective consumption

In recent years, the notion of collective consumption has become intimately linked with the work of Castells (1977), whose ideas have attracted considerable comment and criticism. Unfortunately much of this debate is not particularly illuminating, since many of the protagonists appear to have been talking at cross-purposes, or else moving in ever-diminishing circles of semantic definition. The debate does raise important issues, but since these are bound up with the nature of Marxist explanations of collective consumption, these issues will be held over until Chapter 5, where they will receive extended treatment.

In order to answer the question 'What is the meaning of collective consumption?' a more useful starting point is to consider some of the basic features of advanced industrial societies. In essence, these societies are involved in two basic processes. The first process is that of *production* – making all the goods and services required by the members of the society in order to keep the society in existence. The second process is that of *consumption* – the utilisation of these goods and services by the members of the society. In order to link production and consumption there have to be some criteria for regulating the *distribution* of these goods and services. In advanced industrial societies there are two basic systems used to co-ordinate these processes.

The first system, to be found in communist societies, is usually termed the *command* system within which both production and consumption are regulated by a central bureaucracy under the control of the Communist Party. The criteria used to distribute services may be numerous, such as efficiency, equality, the self-interest of the élite groups, or the long-term survival of the society.

This book is, however, primarily concerned with Western capitalist economies, and in particular Britain and North America, where a second system, based on *market exchange* principles, is dominant. Under the market system, in its extreme form, both production and consumption are left to the 'invisible hand' of the private market. In theory, what is produced is dependent upon consumer demand, which reflects individual preferences for goods and services translated into purchasing power. This demand will, in turn, depend upon the price asked (since the 'law of demand' indicates that people will consume more of a good when it costs little than when it is expensive), and also upon the amount of the good that is supplied so that, in theory, there will be an equilibrium between supply and demand. According to neo-classical theory, markets will therefore automatically adjust to changes in supply and demand to find an equilibrium solution. The distribution of goods and services is therefore primarily based on the ability of individuals to pay.

This approach is based on *consumer sovereignty* – the idea that the individual is the best judge of his or her own welfare. Furthermore, it rests upon a basic philosophy of *methodological individualism*, which assumes that persons are free to make rational decisions to maximise their utility on the basis of their own preferences. Even proponents of the approach would, however, accept that the ability of individuals to maximise their utility is not entirely free. What is produced is often dependent upon the requirements of the producers, and consumer wants are affected by advertising. Thus – as will be elaborated later – individual utility maximisation is inevitably constrained by social and economic forms beyond individual control.

Despite the dominance of market-exchange principles in capitalist societies a substantial – and, until recently, ever-increasing – proportion of goods and services within these economies are now allocated by their public sectors on non-market criteria. In order to understand why this is the case it is necessary to begin by considering the difference between private and public goods.

The pure theory of public goods
Samuelson (1954; 1955) was one of the first economists to discuss in

detail the difference between public and private goods, and, as such, laid the foundations of what is termed the 'theory of public goods'. A *private consumption good* he defined as one which can only be consumed by one person or at most a small group of people such as in a family or household. Food, clothing, housing, and consumer durables such as cars and radios are obvious examples. Consumers have widely differing preferences for these goods, both in terms of quantity and quality, and consequently they are amenable for distribution by private markets.

Public consumption goods, in contrast, have properties which make it impossible for distribution by private markets. Musgrave (1958) elaborated Samuelson's ideas to define three basic criteria which define pure public goods. First, there is the concept of *joint supply* (or *non-rivalness*) which means that, if a good can be supplied to one person, it can also be supplied to all other persons at no extra cost. Second, there is the idea of *non-excludability* whereby, having supplied the good to one person, it is impossible to withhold the good from others so that those who do not wish to pay for it cannot be prevented from enjoying its benefits. Third, there is the notion of *non-rejectability*, which means that once a good is supplied it must be equally consumed by all, even those who do not wish to do so.

It is important to note that the pure theory is based upon the *characteristics of the goods and services themselves and not whether they are produced within the public or private sectors of the economy*. In reality, many goods are produced by nationalised public sector companies but are distributed within private markets (Renault automobiles being a classic example). Conversely, many products – such as medicines and spectacles for example – are manufactured by privately owned companies, but distributed on a non-market basis within the public sector. The Samuelson-Musgravian approach is concerned with those situations where the characteristics of the good lead to market failure so that there is no way of preventing 'free riders', who contribute nothing, from consuming the product. Under these circumstances a rational individual wishing to maximise his utility would withhold from paying anything for a public good. The most commonly cited example of a public good is defence. Despite the creation of 'nuclear-free zones' in over 150 British local authorities, it is impossible for a city to 'opt out' of the added protection or vulnerability engendered by nuclear missiles. Indeed, it is the impossibility of rejecting this type of good which – together with horror at the prospect of nuclear war – has aroused such enormous controversy over the location of Cruise missiles in Britain.

Reasons for a geographical perspective
This immediately brings us to the reasons why geographers are interested in the distribution of public goods and services, for the factors which most commonly undermine this theoretical purity are

of a geographical nature. Drawing upon the pioneering work of Tiebout (1956) and later Teitz (1968), we can divide these factors into three main types.

First, there is the phenomenon of *jurisdictional partitioning*. Most countries of whatever economic system, are divided into smaller local government jurisdictions or administrative areas. For a variety of economic, social, political and administrative reasons, which are described in Chapter 2, these local government units vary enormously in the quantity and quality of public goods and services they provide. Indirectly, then, the amount of public sector resources an individual receives is often dependent upon his or her location.

A second major reason is because of *tapering*. Within these jurisdictions many public services which are theoretically available to all sections of the community, such as parks, libraries, swimming pools and sports centres obviously have to be located at particular points – hence they are often termed 'point-specific' services (Wolch, 1979). Even if these services are provided free at the point of supply, individuals will typically have to bear the cost of travelling to the facility. We know that, in general, costs, together with time and effort, tend to increase with distance travelled. Furthermore, the so-called 'law of demand' suggests that as costs increase so the quantity of a good that is consumed will decrease. All this means is that with a fixed budget of money, time or effort, the amount of a public good, or the frequency with which it is consumed, will decrease with increasing distance from the facility. Eventually a point may be reached where the costs are such that the service is not utilised. Clearly, in these circumstances geography or distance-decay effects undermine the criterion of non-exclusion in the supply of public goods. Similar principles apply if the service is what Wolch (1979) terms an 'outreach' service, that is, one that is delivered to the consumer, such as fire protection or an ambulance service. Here the costs are typically borne by the supplier of the public good so that it costs more to supply recipients distant from the facility supply base. Furthermore, the quality of the service will also vary with distance from the base. Some areas may be less well-protected by police patrols while emergency services will take longer to reach more distant locations. In this case, then, distance also undermines the criteria of joint supply (an identical quality of good for all at no extra cost).

Externalities provide a third reason for a geographical perspective. An externality, in broadest terms, is an unpriced effect. Many activities in advanced industrial societies have side effects which are not reflected in costs or prices. Geography is again important because these activities take place at specific locations, and the side effects will extend outwards from these locations in a *spatial field*. Once again these effects will tend to diminish with increasing distance from the source of the externality. These effects may be positive, producing benefits for the surrounding area, or negative, producing disbenefits. Activities producing negative externalities are sometimes termed *noxious* facilities: typical examples would be the smell from refuse tips, or the noise from roads and airports. Activities with positive externalities are sometimes termed *salutary* facilities, and include the quiet associated with parks and open space, or the social mobility promoted by good-quality educational facilities.

There are many complex issues involved with externalities which are discussed in greater detail in Chapter 3 but a number of points should be noted in this introduction. First, as in the case of jurisdictional partitioning and tapering, the importance of externalities, whether positive or negative, depends upon individual value systems. There may be wide differences between areas, but also between the individuals within the same area, regarding the importance of these side effects. Activities which arouse opposition in some localities may be treated with indifference elsewhere. Frequently it is the impact of these activities upon house-values in owner-occupied areas which is the main preoccupation of local residents. This means that opposition is often greater *before* a new activity is located in an area, or when a valued facility, such as a school, is threatened with closure or withdrawal. Clearly many public sector facilities will have an important impact upon the well-being of local communities.

It should be clear that externalities are related to the tapering effects described earlier. Positive externalities may accrue to an area because of the ease of access to valued facilities such as libraries, sports centres and parks. However, externality effects need not exist only within local government boundaries but may have impacts which extend across jurisdictional boundaries. The term *spillover* is often used to describe a situation in which facilities are provided in a local government area and consumed – but not paid for – by 'free riders' from other political jurisdictions. Major recreational facilities, shopping centres and roads are examples of services provided by large cities but widely enjoyed on a regional basis by those who live outside the city boundaries. Conversely, certain activities may create negative side effects in nearby government units, as when heavy industries produce pollution or when untreated sewage is pumped into the sea and washed along the coast!

Some complications

It takes little thought to appreciate that, given the widespread effects of jurisdictional partitioning, tapering and externalities, few goods will possess all the criteria specified by Samuelson and Musgrave. Even the extent to which a nation is defended can be expected to vary from one area to another; under attack, certain peripheral regions may be sacrificed to preserve a core region from invasion. As Samuelson (1955) himself noted:

> Obviously I am introducing a strong polar case ... the careful empiricist will recognise that many – though not all – of the realistic cases of government activity can be fruitfully analysed as some blend of these two extreme polar cases. (Samuelson, 1955:350).

Table 1.1 is an attempt to present goods and services along such a continuum. At the top of the table (category 1) are the public services which possess many or all of the pure Samuelson-Musgravian characteristics, including defence and the legal system. At the bottom of the table are the pure private goods. Category 2 consists of pure local goods which, generally speaking, are freely available to all individuals at equal cost within particular local government units or administrative areas. From a spatial perspective the main interest therefore focuses upon category 3 which contains various forms of local public goods and services which are made impure through various combinations of jurisdictional partitioning, tapering and externalities. Table 1.1 also attempts to indicate the main sources of this impurity. It can be seen that all the services are likely to display geographical variations because of their administration by decentralised political and administrative units. As will be revealed in Chapter 2, these variations are greater in the case of some services than others. Tapering effects are also widespread irrespective of whether the service is 'place specific' or 'outreach' in character, and some services such as hospitals are a combination of both. Externality effects are also widespread, although in this table we have included only those which are likely to have the greatest effect on public opinion.

Some public facilities such as schools, hospitals and parks, generate pressure groups in favour of their existence, whilst facilities such as public housing or refuse tips are likely to meet resistance from the population of an area if they are proposed in the vicinity. In some cases – roads, for example – there may be groups for and against depending to some degree on the distance of individuals from the facility. Regulatory services such as planning can, of course, have either a positive or negative impact.

It should be stressed that local services are much more extensive and complex than is implied by this list, which is used merely to illustrate the theory of public goods. Although this type of

Key
√ indicates potential source of impurity
PS place specific service
O outreach service
+ generally positive externalities
– generally negative externalities

Table 1.1 A continuum of goods and services ranging from the purely public
to the purely private. (After Bennett, 1980)

Category	Source of impurity		
	Jurisdictional partitioning	Tapering	Externalities
1 Pure public goods			
defence			
legal system			
monetary standards			
social security benefits			
2 Pure local goods			
electricity supply			
local radio and television			
water supply			
3 Impure local goods			
public housing	✓		✓–
schools	✓	✓PS	✓+
old people's homes	✓		
meals on wheels	✓	✓O	
hospitals	✓	✓PS O	✓+
doctors' surgeries	✓	✓PS O	
nurseries	✓	✓PS	
police protection	✓	✓PS O	
fire protection	✓	✓O	
parks	✓	✓PS	✓+
sports centres	✓	✓PS	✓+
swimming pools	✓	✓PS	
refuse collection	✓	✓O	
refuse tips	✓	✓PS	✓–
consumer advice bureau	✓	✓PS	
environmental inspection	✓	✓O	
planning	✓	✓PS	✓+–
roads	✓	✓PS	✓+–
libraries	✓	✓PS	
4 Pure private goods			
food			
clothing			
consumer durables			
cars			

framework is a useful starting point, defining what is meant by collective consumption is much more complex than the theory of public goods would suggest. The crucial point is that there are few *technical* reasons why many goods such as housing, education, electricity supply, roads or health care should be allocated by the public sector in preference to the private sector. This is, of course, revealed most strikingly by comparisons between Britain and the United States.

Indeed, such are the limitations of the theory of pure public goods that Samuelson later abandoned the idea that most services would fall between some mixture of pure private and pure public characteristics. Furthermore, it is of little use to define collective consumption literally, as Lojkine (1976) does, as a good or service that is consumed collectively as opposed to individually. According to this definition hospitals or schools would be defined as part of collective consumption, even if provided by the private sector.

The decision to allocate many services within the public sector has arisen, not because of their technical characteristics, but because of social objectives translated into political action. The pressure for the provision of these services within the public sector has come from many quarters – pressure groups, trade unions, social reformers, moralists, intellectuals, politicians at various levels, public sector bureaucracies and various commercial and business interests – and the relative importance of these agencies and actors has varied over time. Nevertheless, a common theme underlying many of these pressures has been a dissatisfaction with the inequalities in the distribution of services allocated by private markets. Many local services are therefore concerned with the distribution of goods on the basis of social 'need', rather than market forces of effective demand defined by consumers' ability to pay. As such, these services have (in theory at least) important redistributive aims. In consequence, they are not like relatively pure goods, available to all, but restricted to subsections of the population with special needs such as the homeless, poor, elderly or handicapped. Many researchers have made distinctions between these types of service. Richards for example (1970) makes a distinction between personal social services for minorities in need and 'communal' or 'protective' services designed for the whole population. Similarly, Froman (1967) formed a dichotomy between 'segmental' and 'areal' policies, while Boaden (1971) distinguished between needs which are 'narrow' in scope and those which are 'general' in character. Economists concerned with pure public goods theory have tended to neglect such services for those in need, giving them the label 'merit goods'.

Towards a definition
We are now in a position to define more clearly what is meant by the term 'collective consumption'. Dunleavy (1980) has produced a useful

flow chart (reproduced in Figure 1.1) which shows the questions necessary for such a definition. The first question 'Is the process one of consumption?' eliminates the non-consumption activities of the public sector such as monetary payments in the form of welfare subsidies and social security, together with direct action to regulate production. As will be discussed later, pensions, child benefits and social security payments are a crucial part of social policy and essential in any theory of state activity. In some instances direct monetary provision may be an alternative to other forms of collectivised services by the public sector.

The second and third questions, 'Is the object of consumption a service?' and 'Is the service collectively organised and managed?' – exclude commodity consumption such as cars and televisions together with commercial services such as hotels and shops. The

Figure 1.1 Criteria for determining whether a social process can be included within collective consumption (Source: Dunleavy, 1980:53)

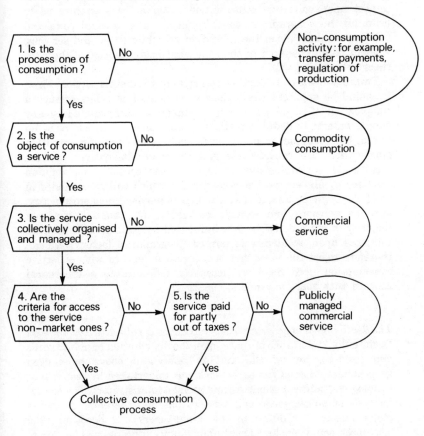

fourth and fifth questions, 'Are the criteria for access to the service non-market ones?' and 'Is the service paid for partly out of taxes?' – eliminate those services provided by state bodies such as gas, electricity or telephone services on a commercial basis.

Essentially then, we are concerned with *those goods and services provided through the public sector on a non-market basis, which reveal variations in both quantity and quality between areas because of jurisdictional partitioning, tapering and externality effects.* This includes those services – such as public transport – which are allocated by public agencies on a non-market basis but are supported by taxes, and also services such as public housing which are allocated on a non-market basis but are quasi-commercial in form (being supported both by subsidies from taxation, and the rents of occupiers). Finally, such a definition must include planning, which is strictly concerned with regulation of land use rather than direct consumption. Nevertheless, given the importance of location upon tapering and spillover effects, this activity obviously has a crucial impact upon collective consumption. Such a focus enables us to examine the geographical contributions to the unequal costs and benefits resulting from the allocation of public goods and services, without being ensnared in the somewhat bogus aspects of the pure theory of public goods.

Two important points are necessary to conclude this section. First, it should be apparent that collective consumption refers to such a complex set of phenomena that it cannot be encapsulated by any simple watertight definition. Much depends upon the questions being asked. For example, in many fields such as housing and education where there are considerable private sector alternatives to state facilities, a comprehensive study must also consider consumption provided by all sectors. The second point, which will be expanded in the following chapters, is that although some aspects of state policy, such as pensions and welfare payments, are aspatial, the vast majority of state activities are influenced by, and in turn have an influence upon, what can be termed 'geographical factors'. We can therefore reject the view that 'a theoretical concern with collective consumption need have no necessary reference to a theoretical concern with space (Saunders, 1981:211).

The development of geographical perspectives in collective consumption
Despite the importance of space upon the distribution of public goods and services, few of the authors referenced above have been geographers. Most of the early work was undertaken by economists, sociologists, political scientists and social administrators. The spatial analysis of public goods and services has not, therefore, formed a major research tradition in the social sciences. Indeed, in 1965 Thompson could conclude that public finance concepts had ' . . . up to

now been largely spaceless.' (Thompson, 1965:257). Prior to the 1970s human geographers were preoccupied with the distribution of phenomena such as industries, offices, shopping facilities and transport networks based upon criteria of locational efficiency such as least cost, maximum profit or distance minimisation. As we have already seen, there are important issues of locational efficiency involved in many public services, but until the last decade geographers paid relatively little attention to services such as schools, personal welfare services, libraries and the like. Previously, most contributions to policy had been at the regional level. The city was certainly the object of frequent analysis by human geographers in the 1960s but they were generally concerned with promoting detailed and sophisticated descriptions of spatial patterns or focusing upon the behaviour of subgroups in the city, rather than focusing explicitly upon problems of social policy formulation and evaluation.

The paper which probably did more than any other to change things was Harvey's brilliant discussion (1970) of the relationship between what he called social process and spatial form. Harvey stressed the ways in which, as we change the spatial form of cities through the relocation of housing, roads, industries and shopping centres, so two important factors are also altered: first, *the price of accessibility* to those facilities which are either desired or necessary; and second, *the cost of proximity* to those noxious facilities which are considered undesirable. Harvey attempted to provide a synthesis of all these tapering and externality effects which he termed 'real income'. One of Harvey's main points was that the distribution of real income may to some degree be independent of, but at the same time reinforce, inequalities of monetary income provided by the occupational market or social security benefits. In the absence of detailed evidence much of Harvey's discussion was intuitive and highly speculative in character, but he maintained forcefully that members of the affluent world organise themselves through political systems to maximise their 'real income'. An important link was thereby forged between the traditional geographical concern with land-use planning and the physical environment on the one hand, and the rapidly evolving field of 'social planning', which involved the welfare services so long neglected from the geographical perspective, on the other.

A similar argument was developed in another influential paper by Pahl (1970). Originally a geographer who became a sociologist, his arguments have had important impacts in both disciplines. He argued that there were two important constraints upon an individual's access to scarce resources in urban areas. The first type of constraint he termed as *spatial*, and it could be expressed by the time or cost involved in overcoming the friction of distance when travelling to a facility. The second type of constraints he termed *social*, and it involved the differential access to scarce resources determined by the bureaucratic rules and procedures employed by the local managers of the urban system, such as planners, housing managers and social workers, whom he labelled 'social gatekeepers'.

As in Harvey's paper, many of Pahl's ideas were speculative and unrefined, and it is not surprising to find that they were considerably modified. Pahl's work gave birth to a number of empirical studies of urban managers, although, as will be described in Chapter 4, this approach became very controversial, and he himself rapidly modified his ideas. Harvey, in contrast, completely abandoned his former 'liberal' approach, perhaps largely in recognition of the enormous difficulties in measuring his concept of real income. He then proceeded within a neo-Marxist framework to examine notions of under-consumption and the growth of suburbs in Western capitalist societies (see Chapter 5). Nevertheless, both Harvey's and Pahl's ideas encouraged the belief that 'local public services bid fair to become the chief means of income distribution in our economy' (Thompson, 1965:118).

Two main questions have been posed in the following decade. The first is concerned with the differential allocation of services between individuals or subgroups. This is often summed up by Lasswell's (1958) now famous aphorism 'who gets what?' In the geographic context, of course, this involves asking the question 'who gets what *where*? (Smith, 1977). The second basic question has been 'What is the most satisfactory explanation for these patterns of service inequality?' In Lasswellian terminology this involves the question 'who gets what where *how and why*?'

Local governments in Britain and the United States

One of the major difficulties facing researchers concerned with the geography of public services is the wide variety of explanatory frameworks that are available. In order to briefly introduce these frameworks it is first necessary to consider the main features of the local governmental and administrative units which are responsible for allocating local public services. The vast bulk of the information considered in this book is Anglo-American in origin, and it is therefore essential to consider the major differences and similarities between the local governmental systems in Britain and the United States. It should be stressed that the following section is concerned with broad generalisations, and inevitably there will be differences of detail between areas. This is particularly true of the United States where there is a tremendous diversity of local governments.

Types of local government
The services under consideration here are allocated by a complex mixture of local governments and administrative units. Nevertheless,

they share in common a responsibility for the distribution of resources within defined geographical boundaries which are part of a larger nation state. They also tend to be one of two main types. First, there are what Stanyer (1976) terms *'primary'* local governments, which have governing political bodies elected by the members of the local area. These tend to be *multi-purpose* authorities allocating a wide range of local services. If they allocate all the services within a local area they are often termed *unitary* authorities. More common, however, is a system whereby power is shared between local authorities in a multi-tiered system. A second main category consists of *'secondary'* units of local government. These also have independent powers of decision-making and taxation but tend to be *single-purpose* or *ad hoc* authorities responsible for only one service, or at most a small group of closely related public activities. In Britain these secondary units of local government are indirectly elected by members of primary authorities, but in the United States they are typically elected directly by the public.

To this classification must also be added various types of administrative authority. These may be responsible for the management of services within a small portion of the local government area, as in the case of local social services areas in Britain. Although these decentralised field offices do not have powers of taxation, or – in theory at least – independent powers of decision-making, as indicated in Chapter 4, they may have a considerable impact on 'who gets what where?' Committees also exist to co-ordinate activities of field workers in these decentralised areas. At the other extreme administrative bodies may be responsible for co-ordinating the activities of various local governments at the regional level.

Viewed against this classification, the major difference between the British and Northern American local government systems is that the latter is much more complex and fragmented, with a large number of secondary units of government. Indeed, such is the diversity that Banfield and Wilson (1963) argue that it is hardly possible to consider anything as a local government in the United States. Nevertheless, below the level of the states four main types of local government unit can be discerned (Johnston, 1982). At the most basic level are the *counties* whose functions vary according to their degree of urbanisation. In the most rural counties without any settlement clusters there is only the legal minimum of service provison – police protection, road maintenance and the administration of public welfare. As one moves closer towards larger urban centres, so there is found a greater combination of all the services necessary to control complex physical environments, such as street lighting, sewage disposal and refuse collection. Certain small rural settlements in the north-eastern states have what are termed *townships*. Although not independent of the counties, they are engaged in a variety of local administrative functions including fire, street-lighting, water and road maintenance. The combination of responsibilities again varies enormously between areas. Of much greater importance within the counties are *municipalities* which consist of more densely populated areas of varying size. They share a variety of names such as cities, towns and villages, but all have undergone the important process of incorporation. This involves the formation of a separate unit of local government which can provide services independently of the county. The process of incorporation usually involves a petition from the local residents, followed by a vote and majority approval in a referendum. The functions of the municipality are specified within a charter and although these tend to vary between areas, within counties municipalities of similar sizes tend to administer similar functions. In the largest cities the municipality may undertake all the functions of the county, but in most cases they provide only a proportion of the county services.

Finally, there are the numerous secondary units of American local government – the *special districts* created on an *ad hoc* basis for the administration of particular services. Most common are the schools districts run by elected school boards with powers over the school syllabus, teachers' salaries and school closures. Their degree of independence from the local states varies from one part of the country to another. Other special districts administer a wide variety of functions including parks, fire services and drainage. These special districts operate within complex administrative boundaries which frequently overlap with many other municipalities.

It is the sheer diversity of this local government system which is the most difficult aspect for the British student to grasp. For example, in 1977 there were no less than 3,042 counties, 18,862 municipalities, 16,822 townships, 15,174 school districts, and no less than 25,962 special districts making a total of 79,862; furthermore, the vast majority of these units are extremely small; only 58 of the 18,862 municipalities had more than a quarter of a million inhabitants and 9,614 contained less than 1,000 (Johnston, 1982). The effect of this fragmentation upon the administrative structure of Chicago is shown in Figure 1.2.

The British local government system can be described much more succinctly. Following the reorganisation of 1974, England was divided into an essentially two-tier structure with an upper tier of 45 *metropolitan* and *non-metropolitan counties* and the lower tier of 332 *metropolitan and non-metropolitan districts*. The division of powers between these tiers is briefly summarised in Table 1.2. In the major cities the bulk of local services are in the hands of the lower tiers of metropolitan district councils, and in the case of London in the lower tier of boroughs. In the non-metropolitan counties however, the balance of power rests with the upper administrative tier. Although differing in some minor aspects, the system is essentially similar in both Wales and Scotland. A third tier consists of *parishes* and

Figure 1.2 Chicago's fragmented local government system (Source: Robson and Regan, 1972)

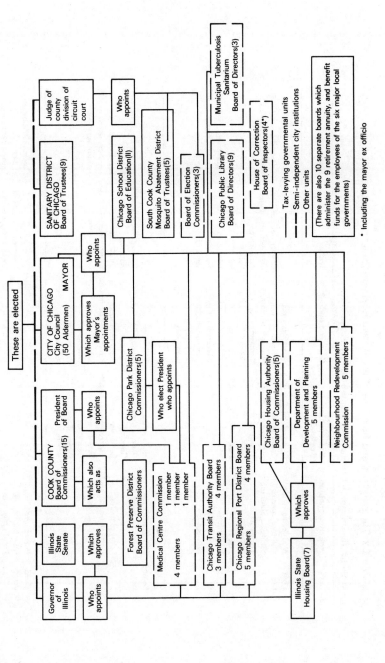

Table 1.2 The structure and functions of the British local government system

Level	Non-Metropolitan England	Metropolitan England*	Greater London*	Wales	Scotland
First tier	*Non-Metropolitan County Councils (39)* Strategic planning Transport Police Fire Education Personal social services	*Metropolitan County Councils (6)* Strategic planning Transport Police Fire	*Greater London Council* Strategic planning Transport Police Fire Education – Inner London Education Authority (Inner Boroughs)	*County Councils (18)* Strategic planning Transport Police Fire Education Personal social services	*Regional Councils (9)* Strategic planning Transport Police Fire Education Personal social services
Second tier	*Non-Metropolitan District Councils (296)* Housing Local planning Environmental health Leisure services	*Metropolitan District Councils (36)* Housing Local planning Environmental health Leisure services Education Personal social services	*London Boroughs (32)* Housing Local planning Environmental health Leisure services Education Personal social services	*District Councils (37)* Housing Local planning Environmental health Leisure services	*District Councils (53)* Housing Local planning Environmental health Leisure services
Third tier	*Parish and Town Councils (7,000)* Local amenities			*Community Councils* Local amenities	*Community Councils (1,343)* Local amenities

* Powers to be transferred to lower administrative tier and new system of joint boards.

community councils and, although by far the most numerous element in the system, their powers are relatively insignificant, being confined to local amenities such as paths and cemeteries.

Councillors and committees

Both the British and the North American systems are governed by local politicians elected for a fixed period by the public and aided in the execution of their duties by a bureaucracy of public employees. A typical example of the British structure is shown in Figure 1.3. The elected members or councillors are collectively known as the council. The chairman of the council (or mayor) is elected by the other councillors and, in contrast to the United States, his or her position is essentially ceremonial rather than political. In most large authorities most councils are dominated by the two major national political parties – Labour and Conservative. The Labour Party tends to derive greater support from the poorer sections of society and is better represented in large cities; conversely the Conservative Party tends to derive greater support from the more affluent middle-class sections of society and is better represented in more suburban and rural areas – the so-called 'shire' counties.

The fully elected council tends to meet somewhat infrequently delegating much of the important decision-making to a set of smaller local committees and sub-committees. The committees may be of various types: 'vertical' committees usually concentrate upon the administration of one particular service such as education or

Figure 1.3 The main elements of the British local government structure
(Source: Byrne, 1983:147)

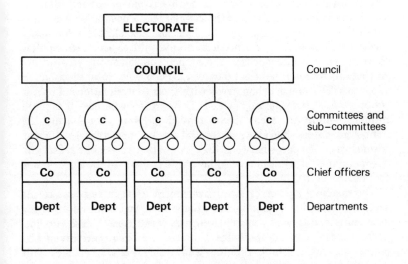

housing; whereas 'horizontal' committees deal with issues such as finance and planning which overlap conventional departmental boundaries. These committees may be more-or-less permanent standing committees, or special *ad hoc* committees designed for a particular short-term purpose. It is in these committees that much of the policy of local government is formulated and scrutinised. The full council is therefore usually concerned with ratifying the decisions of subcommittees or discussing subcommittees' reports which are either approved, amended or 'referred back' to the committee concerned for reconsideration.

Councillors are aided in the execution of their duties by various types of local government official – the permanent non-elected members of the local government bureaucracy. These officials are usually located in specific vertical departments whose prime task is the provision of services, but as with the committee structure, there are horizontal departments which overlap many service categories. Each department is headed by a chief officer who is ultimately responsible for overseeing the execution of policy within his own department, co-ordinating with other departments, co-ordinating with other local authorities and working with the local councillors. A good deal of the chief officer's time is spent in this latter role, presenting reports to the council sub-committees. Below the level of chief officers are various types of local government officer, down to a layer of what in North America has been termed 'street level bureaucrats' – those responsible for the day-to-day delivery of services to the public.

Once again the structure is rather more complex in the United States, with four main types of local administration (see Figure 1.4). The traditional form is known as the *weak-mayor-council* plan, in which the mayor, members of the council and a host of local officials are elected directly. This can lead to complex elections for many positions. However, since American municipalities are much smaller than British local authorities, the council is also usually smaller. As in Britain, national political parties also dominate local elections in the cities. The major urban areas with their concentrations of poorer groups have traditionally voted Democratic whereas the more affluent suburban areas have tended to vote Republican. As Johnston notes, however, these labels do not represent clear ideological differences between their respective voters but reflect the predominance of what is termed 'machine politics' in the major cities (Johnston, 1979).

The machine system of local government grew in response to the tremendous influx of immigrant groups into American cities in the late nineteenth and early twentieth centuries. These groups, including Germans, Jews, Poles, Italians, and Irish, were divided by numerous racial, ethnic, religious and national characteristics. This fragmentation prevented the growth of unified working-class organis-

Figure 1.4 Forms of American city administration (Source: Stanyer, 1976)

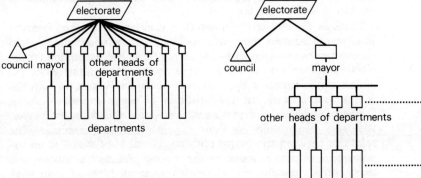

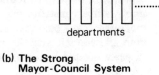

(a) **The Weak Mayor-Council System**

(b) **The Strong Mayor-Council System**

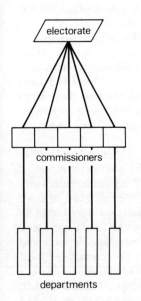

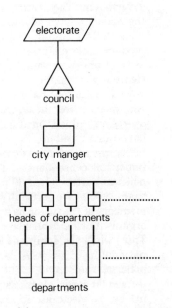

(c) **The Commission System**

(d) **The Council-Manager System**

ations such as trade unions, and the Labour Party in Britain. Instead, various immigrant votes were 'bought' by political leaders with bribes of money, goods and jobs, in a complex system of patronage and corruption.

Towards the end of the nineteenth century three other forms of local administration were advocated by a largely upper middle-class reform movement, who wished to obtain fairer representation for the electorate than under the 'machine' system. One alternative, *the strong-mayor council-plan*, involved the direct election of both the mayor and council but the abolition of many executive offices. Instead, all levels of departments were subordinate to the mayor, who was responsible for their appointment and dismissal. The relations between the mayor and the council were modelled on the separation of powers found in the federal presidential system and many state constitutions. The two remaining types of plan were modelled upon business management. Under the *commission* plan both the council and the mayor were replaced by a small group of directly elected heads of departments. The fourth type of system – the *council-* or *city-manager* plan – is the most centralised and simplified structure of the four. The small council is directly elected and appoints the council manager, who, in turn, appoints all the departmental heads and runs the executive side of the local government. The precise form of this system varies enormously but the majority have adopted non-partisan elections.

As well as eliminating links of patronage the reformers hoped to produce a more efficient, business-like form of administration which at the same time would better represent the wishes of the majority. Generally speaking, however, it is only the medium-sized local governments that have undertaken reform, and in many of the large American cities the mayor-council form of government is still in operation, albeit modified with some aspects of the reformed government system.

The reform of the American local government system has had two important consequences. The first result is the almost total lack of political parties. Over 60 per cent of cities with a population of more than 5,000 are officially non-partisan; the candidates are all members of the major party and election campaigns are contested by organisations established on an *ad hoc* basis by the local candidates. Thus, while the dominant local party may be important for state and national politics, it is largely irrelevant in the context of local policies. The second major consequence is the existence of what are termed 'at large' elections which means that councillors are elected, not by the electorate in small geographical areas such as wards, but by the population of the whole local government area.

Closed and unified versus open and democratic?
It used to be the conventional wisdom that the British local

government system is closed, unified and relatively autonomous, whereas the American system is open, devolved and more democratic in the sense of being responsive to local demands. This judgement arose because of a number of other differences between the two systems. First, at a superficial level, local affairs appear to play a more prominent part in the way of life in American cities. There appears to be much more open and controversial debate over local issues – in which both television and the press play a leading role. Sharpe (1973) even suggests that the press is almost part of the formal process of government and in some cities is the effective opposition, maintaining a continuous flow of information to the electorate. Furthermore, the 'style' of government often appears more participatory than in Britain. There are a great many more pressure groups and formal organisations actively campaigning to get their demands implemented by the local government system. In addition, Americans have to vote for a great many different public positions at various levels. Indeed, it has been estimated that there is one public post for every 441 persons (Johnston, 1982) – a high ratio by any democratic standards. Because so many of the executive posts are subject to election, many would argue that this makes the actions of officials more politically accountable than under the British system. The American tradition of what has been termed 'unfettered individualism' (Wood, 1961), and the prevailing ethos of free-market enterprise also means that there is a general climate of hostility and a suspicion towards the public sector. Local government is seen as a necessary evil and one that should be severely curtailed.

In Britain, by way of contrast, political conflicts are less visible. Arguments are voiced both in council and subcommittee meetings, but only in exceptional cases are they the subject of fervent public debate or widespread and intense reportage by the mass media. Much of the real decision-making in British politics – the bargaining between politicians, senior officers and pressure groups – takes place outside the public gaze. Furthermore, the permanent, non-elected bureaucracies of British local government are larger and more entrenched than their American counterparts. They would seem to have a much greater sense of professionalism and civic responsibility and therefore, arguably, have a greater capacity to play an autonomous role in the formation of policy. As Madgwick has observed, the American professional 'unlike his British counterpart, is not limited by the self-denying rectitude of a corporate profession; he is rather a freelance willing to sell his talents elsewhere' (Madgwick, 1970:95). Finally, it would appear that in Britain there is generally less hostility to the idea of local government; indeed, there is a more widespread public acceptance that public intervention at the local level is essential in a complex industrial society.

The degree of truth in this conventional wisdom will be subject to greater scrutiny in following chapters. For the present, however, it should be noted that certainly the 'style' of local government differs considerably between the two countries. The fragmentation of local powers in the United States means that there is often an absence of unified power to implement change. In order to effect positive action local politicians are often engaged in a 'brokerage' role, organising coalitions of diverse groups to overcome the opposition or inertia of all the other official bodies, authorities and unofficial groups who have the power to resist change (Newton, 1969). However, the diversity of these groups does not necessarily mean that their demands are better represented by the political system. Newton argues that the machine politics of the big cities have encouraged the fragmentation of groups, and have offered immediate material inducements rather than long-term political change (Newton, 1978). The system has encouraged apathy in local affairs, and helped to suppress conflict.

The British system, in contrast, has enabled the demands of various groups to find expression in party politics. In particular, the demands of the working class, and more recently various 'under-classes' such as women, racial minorities and single-parent families, have found expression in the Labour Party. In this context it is important to note that, excluding special districts and school boards in the United States, the number of elected councillors is generally much smaller in American cities than in the case of their British counterparts (Sharpe, 1973). Sharpe suggests that the larger size of British councils has encouraged the representation of pressure groups within the party system. Furthermore, since British councillors are elected on a ward system, this does enable the representation of views from particular localities.

As we shall see later, the representativeness of American pressure groups is also open to serious question. There is evidence that the majority of local pressure groups and voluntary organis-ations are middle class in character, and the low-income groups have a much lower propensity to participate in local affairs. Furthermore, there is also evidence that American councillors are more predomi-nantly middle or upper class in character than in Britain. Newton argues that the reformed system of local government has encouraged this tendency. The non-partisan elections and absence of ward-based representatives who have a greater tendency to support geographi-cally concentrated minorities, give advantages to those with the monetary resources to mobilise support. Hence, reformed local governments encourage middle- and upper-class councillors, lead to the under-representation of low income groups, and generally promote low levels of expenditure. As such, the emphasis upon efficient business management may suppress overt political conflict.

In Britain, the absence of local pressure groups is also partly explicable by their greater focus upon central government where, given the unified system and the power of Parliament, there is often a greater potential to effect major change. All told, this means that the absence of visible group activity in Britain's cities does not necessarily imply a closed, unrepresentative system; indeed, it can well be argued that a flourishing pressure group system indicates the failure of the formal participatory process.

Finally, in this context, we should note that the American suspicion of government does not necessarily mean that their bureaucracies are endowed with less power than in Britain. Where it has been adopted, the American city-manager system generally serves to restrict the opportunities of elected representatives to participate in decision-making, and in the absence of a strong disciplined political party, there may be a vacuum which can be filled by the bureaucrat. In contrast, the British committee system does give elected councillors at least the potential to participate in decision-making. In other American cities without the city-manager system, irrespective of whether the mayor is weak or strong, the devolution of powers does tend to lessen the political accountability of many service agencies and their heads. Furthermore, the United States has a proliferation of special district agencies dealing with issues such as highways, refuse disposal, sewage and planning. As in the case of the less numerous British special districts, the political accountability of such agencies is often questionable.

Constraints on local government activity
The activities of both these local government systems are constrained by law. In Britain, Parliament is the sovereign governing body and there is a *unitary* constitution. All local government activities have to be authorised by Parliament, and if any authorities exceed their powers they are acting illegally or *ultra vires*. In the United States there is a *federal* system, where power is divided between the central federal government and the individual states. Each state has its own constitution and these specify the powers of the various types of local government. The extent to which local governments are autonomous from central governments is a source of enormous controversy which is considered in detail in Chapter 2. Here it should be noted that the local governments are empowered to raise money to support their activities in various ways. Internal sources of revenue are the rents and fees charged for local services, borrowing and local taxation. In Britain the most important source of local tax is that on the property, known as the rates. Property taxes are also important in North America but are supplemented by a wide variety of sales taxes. These internal sources of income are supplemented by various types of central government grant. In Britain it is this latter source of income, mainly embodied in the Block Grant (previously termed the Rate Support Grant) which is by far the most important source of local government income, now accounting for about 50 per cent of the total. In the United States the amount of external funding from

federal and state sources is much smaller on average amounting to 39 per cent (Wolman, 1982).

The net effect of the smaller average size of American local governments and the smaller amounts of external income is that there are much wider differences in the abilities of the local governments to support local services. This has led to two major types of strategy. The first is the attempt to exclude from the local area all developments which would place additional demands upon the revenue base. It is for this reason that the process of separate incorporation from the county is so crucial, for it brings independent control over the pattern of local land use. Municipalities can then engage in what is termed *exclusionary zoning*. This enables the pattern of urban growth and the type of local resident to be effectively controlled by stipulations regarding housing densities, plot sizes and type of building. Low-income residents and patterns of development which would place large demands upon service infra-structures can thus be excluded. High income municipalities can maintain their exclusive character and maximise the value of properties by eliminating negative externalities. A major alternative strategy is to encourage various combinations of domestic, commer-cial or industrial activities into an area to provide additional local revenue generating sources. Where a number of local governments are in competition for sources of income business interests may be able to 'play-off' one authority against another with the intention of obtaining the best deal – namely service infrastructure at minimum cost.

The major differences in fiscal capacity arise between the large cities and their surrounding belts of numerous smaller suburban municipalities. The cities have much greater needs for services, and higher costs, but generally large proportions of low-income residents who, in relative terms, must pay more for their services and/or receive services of lower quality. Furthermore, the major cities have to support a wide range of infrastructures, including public transport, roads, refuse collection and recreational and cultural facilities, which are enjoyed by the members of other areas but not fully supported by user charges. An obvious solution to this problem is to extend the boundaries of cities to incorporate the vast majority of surrounding 'free riders'. It was fear of the increased costs of annexation, together with a desire to avoid the machine politics of large cities, which prompted the desire for both incorporation and municipal reform in suburban municipalities. The wealthier suburban residents can therefore avoid paying taxes which would have redistributive effects in other, poorer income areas. In the late nineteenth century it was the wealthier upper-middle-class residents who first moved to the peripheral areas to avoid the higher costs of city living, but this has also been one of the many factors which has prompted the outmigration of many middle-, and even lower-income groups, from inner cities in the twentieth century. It would therefore be misleading to think of suburban authorities as uniformly affluent, but they do generally exclude the poorest sectors of society, including black residents. Fiscal disparities also exist in other local government units and are especially important in the case of school districts. It benefits the more affluent individual to locate in a middle-class area where good quality education aiding social mobility can be obtained, without having to support additional resources for poorer households. Again, lower-income areas may use industrial property to subsidise the provision of schools.

It is the British case which in this instance is more complex, for the differences between the older city cores and surrounding suburbs, together with their reflection in the local government structure, are less dramatic and explicit than in the United States. It is certainly true that British cities are also 'underbound', in the sense that their administrative boundaries do not encompass the full extent of urban areas as defined in terms of all the people who either work in or make use of, central-city facilities. Although separate incorporations of surrounding towns are unusual in Britain, as in North America, cities have also fought long, hard battles with surrounding rural areas in an attempt to extend their boundaries, and for the most part they have been defeated. This has meant that, despite 'overspill' schemes, British cities have usually had to rehouse their inhabitants at higher densities within their own restricted boundaries rather than on suburban 'green-field' sites. Although the claim is questioned in certain quarters, it is generally accepted that the imposition of green belts around British cities and associated land-use controls have effectively led to the containment of urban England since the Second World War (Hall *et al.*, 1973). Under the reorganisation of 1974, many cities which previously undertook all local functions had many of their powers – including strategic planning – taken away, and allocated to an upper tier of counties. Nevertheless, the assumptions incorporated into the new strategic plans have generally maintained the previous patterns and, together with powerful conservationist lobbies, these have continued to contain urban sprawl. The satellite commuter belts of the cities are certainly growing rapidly, but this growth is concentrated into particular centres, and consists predominantly of the more affluent sections of British society who can afford to buy their own homes.

The meaning of 'urban'

Implicit within the previous discussion has been a spatial framework for the analysis of collective consumption. Since this is primarily a book about services within *cities*, and the terms 'city' and 'country-side', 'urban' and 'rural' have undoubtedly aroused even more controversy than the term 'collective consumption', it is necessary to make the spatial framework explicit and consider the meaning of 'urban'. In recent years sociologists have tended to argue that the terms 'urban' and 'rural' have ceased to have any significance, at least in terms of sociological processes within advanced industrial societies. Thus, if one seeks to explain differences in life style between individuals, better explanations can be achieved in terms of their class position or age, than whether they live in the 'town' or the 'countryside'.

In the past, geography has been stricken by a complex set of largely semantic debates over the definition of 'hamlet', 'village', 'town' and 'city'. Today the term 'urban' is usually defined in relation to one of three sets of criteria. The first and most simple definition is a *physical* one, in terms of the extent of continuously built-up residential areas that are surrounded by green fields, or other form of non-built environment (such as scrub or desert in parts of the United States). Equally straightforward are *administrative* definitions, in terms of the boundaries of political jurisdictions of the type described in the previous section. Most complex are the third type of *functional* criteria, which define urban centres as substantial agglomerations of persons engaged in predominantly non-agricultural occupations. Such definitions usually involve allocating to older inner-city areas their surrounding suburban commuter hinterlands which contain large numbers of inhabitants who engage in industrial and commercial occupations, often in the city centres. Although many of those who have moved outwards from the decaying, high-density inner-city areas towards the newer, low-density suburbs and surrounding smaller settlements have perceived this as a 'flight from the city' – and in administrative terms this is the case – in functional terms they remain within a 'daily urban system'.

Clearly, there need be little overlap between these types of definition. In Britain the physical and administrative definitions often overlap, since the districts encompass the continuously built-up older parts of cities within the green belts, but both in Britain and in the United States functional definitions do *not* accord with the other types of definitions. The relationship between physical administrative and functional definitions of 'urban' in the Southampton area is shown in Figure 1.5.

For most academic purposes, such as considering urban growth processes or patterns of resource allocation between 'inner' and 'outer' city areas, the functional definitions are of most use. Furthermore, despite recent evidence of 'counter-urbanisation' – the move towards smaller settlements in the urban hierarchy – most people still continue to live within the major 'daily urban systems'. These cities are the major centres of social problems in advanced industrial economies, and contain the largest absolute – if not relative – concentrations of social problems. This does not imply that

Figure 1.5 Physical, administrative and functional definitions of 'urban' in the Southampton city region

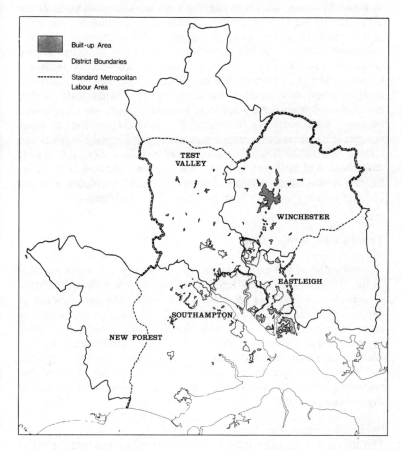

problems are necessarily less extreme outside the major urban centres. There is an urgent need to redress the balance of research, which is overwhelmingly urban in character, in order to examine conflicts over collective consumption in (for want of a better term) 'rural' areas. Indeed, there is already evidence for believing that problems of accessibility to facilities such as schools and hospitals are likely to increase with distance from major urban centres. Nevertheless, ever since the Industrial Revolution (and even before this time) the major cities have been the major sources of both positive and negative externalities, the greatest concentrations of poverty and wealth, and the sources of most intense political conflict.

Clearly our definition of 'urban' will vary with the problem under examination. The analysis of jurisdictional partitioning will involve large administrative districts, such as states and counties, which incorporate urban centres of varying size, together with rural areas; although the big cities are likely to have a major impact upon many of the results. In the case of tapering effects, the analysis will frequently involve an administrative definition of urban areas, although some studies look at patterns of accessibility within a broader functional urban context. Finally, studies of locational conflict frequently involve incidents at the micro-scale within jurisdictional boundaries, but also involve conflict over 'spillovers' between administrative districts. As stressed in the previous description of local government systems in the United Kingdom and United States, the fragmentation of responsibility inevitably means that there will be a gap between the political agencies responsible for the execution of services designed to meet problems, and the broader urban systems which generate these problems.

Theoretical perspectives

Having outlined the main elements of the local government systems in the United States and United Kingdom, we are now in a position to consider the various theories which have been put forward to explain patterns of service delivery. These theories are many in number, but can be conveniently grouped into three main types: the *public choice approach*, the *neo-Weberian approach* and the *neo-Marxist approach*. In essence, the differences between these theories boil down to disagreement over: first, who makes the decision regarding service allocation in cities: and second, whose interests these decisions serve.

Public-choice theories
The first set of theories used to explain service allocations in cities can be collectively termed 'public-choice theory'. These theories are the modern embodiment of the liberal-democratic representative view of local government, which can be traced back to the ideas of John Stuart Mill. He recognised that in modern industrial societies with a complex division of labour, a comprehensive system of participatory democracy, in which all members of society had their say about all decisions, would be impossible. He therefore argued that it is necessary to delegate political power to representatives, who are accountable to an informed and educated electorate at periodic elections in which all members of society are able to vote for the politicians of their choice, free from coercion (Goldsmith, 1980).

According to this approach, it is the local politicians who make the decisions regarding the allocation of services in cities, but they do so in the interests of their voters. This public-choice view is derived from an analogy with private markets. Local politics are envisaged as a political 'market-place', in which politicians respond to the demands of the public in a similar manner to the way in which it is maintained that entrepreneurs respond to the preferences of consumers. The crucial issue is how, in the absence of a system of direct participatory democracy, are these preferences revealed in the political context?

One influential approach by economists substitutes political parties for market processes as the means of linking individual preferences to public expenditures (Downs, 1957; Buchanan and Tullock, 1962). These models assume that politicians offer tax and expenditure options to voters to maximise the votes they receive, and in their search for public support to obtain and stay in office they will discover the preferences of voters. Political parties are thus seen as analogous to entrepreneurs in a profit-seeking economy, in that they formulate those policies which attract most votes, just as entrepreneurs produce the products they believe will gain the most profits. Although this work had antecedents in Hotelling's (1929) work on the location of ice-cream sellers on a beach under conditions of competition, a major limitation of the work in the context of local governments is that the models are essentially aspatial in character and have been applied to the national level.

The most explicitly geographical attempt to provide a conceptual bridge between the private and public sector solutions to the market allocation problem was that of Tiebout (1956). He postulated that the demand for public goods is registered by the process of residential selection. He claimed that, by his choice of administrative district, the 'consumer-voter' expresses his preference for a particular tax mix. The individual will thus choose to reside in the local government area whose range of services and taxes best fit his own preferences. Tiebout later collaborated with Ostrom and Warren (Ostrom *et al.*, 1961) to produce a more general theory, in which local governments were also considered to be in competition with one another for residents and/or industry and commerce. The decentralised structure of metropolitan governments is according to this approach, the result of market-like competitive forces which sustain the existence of separate types of communities to fulfil particular functions (see also Warren, 1964). (Although it is based upon an analogy with international politics rather than economics, the work of Holden (1964) is similar in its emphasis upon the competitiveness of local governments.)

Tiebout's model is an idealised abstraction and involves a large number of restrictive assumptions in order to achieve an optimal solution. These assumptions include omniscience on the part of voters, perfect mobility of households, no economies of scale in the supply of services and, of course, an enormous range of municipalities. There is limited evidence for the existence of 'voting with one's feet'

(Aronson, 1974) and certainly escalating costs and diminishing levels of service provision have been amongst the important reasons encouraging the outmigration of persons from inner-city areas. However, the bulk of literature on residential relocation suggests that while the quality of local services – in particular the nature of schools, and to a lesser extent the level of local taxes – may have some impact upon the eventual destination of the move, the decision to move is more often the result of pressures generated by changes in the life cycle or socio-economic status. Although the decision to move into the newer suburbs seems to have been encouraged by a general disaffection with many aspects of inner-city living such as high crime levels and congestion, these are factors which are only indirectly affected by public services *per se*. Arguably, the choice of dwellings in the new suburbs is also influenced by the greater availability of mortgages on newer properties; by way of contrast, many banks and building societies are reluctant to provide loans on properties in inner-city areas which they feel have an uncertain future. The Tiebout model also ignores the fact that certain households have relatively little choice in their location and indeed all persons are restricted in varying degree by constraints of income. In view of all these limitations it is not surprising that Tiebout's approach has been less influential than the other main type of public-choice theory – the pluralist models of Dahl (1956) and Polsby (1963).

This approach argues that politicians reflect the preferences of voters through their responses to the demands made by pressure and interest groups in a pluralist society composed of many complex groups. It is argued that the stronger the group's preferences the more likely it is to take political action to get its view heard, and the stronger these actions are, the more likely it is that politicians will respond. However, pluralists argue that these responses will not favour or discriminate against any particular section of society, because the state's role is one of a neutral arbiter or referee between competing groups. Pluralists maintain that pressures come from a wide range of groups which cut across conventional class lines and this guarantees broad equality of political outcomes (and service provision). Thus, individuals find themselves in many different and non-overlapping groups according to different issues. Furthermore, overriding all of these activities are the ever-present elections through which politicians may be brought to account.

The difference between the Tieboutian and pluralist public-choice approaches can neatly be summarised in the terminology of Hirschmann (1970). He observed that, when faced with a problem, the inhabitants of an area have three broad courses open to them. The first course is termed the *exit* option, and is again based upon an analogy with private markets. Just as when a consumer is dissatisfied with a product he or she can cease to purchase the commodity, so it is argued that an individual can move to another jurisdiction if dissatisfied with the level of services provided in the existing locality. However, in the same way that consumers may be stuck with an expensive purchase so, as noted above, many persons may not be able to afford the cost of moving to another district. A second, *voice* option is then available to overcome the problem. This can involve various forms of political representation ranging from petition-gathering, lobbying, letter writing and forming a residents' association, through to protests and demonstrations. Dear and Long (1978) argue that the latter type of activity, if illegal, can be defined as a particular subset of the voice option. Protests may escalate into violence against persons or property, and while such actions are undoubtedly successful in drawing attention to a cause, they are generally socially unacceptable and run the risk of alienating both official and wider public support. Dear and Long also draw attention to another form of group representation which is undertaken in *formal decision-making* processes. In Britain land-use planners are obliged at various stages of plan construction to engage in formal consultation with the public over structure plans. Since such participation procedures are initiated by government they may be distinguished from the more 'pure' form of voice option which arises almost spontaneously in response to some local threat. Formal participation approaches may of course divert informal political representations.

The final option available to an individual, household or community under threat is that of *loyalty* or *resignation* – or in other words to do nothing and accept the problem. As will be elaborated in Chapter 3, there are a number of reasons for believing that this is quite a common course of action in both British and American cities; but it is an option which is almost totally ignored by public-choice approaches. The Tieboutian model emphasises the exit option to the exclusion of all other possibilities, while the pluralist approach is firmly fixed upon the voice option.

In the light of the previous section it should be evident why public-choice theories have generally originated in the United States and found greater acceptance there than in Britain. The diverse nature of local groups (perpetuated by the old machine system), the overt role played by pressure groups and local politicians, the smaller size of public bureaucracies, the relatively restricted scope of local government and of course the much greater fragmentation of administrative units – have all encouraged these theories. Indeed, in various ways these provide rationalisations and justifications for these aspects of the American system portraying them as essential ingredients in a democratic system.

Like the neo-classical economics from which they obtain their inspiration, all of these public-choice theories are based on the assumption of methodological individualism – the idea that individuals are free to make rational decisions on the basis of their preferences. In reality, of course, individual preferences are strongly influenced by previous experience, and individual attempts to maximise utility are subject to considerable social economic and political constraints.

Weberian perspectives

The merits of these theories will be considered later but it should be noted that conspicuous by its absence in these perspectives is any mention of the role of public bureaucracies in decision-making and service delivery. Given the larger size of non-elected government employees in British local government, it is no mere coincidence that the neo-Weberian approach, with its emphasis upon the independent powers of bureaucratic forms of organisation, has had much greater impact in Britain than public-choice theory.

Following the ideas of the pioneering German sociologist Max Weber, this perspective suggests that decisions regarding service allocations are made by officials in the permanent bureaucracies of local government in the interest of their own self-preservation. Weber argued that modern industrial societies were becoming increasingly bureaucratic in their form of organisation, and this reduces the possibility of effective political control over decision-making. This approach may be compatible with a wide range of different service distributions; services may benefit many differing sections of society from rich to poor, depending upon the way in which the organisation operates. The bureaucracy may respond to local pressures, or may employ strict technical criteria in the interests of fairness or efficiency, but all stategies will be destined in the interests of the long-term survival of the organisation. Clearly, whereas the pluralist perspective emphasises the role of politicians in the decision-making process the Weberian approach – at least in its early forms – reduces their role to one of virtual insignificance.

Marxist perspectives

Marxist perspectives say nothing directly about who makes the decisions regarding local service allocations, and whether local politicians or local officials are most important. This approach also says nothing directly about what groups in society have most influence upon these decisions, whether they be pressure groups, trade unions, industrialists or the central state government. It is therefore incorrect to interpret Marxist approaches as suggesting that local government will be unduly influenced by, and will inevitably act in the interests of, particular groups such as industrialists or local owners of property. Local government is not regarded as a 'thing' which is controlled by a particular group for their own interests, but is a set of social relations which is functional for the overall maintenance of the capitalist system.

As will be described in Chapter 5, Marxism is above all a holistic way of examining social issues. It is vitally important to place any particular set of observations within the context of the wider whole of which they are a part. Marxists see conflicts in the sphere of production as the most important struggles in society and this means that their perspectives tend to downgrade conflicts in the sphere of consumptions.

Conclusions, and framework of this book

There are three basic reasons for a geographical perspective upon collective consumption: because of jurisdictional partitioning; distance-decay or tapering effects; and the widespread existence of positive and negative externalities. There are, in turn, three major theoretical perspectives available for explaining these factors: public-choice theories; neo-Weberian theories; and neo-Marxist theories. The interrelationships between these processes and theories forms the basis for the rest of this book.

The study of jurisdictional partitioning is now the oldest geographical approach to the study of public services, but it has been somewhat neglected by geographers. This approach therefore forms the focus for Chapter 2. Since tapering effects and externalities are closely related these are treated together within an intra-urban focus in Chapter 3. Public-choice theories have either implicitly or explicitly been the dominant theoretical perspective used throughout much of the 1960s and 1970s to explain patterns of service delivery and this perspective is integrated into Chapters 2 and 3. Chapter 4 considers the neo-Weberian perspective; while the various types of neo-Marxist theory provide the focus for Chapter 5. As will be revealed, none of these theoretical frameworks is without limitations, and in the final chapter, entitled 'Beyond locational analysis and structuralism', there is an attempt to specify how these limitations can be overcome without resorting to some bland form of eclecticism.

2 Jurisdictional partitioning and the 'outputs' approach

Introduction

Practically all nations find it necessary to decentralise the administration of government. This decentralisation can take many forms,
the most simple being the creation of some local centre, such as a tax
office, responsible for the execution of central government functions
within some limited area of the larger nation state (Byrne, 1981). An
alternative approach is to hive off the service from central
government completely to form a semi-independent organisation
such as the Post Office or Housing Corporation in Britain, or the
New York Port Authority in the United States. A third, and more
complex approach is for the central government to transfer the
administration of certain aspects of government to some local
political jurisdiction responsible for a defined geographical area. The
bulk of services considered in this book are administered by semi-
independent organisations and local governments.

This decentralisation of powers is usually justified by two main
types of argument. The first argument stresses the benefits of such a
system for the efficient administration of services. Obviously, a
single central government office would have immense difficulties in
dealing with even a relatively small country, and local governments
also have numerous small field offices for the administration of
services.

The second major justification for a decentralised system stresses
its contribution to local democracy. Precisely what is meant by this
term is often not clear, but local bodies with political representation
are often seen as a way of enabling decision-making units to be in
close contact with the wishes of their electorate and responsive to
their needs. At the same time, it is often maintained that local
governments encourage public participation in decision-making, and
act as a bulwark against the tyranny of an all-powerful central
government. The independence of local governments is also seen as a
way of encouraging diversity and experiment in the administration
of services.

The so-called 'outputs' approach involves analysing the consequences of this jurisdictional partitioning by comparing the quality

and quantity of local services allocated by differing local governments. It concentrates on what local governments actually provide – hence the term 'outputs' – rather than concentrating upon 'inputs' to the system, such as voting- and interest-group representations. This approach has, in turn, been prompted by two criteria. The first factor is the desire to ensure greater *efficiency* in the administration of local affairs. It has frequently been observed that local authorities vary considerably in terms of the *per capita* cost of the services they provide. Thus, over the years, a great deal of effort has been expended in an attempt to find the optimum or most efficient local government unit in terms of the ability to provide equal units of service output at lowest cost.

The second major reason for the external scrutiny of local government service allocations has been the desire to promote greater *equality* of treatment for individuals, irrespective of their location. Studies comparing the services provided by different local authorities have revealed wide variations, both in terms of quantity and quality. Individuals may, therefore, receive substantially different amounts and combinations of public sector goods and services depending upon the administrative authority in which they are resident.

Outputs studies may be grouped into two broad types, depending upon the extent to which they share this concern for equality of service provision. On the one hand, there is a set of studies, predominantly North American, known as *'expenditure determinant'* studies, which are *not* overtly concerned with issues of equality. As their name suggests, the main concern of these studies has been to explain variations in local government expenditures usually by reference to the internal characteristics of the authorities. As will be described later, these studies have been strongly influenced by public-choice theory and refer to 'demands' and environmental 'inputs' rather than needs. Nevertheless, whatever the label used, a characteristic of many of these studies, especially the early ones, is the superficial manner in which they have measured many of the variables of interest.

A second type of study, almost exclusively British in character, is explicitly normative in orientation, and is concerned with the criteria which *ought* to govern the allocation of resources between areas rather than explain the patterns which actually exist. These studies have been influenced by Davies's (1968) notion of territorial justice – the idea that in a set of local authorities, each area should allocate an amount of resources for a service in direct proportion to its needs for the service. In general, this second type of study has revealed a much greater concern to provide detailed measures of needs and service outputs, rather than focus exclusively upon expenditures. The British concern with needs undoubtedly reflects the greater scope of welfare services in Britain than in the United

States. However, in more recent 'outputs' studies the differences between British and American approaches are less noticeable.

Whereas efficiency is often portrayed as compatible with a decentralised local government system – indeed, in the Ticboutian model outlined in Chapter 1, efficiency is used as a justification for a fragmented system – the democratic function is increasingly seen as incompatible with the attainment of greater equality for individuals. Rather than a healthy democratic response to local conditions, variations in service provisions are seen as an inegalitarian outcome, which is incompatible with the ideals of the welfare state, and which should be remedied by central government intervention. In fact, the relationship between decentralisation and efficiency has also been seriously questioned in recent years. During the late 1960s and early 1970s there was a strong movement in Britain in favour of larger local authorities; these, it was argued, would be better placed to take advantage of economies of scale and provide extensive and diverse services more efficiently.

Spurred by these twin criteria of efficiency and equality, the study of jurisdictional partitioning is now one of the oldest approaches concerned with geographical variations in service allocations. However, it is important to place the origin of these studies in their historical context; for, by comparing large numbers of local governments, using multivariate statistical techniques, the exponents of this approach were attempting to escape from the limitations of much older traditions of analysis. On the one hand, there is an extensive British literature dealing with local government from a formal, legalistic viewpoint. These studies have tended to ignore the ways in which local governments actually act in practice, and Dunleavy (1980) calls them 'pre-behavioural' in the sense that they have eschewed the approaches of 'mainstream' social science. One form of this institutional analysis has focused almost exclusively upon what is regarded as the undesirable erosion of autonomy in local government through central intervention (Robson, 1966). Although, typically, little scientific evidence is used to support this hypothesis, the work has had a powerful influence on studies of local government behaviour.

The growth of comparative studies in the United States in the 1960s was also a response to the dominance of the 'community-power debate' which had established a powerful grip upon North American political science ever since the Second World War. The basic question posed by these studies was 'who rules?', or, in other words, 'who makes the crucial decisions that affect people's lives in local communities?'

Much of the impetus for this debate had come from the work of Hunter (1953) in Atlanta, Georgia. He wanted to discover who had power in the city and refined his 'reputational methodology' in order to answer this question. This involved asking local experts who they thought were the main 'community influentials', and plotting the networks of power groups so revealed. This approach suggested a hierarchical power structure dominated by local businessmen. Hunter's approach was, however, widely criticised by the pluralists who argued that this approach defined power as an attribute of individuals, rather than as the behaviour of individuals in attaining particular ends. Thus followed the pluralist focus upon overt political conflict where power was defined in terms of an ability to affect outcomes. The pluralist approach was, however, criticised in turn for its focus upon overt political conflict over issues such as roads and urban renewal programmes to the neglect of the less dramatic, but nonetheless important processes of mainstream service allocation. Furthermore, the pluralist studies concentrated on isolated case studies of local authorities in which the generality of processes was often difficult to observe and evaluate. By examining aggregate expenditure patterns in a large number of local authorities it was hoped that outputs studies would escape the limitations of the community-power debate.

It should be apparent, even from this brief introduction, that the term 'ouput' is susceptible to a variety of interpretations, and this requires some clarification. This can best be achieved by considering the 'territorial justice' tradition of outputs studies, which has given greater attention to definitional problems.

Territorial justice

In broad terms, the idea of territorial justice may be construed in two ways. The first approach is concerned with the just distribution of *territory* between competing parties – the type of conflict which has traditionally been studied by political geographers in their analysis of boundary disputes and political settlements. The second interpretation of the term 'territorial justice' refers to the just distribution of *resources* among political or administrative units in accord with some normative criteria.

This second interpretation has only been a major source of interest for geographers in the last ten years, largely because it is only in this period that they have begun to examine social policy defined as 'the policy of governments with regard to action having a direct impact upon citizens by providing them with services or income' (Marshall, 1970:9). This is not to deny that much earlier work was concerned with needs – especially after Thompson (1964) asked 'What about a geography of poverty?' Such studies included examinations of the spatial patterns of housing needs (Smith, 1970), forms of mental illness (Giggs, 1970), and the economic health of regions (Smith, 1968). Furthermore, practitioners of factorial ecology were, through their derivation of dimensions of social rank and ethnic status, implicitly concerned with measures which differentiate urban areas and their subpopulations according to various needs. However, the majority of geographers working within this school have sought to describe these patterns in order to provide some theory of urban spatial structure, or else explain the behaviour of subgroups within the city – tasks they conspicuously failed to achieve – rather than use such information as a further input to the evaluation of social policy. The spatial allocation models most frequently used by geographers have been concerned with simulating the growth of employment, tertiary and residential activity in urban and regional systems. The main use of these models has been to predict the patterning of future land uses on the basis of locational criteria such as land availability and journey-to-work distances. Consequently, such work has tended to rely upon mechanistic and stochastic principles derived by analogy from the physical sciences, and has tended to ignore factors such as income effects, social impacts and service inequalities.

Thus it was in the field of social administration that the scrutiny of service allocations by local authorities was first formalised by Davies (1968). His concept of territorial justice is essentially a spatial extrapolation of the normative principle derived from Marx, 'to each according to his need'. Davies claims:

> In the services for which the most apparent distribution between individuals is 'to each according to his need', the most appropriate distribution between areas must be 'to each according to the needs of the particular area'. Since the former term is synonymous with social justice we can call the latter term territorial justice. (Davies, 1968:16)

Since the analysis deals with local administrative areas, which are aggregates of individuals, territorial justice is defined as: 'An area distribution of provision of services such that each area's standard is proportional to the total needs for services of its population' (Davies, 1968:39).

The extent of territorial justice can thus be gauged by the extent of a positive linear relationship between indices of needs and service provision, as revealed by correlation coefficients. In theory, a situation of territorial justice should be reflected in a coefficient of $+1$; and conversely a situation of territorial injustice would reveal a coefficient of -1. In reality, of course, actual values are unlikely to reach these extremes.

It is important to stress that this approach does not involve treating all people (or administrative areas) the same, irrespective of their circumstances – what is sometimes termed the principle of *arithmetic equality*. Instead it is based on the principle of *proportional equality*, the notion that individuals experiencing the same conditions, or with the same characteristics, should receive the same proportion of resources (Smith, 1977).

The concept of territorial justice should also be distinguished from the ideal of *positive discrimination* (contrast diagrams A and B in Figure 2.1). Positive discrimination, as the name suggests, is an attempt by policy makers to positively discriminate in favour of certain individuals or areas who have experienced disadvantage, for whatever reason, over a considerable period of time. It thus involves providing additional resources to the most deprived areas. In Britain such policies in the realm of education, race and housing have frequently been criticised as cosmetic exercises which do little to remedy the underlying causes of disadvantage. In this context we should note that a policy of positive discrimination differs from the idea of territorial justice in which *all* areas receive resources in direct proportion to their needs. Positive discrimination usually involves making a distinction between deprived and non-deprived areas, and will only lead to a distribution of resources similar to that which would be achieved by the concept of territorial justice if needs are highly concentrated.

Another feature of the approach is that although relationships between needs and resources may be strong and positive, one of the variables may exhibit a wider range of values than the other. This could lead to either of situations C or D in Figure 2.1. In case C a large variation in needs is associated with a small but strongly correlated amount of resources, whereas in case D small variations in needs are associated with considerable variations in resource allocation. In case C the high-need areas will tend to suffer relative to the low-need areas; conversely in case D the high-need areas will gain at the expense of other areas. Case D is closest to the concept of positive discrimination, and in some circumstances may be preferable to strict proportional equality. If, for example, an area has been deprived of services for a long period it may be necessary to compensate for the previous lack of provision.

Culyer (1976) has pointed out that if one considers the costs of meeting unmet needs then numerous complications can arise. A policy of minimising the total unmet need in the system would involve directing resources to those area where the unit cost of meeting needs was least. It might be, however, that for various reasons the unit costs of meeting needs is much greater in the high-need areas so that inevitably such areas would be left with a greater amount of unmet needs. Conversely, a policy designed to equalise the total amount of unmet need in each area would restrict the aggregate amount of need in the system which could be met. Policies based on territorial justice can therefore raise many complex ethical problems, although it should be noted that usually we do not have sufficient knowledge to be able to make the fine judgements implied above.

It is also important to note that, because of the ecological fallacy, a pattern of territorial justice *between* a set of administrative areas

Figure 2.1 Possible relationships between needs and resources
(Source: Pinch, 1980)

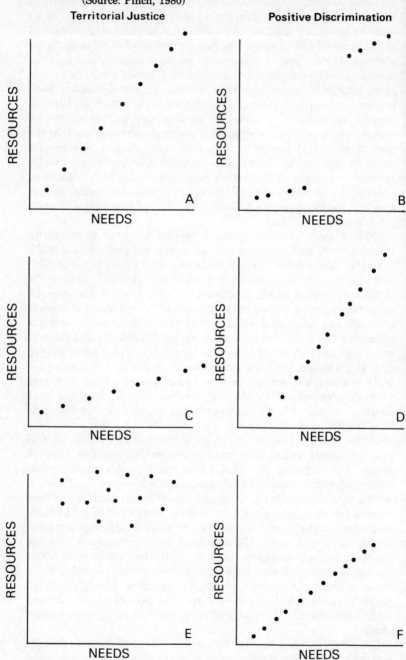

does not necessarily imply a situation of social justice amongst the individuals *within* the areas. Furthermore, it has been pointed out that often externalities and indivisibilities in the provision of public goods and services lead to situations in which geographical or areal need may not be the same as the aggregate of individual needs (Bennett, 1980). However, Davies's approach was specifically tailored to evaluate the distribution of British personal services which are delivered at the individual level – hence the needs indices are the aggregates of the needs of all the individuals in the area. Nevertheless, the correlational methodology of the approach does mean that it is concerned with *relative* variations in resource provision between areas, and says nothing about the overall deficiency in service provision. It is therefore most suitable for application in contexts in which inequality in provision between areas is large in relation to the overall shortfall in service provision. If we compare situations E and F in Figure 2.1, the former is preferable despite the lack of territorial justice, because overall each area has a greater amount of resources than in case F. However, in most areas of social policy resources are limited, and ideally territorial justice should be applied in all situations.

In practice, most researchers have ignored many of the theoretical complexities discussed above and have been merely concerned that there should be some broad correspondence between needs and provisions across a set of local government areas, since this is a situation that is not often found in reality. The evaluation of territorial justice has therefore been on a conceptually simple basis. However, this does place a great emphasis upon the manner in which the key variables – needs and resources – are measured, and these complex issues are considered in the next section.

Needs
The idea that society should be organised in order to satisfy human needs is a noble sentiment with a long history. Although Marx never made clear what society would be like after the revolution, his writings suggest that under socialism 'need' would become the central criterion governing production, distribution and consumption. Indeed, economists have long made a distinction between the *use value* of goods and services – the extent to which they satisfy human needs – and the *exchange value* of these items – the prices they can command in the market. The neo-classical theory referred to at the beginning of Chapter 1 argues that consumers will satisfy their needs by purchasing those bundles of goods and services which satisfy their preferences. However, in capitalist economies production is often directed towards those items which will make the most profits, rather than towards the satisfaction of fundamental but expensive and therefore unprofitable, human needs, such as shelter, health care and education. Indeed, as described in Chapter 1, there

are some fundamental needs – such as defence – which are impossible, or at best extremely difficult, to satisfy through private markets. While prices can be determined and measured easily, human needs are therefore much more complex and controversial.

At the root of much of this controversy is the fact that there can be no absolute definition of need. It might theoretically be possible to determine the minimum level of nutrition and shelter necessary to keep an individual alive. Indeed, there is growing evidence that following the recession, public expenditure cuts and unemployment have hit the poorest groups in Western societies, such that standards of nutrition and housing have become extremely low for a large minority, but the majority live at levels far above those of mere subsistence. The concept of need is therefore inherently relative in character and refers to the adequacy of existing conditions in society in relation to some socially acceptable norm. Needs thus involve perceptions of conditions, and individual judgements regarding the nature of those conditions which constitute need.

It is therefore important to recognise that those involved in local decision-making processes which affect collective consumption – politicians, professionals and the public – may have widely differing attitudes regarding the nature of needs. One way of analysing this problem is to recognise the typology of need definitions put forward by Bradshaw (1972). He distinguishes between four main types of need. First, there are *normative* definitions of need, as made by professionals such as social workers, local administrators and housing managers – in other words Pahl's social gatekeepers. These definitions may contrast with the *felt needs* of the public if they are expressed in some way through questionnaires or interviews. These felt needs may be latent, or else become *expressed needs* if turned into action of some form such as complaints, petitions for a facility, applications for a service or even demonstrations. Finally, *comparative needs* may be ascertained by examining the characteristics of those actually in receipt of a service.

There may be wide variations in definitions of needs amongst the members of these various groups, but a crucial dichotomy which emerges from this classification is that between the values of local gatekeepers, which are likely to be reflected in comparative needs, and the values of the public, which may or may not be expressed. The values of these two sets of actors will interact in complex ways to affect the level of service delivery. It is likely that the demand for services (as defined by expressed needs) will be influenced to some degree by the supply of these services (defined by the normative needs of local administrators). A classic strategy of local authorities who are short of resources for a particular service is to restrict publicity so that they will not be inundated with demands that cannot be met. Conversely, the provision of services can turn felt needs into expressed needs. A good example of this is the way in which applications from the elderly for residential accommodation often follow the location of an old people's home in an area.

It is, no doubt, the value-laden nature of needs indices that has tended to inhibit explicit studies of needs, for it would seem to undermine the academic goal of objectivity. However, recognition of the importance of values in needs indices does not imply a cul-de-sac for the researcher, provided that the values inherent within the needs index are made explicit. The index can then be used as a yardstick against which to gauge the allocation of services, for it may be that deviations from territorial justice result because of differing perceptions of needs in particular areas to those incorporated into the aggregate needs statistics.

Resources

The measurement of local government resource allocations is almost as complex as the measurement of needs. A major difficulty, apart from the inherent difficulties of obtaining reliable and accurate information, is the fact that numerous authors have produced many complex and contradictory classification schemes. There is little consistency of usage, and the same term is used to denote quite different things. The scheme adopted here is a combination of the most commonly accepted and least confusing terminology.

Fortunately, when reduced to essentials, it is possible to envisage resources as consisting of three interrelated elements (see Figure 2.2.). All three of these elements have at various times been termed 'outputs', so this term is best abandoned in this context. At one extreme on the left of Figure 2.2 are the financial *inputs* allocated to a service by a local authority or administrative agency. (These are the resource measures which expenditure determinant studies usually term outputs.) These expenditures may be of two main types:

Figure 2.2 Elements of resource allocation in local social services
(Source: Pinch, 1979)

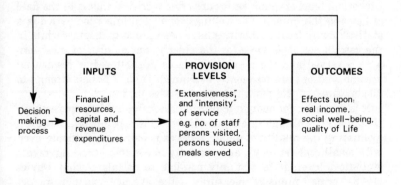

revenue- and capital-based. Both are the result of a complex decision-making process reflecting the interaction of professionals, administrators, local councillors, pressure groups and central government.

There are many good reasons for examining expenditures since these may indicate the relative priority that is attached to a service. Many, though by no means all, social reforms ultimately boil down to the allocation of more financial resources to meet particular social problems. However, expenditures may be a poor index of actual service provision levels to individuals. The cost of providing services is likely to vary between administrative areas, and councils are likely to vary in their efficiency, i.e. their ability to provide units of service of equal quality at least cost. Finally, the complexity of many of the financial transactions involved in the allocation of services makes rigorous accounting procedures, and hence strict data compatibility between areas, difficult to achieve. In Britain the publications of the Chartered Institute of Public Finance and Accountancy have a number of limitations. In particular, items classified under 'administration' are difficult to incorporate consistently, including as they do the costs involved with central administrative departments and pooled administrative buildings.

Despite the considerable efforts that have been made in recent years to improve the quality of financial statistics, it is therefore necessary to supplement measures of financial inputs with the second main element of Figure 2.2 – *physical indices* of the services procured by the expenditure. Davies (1968) uses the term 'extensiveness' of provision to denote the proportion of a population which is in theory eligible for a service, and actually receives it (such as the proportion of old people who receive home helps). Other physical indices are the number of units of service provided, or the number of staff or items of equipment used in a service category.

The nature of these indices of service provision will vary with the type of service under examination, and the nature of the data available for that particular service category. In the sphere of education, teacher–pupil ratios are often a critical index; in the field of housing the number of dwellings completed in a time period is a statistic many local authorities have been proud to display; while in the case of social services for the elderly, the number of meals-on-wheels served and the number of places in sheltered or residential accommodations are frequently examined. Table 2.1 is an attempt to display some of the main indices of service provision.

It is of course not enough to provide extensive public services: they should also be of high quality. As Hirsch (1968) points out, however, evaluating the quality of public services is extremely difficult, even with small scale surveys, and virtually impossible at the aggregate statistical level. It is certainly possible to calculate what Davies (1968) terms 'intensity' measures – the average expenditure per

Table 2.1 Typical indices of service provision used in 'outputs' studies

Service	Indices
Housing	Number of buildings completed or renovated
	Average level of local authority rents
	Level of rate subsidy to housing account
	Proportion of properties high-rise
Education	Teacher–pupil ratios
Police	Number of policemen per head of population
	Average response time to public calls
	Arrests as proportion of crimes ('clear-up rates')
Libraries	Number of books per head of population
	Book circulation rates
Local welfare services	Number of places available in residential or sheltered accommodation
	Number of elderly visited by health visitor
	Number of elderly served with meals-on-wheels
	Number of domestic helps employed
	Number of home nurses employed
	Average size of residential homes
	Average charges for services

recipient of a service – but it is difficult to gauge whether such variations between local authorities result from differences in the quality of services or simply reflect variations in costs or efficiency of councils. In many of the labour-intensive services the quality of care is often dependent upon a complex set of factors not necessarily related to material standards, but involving, for example, the attitudes of service personnel.

The third element of Figure 2.2 is again often termed 'outputs' but is best described as *outcomes* : the effects of these services upon the well-being of individuals and the physical fabric of their local communities. Here we are concerned with the effect of services upon the notion of real income discussed in Chapter 1. The major problem in this context is that an individual's total well-being is often dependent upon many factors other than simply the quantity and quality of local public services. For many groups, especially in inner-city areas, the major problems stem from a lack of income either through the formal economy or social security system, together with general forces of environmental deterioration which existing public services are unable to counteract. Thus, many elderly persons may be eligible for home helps or meals-on-wheels but their main problem is a lack of income through limited pensions. New dwellings have been provided for many slum dwellers but they have lacked the income to maintain and furnish them adequately.

This does not mean that public services are unimportant. Although in some cases such as housing they have sometimes exacerbated problems, and in others they are allocated in such a way that they stigmatize the recipients, in many instances there is a strong need for more public provision. It does mean, however, that in many cases it is extremely difficult to separate the effects of public services *per se* from all the other processes at work in the urban environment.

The evaluation of territorial justice 1: Social services in London
At this point the concept of territorial justice can best be illustrated with an example. The author undertook an evaluation of territorial justice amongst services for the elderly within the greater London local government system (Pinch, 1978; 1980). Following the local government reorganisation of 1965, London was divided into 32 boroughs who were given responsibility for the administration of local social services for old people. These services include residential accommodation, home helps, meals-on-wheels, home nursing and health visiting. (A description of responsibilities following the reorganisation of London local government in 1965 can be found in Table 1.2.)

These services are intended to help those elderly persons who are too frail or feeble to look after themselves; but, given overall shortages of resources, it is the inability or absence of relatives to look after an elderly person which in practice is the prime factor determining whether an elderly person will receive these services. A second characteristic affecting the likelihood of receiving such services is the presence of debilitating social circumstances such as poor housing or bad health. However, as might be expected, there is no detailed information on areal variations in the availability of family care among the London boroughs. Fortunately, detailed case studies have examined this issue in areas of widely differing social status in London. A comparison of results from Wilmott and Young's study of Bethnal Green (which is now part of Tower Hamlets) and the middle-class area of Woodford (now part of the London borough of Redbridge) revealed that in neither area were the elderly deserted by their offspring in times of need. These studies confirm the view that, despite the extension of the Welfare State since the Second World War, it is still the family which provides the main source of care for the elderly in times of need.

In the light of these results in the London boroughs and the fact that there are few variations in the age structure, it was decided that the availability of family care could be held as a 'constant' in London, and that differences in living conditions should indicate the relative differences among London boroughs in the need for care amongst their older populations. There are some grounds for believing that the availability of family care is reduced in some of the inner-city areas that have lost population but this should also be correlated with poor social conditions.

A number of factors reflecting poor social conditions were extracted from various sources to reflect bad health, immobility and social isolation (see Table 2.2). The pattern of variation in these factors is very strong in London, such that it was possible to summarise most of the data with a single social conditions index using principal components analysis (for a full description of the approach see Pinch, 1979). Figure 2.3 shows the resulting concentration of high need in the inner-London boroughs, particularly in the East End boroughs of Tower Hamlets, Newham, Hackney and Lewisham.

Table 2.2 Variables used to construct social conditions index for London boroughs

Variable	
1	Percentage of economically active and retired males in socio-economic groups 7, 10, 11 and 15 (personal service, semi-skilled manual workers and unskilled manual workers) in 1966.[*]
2	Standardised death rate (Triennial average 1970-71).[I]
3	Bronchitis mortality rate in 1971.[I]
4	Infant mortality rate in 1971.[I]
5	Percentage of males of working age employed in 1971.[‡]
6	Percentage of households without a car in 1966.[*]
7	Percentage of households without exclusive use of hot water tap, fixed bath and inside WC in 1971.[‡]
8	Percentage of persons above pensionable age living alone.[‡]

Sources
[*] 1966 Sample Census
[I] 1971-72 Statistical Review of England and Wales
[‡] 1971 Census

Figure 2.3 a. Key to the London boroughs

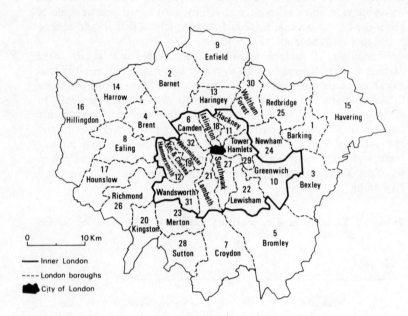

This needs index was correlated with a variety of indices of service provision, a sample of which are shown in Table 2.3 (for more detailed results see Pinch 1979; 1980). The main pattern is remarkably clear: the variables relating to the local welfare services for the elderly – residential home, home-helps and meals-on-wheels – have high correlations with the Social Conditions Index; whereas the variable relating to the local health services – home nursing and health visiting – have either small or negative correlations. This applies to both expenditures and physical indices of service provision.

These relationships are shown graphically in Figure 2.4. Expenditures on residential accommodation (diagram A) reveal a much wider degree of scatter than expenditures on home helps (diagram B). The number of persons visited by home helps and meals-on-wheels (diagrams C and D) also display high degree of linearity, although in the latter case there is relatively little variation in overall provision levels between the various boroughs. The number of persons visited by home nurses displays a wide scatter of points

Figure 2.3 b. Standard scores of social conditions index for London boroughs (Source: Pinch, 1979)

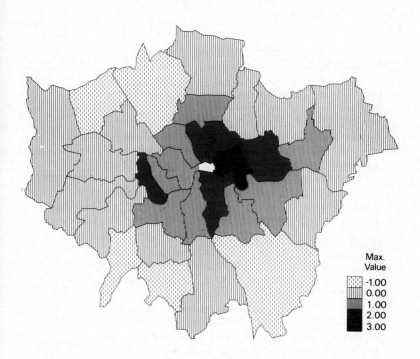

Max.
Value

-1.00
0.00
1.00
2.00
3.00

with little association either positive or negative, while the number of persons visited by health visitors displays a negative association with the needs index.

The evaluation of territorial justice 2: Housing in Greater London
The second case study of territorial justice evaluation concerns housing in the London boroughs. This service is used because it raises a number of different considerations from the personal social services considered previously. The latter are heavily labour-intensive in character, and the bulk of expenditures in these service categories is devoted towards the employment of staff. This can in some circumstances lead to strong associations between indices of expenditures and staff employed or units of service performed. In contrast, housing services are predominantly concerned with the provision of an expensive and durable physical product. Although considerable numbers of people may be involved in the construction and management of these housing units, the service is largely capital-intensive in nature. Expenditure on housing is therefore

Table 2.3 Correlations between social conditions index and indices of service provision for residential accommodation, home helps, home nursing and health visiting in the London boroughs

	Social conditions index
Expenditures	
Average net expenditure on residential accommodation for the elderly and disabled provided by London boroughs and registered voluntary and private agencies on their behalf between 1965 and 1968 (per 1000 population).	0.45
Average net expenditure by London boroughs on home helps between 1965 and 1968 per 1000 population.	0.79
Average net expenditure by London boroughs on home nursing between 1965 and 1968 per 1000 population.	0.15
Average net expenditure by London boroughs on health visiting between 1965 and 1968 per 1000 population.	0.55
'Extensiveness' indices	
Number of persons (excluding staff) in residential accommodation for the elderly and disabled provided by London boroughs and registered voluntary and private agencies on their behalf on 31 December 1971 per 1000 population of pensionable age in 1971.	0.65
Number of persons aged 65 or over first visited by a home help during 1971 per 1000 population aged 65 and over.	0.81
Number of persons aged 65 and over served with meals-on-wheels by London boroughs and voluntary agencies in a one week period in 1970 per 1000 population aged 65 and over.	0.72
Number of persons aged 65 and over first visited by a home nurse during the year 1971 per 1000 population aged 65 and over.	0.25
Number of persons aged 65 and over first visited by a health visitor in 1971 per 1000 population aged 65 and over.	0.44
Staff employed	
Number of home helps employed by London boroughs per 1000 population of pensionable age in 1971.	0.68
Number of home nurses employed by London boroughs in 1969 per 1000 population aged 65 and over.	0.03
Units of service delivered	
Number of meals-on-wheels served to persons aged 65 and over by London boroughs and voluntary agencies in a one week period in 1970 per 1000 population aged 65 and over.	0.72

Sources Welfare Statistics, Local Social Services Statistics and Local Health Services Statistics.

Figure 2.4 Relationships between needs and selected indices of service provision (Source: Pinch, 1980)

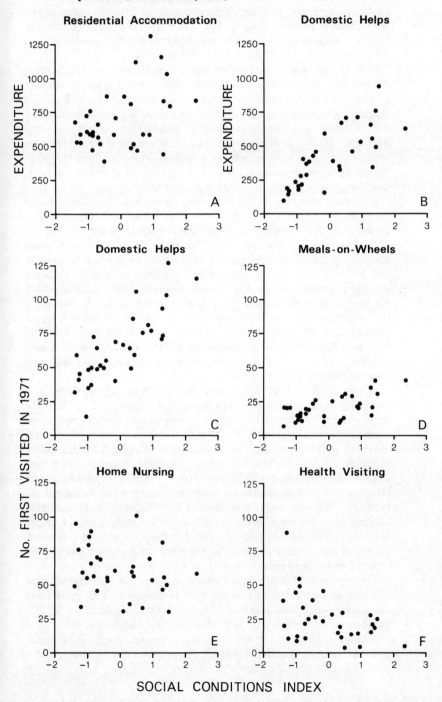

largely concerned with the repayment of long-term loans, and the varying rates of interest and costs prevailing at the time of construction mean that expenditures may be a crude index of the magnitude of physical output. For this reason the housing study in London concentrated upon the number of dwellings produced in a given period (Pinch, 1978).

One of the main features of these construction totals is that, within any given local authority, they are likely to display considerable fluctuations from year to year because of factors such as difficulties in obtaining suitable building sites, shortages in construction capacity, and short-run financial difficulties. Even if there are no major delays, it takes some years for the building cycle to be completed through from planning to construction. It is therefore necessary to measure totals over a longer period than the triennial averages usually used in the case of expenditures.

A factor analysis of housing-need variables for the London boroughs revealed two basic dimensions. The first index was a measure of overcrowding in those areas where there was considerable pressure on the available housing stock, and consequent shortage of dwellings and amenities. The second dimension isolated the housing which was essentially obsolete in quality, lacking standard amenities. As Figure 2.5 demonstrates, although both housing-need variables are concentrated in the inner-city boroughs, the worst conditions were in different areas. Overcrowding is concentrated in some of the western inner boroughs, including Camden, Kensington and Chelsea and Hammersmith, while obsolescence is greatest in the eastern inner boroughs of Tower Hamlets, Newham and Hackney.

It was decided that rebuilding was the most appropriate local authority response when properties were obsolete, but that the improvement of properties with improvement grants was more appropriate where properties were fundamentally sound but overcrowded. However, no such strict demarcation of problem and policy response can be maintained, so a composite housing index was formed and correlated with the combined total of new buildings and total renovations completed. During the period under examination, between 1966 and 1971, responsibility for housing in London was divided between the lower tier of London boroughs and the upper administrative tier of the Greater London Council. The housing powers of the Greater London Council were subsequently transferred to the London boroughs.

The relevant correlations are shown in Table 2.4. As expected new building is positively associated with obsolescence, but negatively associated with overcrowding. Private sector construction is also negatively associated with the obsolescence dimension, being concentrated in suburban low-need areas. However, the local boroughs and the Greater London Council, the upper level of government,

Figure 2.5 Dimensions of housing need in the London boroughs a. standard
scores from Promax Overcrowding dimension; b. standard scores
from Promax Obsolescence dimension
(Source: Pinch, 1978)

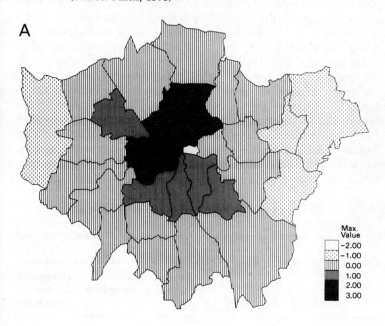

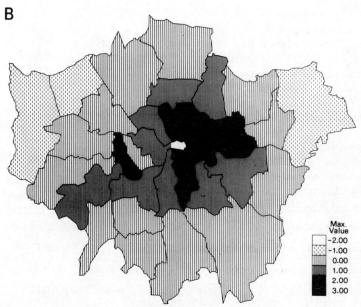

have focused their building efforts in the inner high-need boroughs. Considerable demolition is necessary before rebuilding can begin in some of the boroughs which are short of land, and when the net rebuilding rate between 1966 and 1971 is calculated, the correlations between the construction variables and the housing needs variables are considerably reduced. As expected, the rate of renovation is most strongly associated with the overcrowding dimension, but when added to the net construction rate and correlated with the composite housing need index the coefficients, though positive, are not large.

It should be apparent from these examples that evaluation of the degree of territorial justice involves considerable care both in the construction of the variables, and the interpretation of the scatter diagrams. However, the approach has been criticised for much broader reasons than deficiencies with respect to such methodological problems. The most common charge is that, in focusing upon relative variations between areas, the approach perpetuates the geographers'

Table 2.4 Correlations between indices of housing need and construction and renovation policies in London boroughs between 1966 and 1971 (Source: Pinch, 1978)

	Obsol-escence	Over-crowding	Composite housing need index
New construction			
Total constructions	0.31	−0.10	0.13
Private sector constructions	−0.59	−0.44	−0.52
Local authority constructions	0.50	−0.17	0.30
GLC constructions	0.67	0.20	0.53
Total public sector constructions	0.73	−0.17	0.48
Demolition and closures	0.28	0.28	0.31
Net constructions			
Total net construction	−0.15	−0.31	−0.23
Net local authority construction	0.10	0.17	0.30
Net GLC construction	0.27	0.20	0.27
Net public sector construction	0.47	0.26	0.41
Improvement grants	0.45	0.66	0.58
Net constructions and improvement grants			0.17
Net local authority constructions and improvement grants			0.38
Net public sector constructions and improvement grants			0.44

'fetish over space', and is concerned with relatively small inequalities in society rather than focusing upon the fundamental determinants of deprivation. Smith (1979) argues that we may achieve territorial justice in the provision of existing welfare services, but this would still leave a society in which many pensioners lack sufficient income to keep themselves sufficiently warm in winter. The concept of territorial justice is thus seen as a 'reformist' tool.

It takes little thought to appreciate that such critics have been attacking a straw man of their own creation. Much of course depends upon the use to which the approach is put. It *can* be used as a tool for policy-making and social reform in situations where inequalities between areas are large. In such circumstances, the changes suggested by the approach to achieve a greater degree of territorial justice may be by no means marginal or insignificant. What *is* a major limitation of the approach, however, is that by correlating needs with existing services it says nothing directly about the relevance of those services to the problems under investigation. It does not directly question whether existing systems of health care, housing or welfare are more appropriate for people's needs. It may be that there is so little territorial justice that alternative approaches are indicated, but what these approaches are is not directly revealed.

To be widely applicable as a prescriptive tool there needs to be a broad consensus over definitions of problems, and the most appropriate policies to overcome these problems. The bulk of evidence from social research in the last two decades would indicate that such conditions are often not present in society (although the extent of disaffection with existing services should not be exaggerated, since many groups are campaigning to preserve the existing structure of the Welfare State in the face of cuts from the present (1985) Conservative government). Housing is, of course, the classic example of conflict over solutions to social problems. The statistics published at the aggregate local authority level reflect the legacy of the Victorian 'public health' approach to housing. The aggregate housing-need indices are those dominated by measures of overcrowding and the absence of standard amenities such as hot water and inside toilets. However, housing is so fundamental to individual life styles that it has to satisfy an enormous set of criteria, ranging from the internal character of the dwelling through to its location and proximity to desired facilities. Numerous studies have shown that slum dwellers are often less concerned with issues such as amenities than planners and social reformers. In many cases there is a desire for home-ownership even if the property is substandard in some respects. It is because of these clashes over definitions of needs that public housing schemes have fostered such dissatisfaction amongst the inhabitants of the new dwellings, even if they have had a major impact upon aggregate housing statistics. Investigating these conflicts clearly requires a level of local investigation below the aggregate level of comparing jurisdictions.

Nevertheless, it is at the jurisdictional level that many of the important decisions concerning resource allocations are made and become manifest. Provided the above limitations are borne in mind, the concept of territorial justice can be employed as a first step to uncovering these patterns and processes without diverting attention from fundamental sources of inequality. Although the concept of territorial justice is concerned with spatial variations between jurisdictions it does not imply – as do some geographic theories – that space is an independent determinant of these variations. The spatial boundaries of local governments are simply a mesh which reflects broader political and social processes. It is now appropriate to consider these processes in the second main type of 'outputs' study which has focused upon explaining variations in local government service allocations.

Outputs studies

North American literature

The origins of American outputs studies are much older than studies of territorial justice, and the amount of literature is now vast in scope. In order to make the following discussion manageable the work is therefore classified according to different time periods, types of approach and empirical contexts. American research was initially prompted by a series of 'expenditure determinant' studies undertaken by a group of urban economists between the early 1930s and the early 1960s.

It is difficult to pinpoint in any precise manner the origin of these quantitative comparative studies of local public expenditures in the United States. As early as 1926, D.A. Davenport noted a strong and positive relationship between *per capita* municipal expenditures and population size, and similar observations were made by M.L. Walker in 1930 (see Brazer, 1959). However, the classic paper which seems to have prompted the spate of following studies was that by Colm and his associates (1936). They examined the effects of population density, urbanisation, industrialisation and *per capita* incomes upon *per capita* municipal expenditures on highways, education and public relief in American states. The study concluded that increasing *per capita* expenditures were associated with all of these environmental variables. This approach was replicated on 1942 data by Fabricant and Lipsey (1952), and on 1952 data by Fisher (1964). Both of these studies also found that, using multiple regression models, population density urbanisation and *per capita* incomes were positively associated with a range of *per capita* expenditures. However, it was also observed that over this twenty-year period, the explanatory power of the environmental variables (as measured by R^2 values) declined considerably. Sacks and Harris (1964) hypothesised that this progressive decline in explanatory power was a consequence of the increasing importance of federal aid to local governments, and when this was included as an explanatory variable, the R^2 values for total expenditures, and highways and welfare expenditures increased considerably.

Quite apart from compounding dependent and independent variables, the Sacks and Harris study would seem to suffer from the same deficiencies as other studies of this type at this time (e.g. Brazer, 1959; Kurrow 1963): namely, a lack of any rigorous theory to explain these patterns. Indeed, Colm and his associates argued that their 1936 study did not establish whether increased expenditures in highly urbanised, densely populated, high-income areas were due to either greater *needs* in these areas, increased *demands* for more services, greater amounts of *resources* to meet either the needs or demands, or increased *costs*. Although Fabricant and Lipsey claimed that income was the most important environmental variable, for 'any given level of income (or density) even fairly pronounced differences in degrees of urbanisation are associated with only slight differences in *per capita* expenditures' (Fabricant and Lipsey, 1952:127) – their study, like the majority of empirical studies by urban economists in the 1950s and early 1960s, did not answer the questions posed by Colm. Thus, it is perhaps not surprising that Fisher (1961), when commenting upon the decline in the explanatory power of his environmental variables, called upon political scientists to explain these results.

In fact, throughout the 1960s and 1970s there was a considerable amount of quantitative comparative analysis of local government undertaken by political scientists in North America. Most political scientists adopted what could be loosely described as a 'systems' approach, following the fashion set by Easton (1957). A system is usually defined as an integrated group of interacting elements or variables designed to perform a particular function. The local political systems outlined in Chapter 1 may thus be regarded as the group of functionally interrelated variables whose task is to allocate resources. The general framework that has been adopted is similar to that outlined by Dawson and Robinson (1963), which is reproduced in Figure 2.6. Moving from left to right across the diagram, it may be seen that the political system is seen as a major 'filter' through which needs are perceived, forming a key intervening variable. However, the model also allows for the possibility of external conditions affecting outcomes directly. It also incorporates feedback since the nature of public policy at any particular point in time should have a subsequent effect on environmental conditions which, in turn, should affect the political process and public policy.

In practice most of the quantitative studies by political scientists have been static and cross-sectional in character. One of the first of

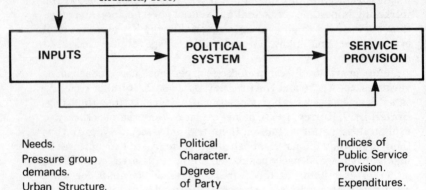

Figure 2.6 A model of the local government system (After Dawson and Robinson, 1963)

Needs.	Political	Indices of
Pressure group	Character.	Public Service
demands.	Degree	Provision.
Urban Structure.	of Party	Expenditures.
Size of	Competition.	Physical
Authority.	Bureaucratic	Indices.
Rateable Value.	Influences.	

these studies was that undertaken by Wood (1961) in which he examined the behaviour of the numerous local governments in metropolitan New York. His broad 'challenge–response–consequence' approach is similar to the 'inputs–political-process–outputs' framework, and Wood placed great emphasis upon the difference between the environment as may be measured and the environment as perceived by local politicians. He illustrated this difference with case studies of the various strategies employed by municipalities in New Jersey to change their environment. However, there were no variables explicitly measuring the political process and, despite his theoretical outline, his work must be regarded as similar to that of the economists noted above, albeit with a wider range of environmental variables.

One of the first papers which did explicitly introduce political measures was that by Dawson and Robinson (1963). They tested the hypothesis that the degree of competitiveness amongst political parties had a positive impact upon the extent of expenditure on welfare policies by American states. This hypothesis was derived from the work of Key (1949), who argued that since politics was a struggle between the 'haves' and the 'have-nots', the degree of competition between parties was important for the way in which it forced parties to become organised in order to implement reform policies. This view was derived from observation that welfare policies were better provided in the southern states of America, which had competitive party systems. Dawson and Robinson found that indices of party competitiveness were associated with higher expenditures on a range of welfare services, but were also related to a number of environmental variables including wealth, urbanisation and industrialisation. However, when they attempted to control for these environmental variables, the results suggested that the correlations between inter-party competition and welfare policies were a result of *per capita* income and its relationship with inter-party competition, rather than the effect of competitiveness *per se*. The similar studies by Hofferbert (1966) and Dye (1966) also corroborated the fact that political variables did not intervene between the environment and expenditures in the American states but were, like the expenditures, the result of environmental factors (see also Dawson, 1967; Dawson and Gray, 1971).

These negative findings understandably provoked responses from other political scientists. It was suggested that political factors *were* important but not in the manner in which they were measured in these studies. Jacob and Lipsky (1968) argued that many of the most significant features of the local political system were not incorporated into these studies. Sharkansky and Hofferbert (1969) collected a larger number of variables reflecting political influences and public outputs, and did manage to correlate their political factor with welfare and education policies, after controlling for their socio-economic factor. Political dispositions seemed unimportant, however, in the case of highways and natural resources expenditures. Fry and Winters (1970) devised measures of the net redistributive impact of tax burdens and expenditures across income classes, and found that redistributive policies were explained by political rather than socio-economic factors. This prompted a formulation from Booms and Halldorson (1973) which, the authors claimed, raised the explanatory power of socio-economic variables as determinants of redistributive policies. Yet again, Uslander and Weber (1975) argue that political variables have much to offer as explanations of welfare policies.

Despite such exchanges, much of the momentum began to disappear from inter-state comparisons in North America in the early 1970s. This may have been prompted by a recognition of the diminishing marginal returns with each further outputs study. The status of these papers was also damaged by a series of critiques which revealed some fundamental methodological and conceptual limitations. Many concluded that the work of political scientists did not make the way in which environmental inputs were translated into policies any clearer than the work of economists had done. (These weaknesses are considered in detail below.)

British comparative studies
Ironically, just as quantitative comparative studies began to decline in the United States they were beginning to gather pace in Britain. Once again the methodology and terminology were heavily dependent upon Easton's systems framework. In essence, it is assumed that the role of local authorities is to respond to the need or pressures generated by the local environment, but that the nature of this

response is determined by a number of other factors.

Elected councillors are in constitutional terms the final decision-makers, and a number of writers have asserted that their attitudes are an important determinant of policies and service provision levels (Boaden, 1971; Davies *et al.*, 1971). More specifically, since local councils in large urban areas are usually dominated by the major national political parties, Labour and Conservative, it is argued that the party which has overall control will have an important impact upon policy outcomes. The argument suggests that the broad outlines of policy will be inspired, as at the national level, by the broad class divisions represented by these parties. Thus, Labour-controlled councils, deriving their support from the working classes, should administer policies which will assist the poorer sections of the community and are therefore more likely to spend additional sums on redistributive local services. In contrast, the Conservatives, deriving their support mainly from the more affluent middle-class sections of society are, the argument proceeds, less likely to engage in relatively large expenditure; but in the interests of local ratepayers are more likely to keep public spending to the minimum possible. These two broad orientations to public policy correspond with the ideologies of the two parties – the Labour Party favouring public provision and the Conservative Party placing greater faith in the ability of the private sector to allocate resources. This is sometimes termed the *adversary model*, in which a political party proceeds to implement its policies whatever the margin of its electoral success (Johnston, 1979). Clearly, in the British context ideological cleavages between the major political parties would seem to play a much greater role than in the United States. Although the Democratic Party has been generally more in favour of welfare expenditure, attitudes towards the private sector are not polarised in the manner they frequently appear to be in British local politics.

However, a number of writers have disputed the line of reasoning described above. They argue that, while the distinction between the Labour and Conservative Party may affect the postures made in council debate, in practice, as at the national level, political parties have relatively little effect upon levels of service provision (Griffiths, 1966). Numerous arguments have been forwarded to support this view; these include the fact that both major parties are committed to the concept of the Welfare State (an argument which perhaps needs revision in the light of Thatcherite policies), the fact that central government plays an important role in monitoring and maintaining local authority standards, and the increasing importance of professionalism in local authority departments. Indeed, it is a view held by a number of writers on local authority affairs that local governments are mere 'agents' of central government (Green, 1959; Robson, 1966). This, it is claimed, is the consequence of the increasing financial dependence of local authorities upon central government, and the fact that the latter has, since the Second World War, made increased efforts to scrutinise local government behaviour. Usually allied to such claims has been the attitude that these developments are undesirable since they are deemed to have eroded local initiative and democracy. By implication these authors assume that local political parties are powerless to intervene with any major effect upon local policies.

Financial considerations might also suggest that political dispositions are relatively unimportant, for in relative terms local authority expenditures display little variation from year to year. This inertia arises because of the nature of the budgetary process which has been described in detail by Wildavsky (1964). He shows that budgeting is a highly incremental and conservative process which takes place in an environment dominated by constraints. Existing obligations have to be met each year which tends to leave participants with relatively little room for manoeuvre. Consequently:

> The largest determining factor of the size and, context of this year's budget is last year's budget . . . The budget may be conceived as of an iceberg with by far the largest part below the surface outside the control of anyone. (Wildavsky, 1964:13.)

While capital outlays by local governments may vary enormously from year to year, there is frequently relatively little leeway for changes in revenue expenditure, apart from general increases in overall levels due to inflation. Existing employees have to be paid on nationally agreed scales and loan charges on existing debts must be met (Oliver and Stanyer, 1969). From the viewpont of political representation this means that, even if an authority changes political hands there is frequently little that can be done in any radical manner to affect overall expenditure levels.

Another argument which would tend to undermine the value of political control as an important explanatory variable is the view that the degree of marginality of the council will affect the receptivity to needs within an area. It is argued that, in an attempt to gain political control, each political party will listen intently to the demands and preferences of the electorate and formulate policies accordingly. This line of reasoning suggests that political instability does not frustrate attempts to meet local needs, while stability and one-party domination does not necessarily enhance the differences in receptivity to local needs. In other words it is quite possible for a stable, one-party majority to be comparatively apathetic and irresponsive rather than rigorously pursuing policies in keeping with its own ideological stance.

The most developed form of this *vote-buying* model is that put forward by Downs (1957), as outlined in the first chapter. The Downsian model is based on the simple assumption that politicians are primarily interested in staying in political office. Hence they formulate policies to win elections, rather than win elections to implement policies. It is also assumed that the voter will cast his vote for the party which he or she believes will provide more benefits than any other. In order to win office and stay in power, politicians will therefore promulgate policies which they feel will win the maximum votes. The logical consequence of this is that policies will converge towards the mean, and towards the desires of the average voter. Since the poor are more numerous than the rich, redistributive policies might be expected in a competitive political environment. An obvious flaw in this argument is that deprived minorities might be neglected by the demands of a relatively affluent middle-class majority upon whom politicians target their policies.

Whatever the perceptions and attitudes of local councillors, it is frequently asserted that their ability to enact policies will be dependent upon a number of other factors. Prominent amongst these factors have been the advantages conferred by a large *population* size (Davies, 1968). Amongst these supposed advantages are the ability to administer large indivisible resources which can only be provided economically to large populations; the ability to provide specialised services and staff; more effective planning; and the ability to attract staff of high calibre (Davies, 1972).

Such arguments were important in leading to the reform of the English and Welsh local government systems in 1974, but they are also the source of some of the most severe criticisms of the new system. Indeed, it can be suggested that few arguments are likely to gain as much widespread popular support as the idea that large local governments are bureaucratic, inflexible and insensitive to individual needs. Thus one finds frequent assertions that smaller authorities enable councillors and permanent officials to be in close contact with the needs of individuals. It is also argued that the problems of internal communication both within and between local authority departments are increased in large authorities (James, 1966).

Often implicit (and sometimes explicit) within the arguments supporting relatively large local authorities is the assumption that such units will possess greater *resources* to finance their activities. This, it can be suggested, is an important determinant of service provision levels and the extent to which local needs are met. Certainly the main source of revenue in Britain – rateable values – shows considerable variations in *per capita* values among local authorities (Oliver and Stanyer, 1969), and studies have found an inverse relationship between the level of local resources and the rate of tax, known as the rate levied, or poundage (King, 1973). This suggests that relatively poorer authorities have to make greater efforts to meet their obligations and that variations in wealth are a strong possible influence upon service provision levels. However, the issue is complex because in Britain about 50 per cent of local authority spending is now financed directly by central government. This central funding has numerous objectives, but one of the most important is to compensate poorer authorities for their relatively small rate-base. Thus, to argue that the level of internal resources possessed by an authority is an important influence upon service levels is to incorporate the assumption that central government funding is ineffective in overcoming inequalities in local wealth. If this is not the case then, as King (1973) suggests, the high rate poundages in areas with poor rateable values may be a reflection of a desire to obtain higher standards, rather than a reflection of the ineffectiveness of central government policies in wealth equalisation.

Results from British comparative studies
As in the case of American studies, British output studies have produced a complex set of regression and correlation coefficients which make comparisons difficult; but it is possible to extract some general conclusions.

Most attention has focused upon the impact of party control upon spending levels. This is usually measured by the proportion of seats held by the Labour Party. The rationale for concentrating upon the Labour Party lies in the fact that the Labour/others dichotomy is considered to be the most important one, since many independents and members of Ratepayers Associations have views which accord more closely with the Conservatives (Alt, 1971). There are, in fact, relatively few independent councillors in the major British cities. The focus upon the number of seats held rather than some binary measure of whether a party has political control is justified on the grounds that the stronger the nature of the control, the more support the policy is likely to have from local inhabitants, the longer the party is likely to have been, or will remain, in power, and the easier it is for the party to implement its policies.

Table 2.5 is an attempt to summarise some of the main findings from the early outputs studies regarding the influence of Labour control on *per capita* expenditures. These studies focused almost exclusively upon results from the English county boroughs in the 1950s and 1960s. Although the strength and character of the results varies with the variables and methodologies employed, overall, there is a high degree of consistency which would seem to support the adversarial model. Even when controlling for indices of needs and local resources, Labour Party strength appears to have a positive independent effect upon *per capita* expenditures on education, housing and local welfare services. These are services which affect particular subsections of the population and have a potentially redistributive effect. These characteristics, together with their relatively high cost, and the availability of private sector alternatives in certain instances, make them politically sensitive. In contrast, services such as parks, libraries, refuse, fire and sewage which affect

Table 2.5 Some results from British 'outputs' studies

Study	Services upon which Labour control has a positive impact
Alt (1971)	Expenditures on: education child care local health authority housing (revenue account)
Boaden (1971)	Expenditures on: education health services children's services Percentage of housing built by council Level of rate subsidy to housing account
Danziger (1978)	Expenditure on: secondary education primary education Council housing rent subsidies
Davies, Barton McMillan and Williamson (1971)	A variety of indices of expenditure and service performance amongst services for the elderly
Davies, Barton and McMillan (1972)	A variety of indices of expenditure and service performance amongst services for children
Pinch (1978)	Rate of council house building and renovation in London boroughs
Pinch (1980)	Expenditure on domestic helps, and health visiting for London borough No. of persons visited by health visitor or served with meals-on-wheels in London boroughs

all the population are not significantly different between Labour and Conservative cities. Boaden (1971) and Alt (1971) also found that Labour strength was negatively associated with *per capita* expenditures on police services. This again can be explained by the ideological cleavages of the parties, the Conservatives being more in favour of the preservation of law and order and the status quo.

The major exceptions to these findings are the studies of Nicholson and Topham, which examined housing (1971) and roads (1975). When reduced to essentials, their analysis revealed that investment in houses and roads was primarily determined by social conditions in the authorities – the extent of poor housing and rush-hour congestion – such that the political complexion of authorities was not important in either case. The discrepancy with the other studies is no doubt explained by the fact that they were dealing with capital rather than revenue account expenditures. Whereas the latter reveal relatively small variations from year to year, the former are subject to considerable yearly fluctuations as various building projects are implemented. Variation also results from central government's use of loan sanctions to regulate the economy. For these reasons Nicholson and Topham used capital expenditures averaged over a decade, and it may be this fact, combined with central government intervention, which undermined any political association in this case. Political variables were in fact given relatively low priority in these studies, in each case comprising no more than 2 of the 37 independent variables.

The vote-buying model and the impact of marginality has been subject to much less analysis in Britain. A typical measure of marginality is that used by Alt (1971) in his study of county boroughs. The index was constructed by subtracting from 50 the differences between 50 per cent and the total percentage of seats on the council which are held by the Labour Party. In simplest terms the index is designed to measure the extent to which the percentage of seats held by the Labour Party is close to 50 – a situation of maximum competitiveness between the parties with a score of 50 (i.e. 50 – (50–50)). Total control brings a score of 0 (i.e. 50 – (100–50)), while percentages of 30 and 70 produce identical competitiveness scores of 30.

Alt (1971) found that his marginality index had an effect upon *per capita* expenditure on education, housing and children's services, but generally this variable was not as important as the impact of Labour Party control. Danziger (1978) and Ashford, Berne and Schramm (1976) also found that marginality indices were relatively unimportant in county boroughs.

The influence of local authority size has proved much more intractable. The idea that large local governments could take advantage of scale economies in the provision of local services was one of the arguments used for the reform of the British local government systems in 1974, and the Royal Commission on local government established studies to investigate these matters. Gupta and Hutton (1968) investigated the impact of various measures of size and scale upon cost per unit of output for selected local services, but with generally inconclusive results. Similarly, in Boaden's (1971) analysis, local authority population size was relatively unimportant compared with needs and party control, a finding replicated in most other British output studies (Alt, 1971; Danziger, 1978).

One major exception is the set of studies which have shown that size affects the scale and diversity of specialised services available to minorities with particular needs. There is some evidence that larger local authorities promote more specialised institutional care for children (Davies and Barton, 1968; Davies, Barton and McMillan, 1972) the elderly (Davies, Barton, McMillan and Williamson, 1971) and the mentally handicapped (Danziger, 1978). There is also evidence that smaller local authorities have greater difficulty in running an adoption service (because of a smaller range of potential adopters and the difficulties of maintaining confidentiality); that the proportion of teachers released for advanced training courses is reduced in smaller authorities; and that larger authorities find it easier to sponsor students on courses for health visitors, social workers, nursery nurses and workers in old people's homes. It appears from these results that below a certain size threshold there is insufficient scope or resources to provide more specialised services.

Newton (1974) draws attention to one other correlate of local authority size – *per capita* police expenditure. This is a finding which, curiously, has been somewhat ignored by those who have discovered it (Alt, 1971; Boaden, 1971; Danziger, 1978). Whether this results from increased costs in cities, or increased pressures upon the police through increased rates of crime and traffic management problems, is not clear.

The influence of local authority wealth is also difficult to untangle. Oliver and Stanyer (1969) found a positive association between Labour representation and the rate levied but attributed this to the fact that Labour control is generally stronger in areas where rateable values are less. As they found little association between Labour control and total rate receipts or current expenditure per head, they concluded that in order to raise roughly equal revenues in poorer areas Labour-controlled councils are compelled to levy high rates. The implication of this is that central equalisation schemes are inadequate in compensating local authorities for variations in levels of local wealth. However, using somewhat different data, Boaden's (1971) analysis did indicate that Labour control had an independent effect upon the rate levied, irrespective of local wealth. This might however, suggest a desire for higher standards rather than the inadequacy of equalisation schemes. In this context there are likely to be considerable variations between types of service. Alt discovered a negative correlation between local wealth and education spending, but when controls were introduced via partial correlations the greatest source of the variation was due to the positive association with Labour control (these also being the poorer areas).

Limitations of outputs studies

Generally speaking then, there is a somewhat inconclusive character to the early British outputs studies. They have revealed that, in sharp contrast to the United States, political measures do appear to have an important impact upon expenditures, as do socio-economic conditions or 'needs', but the influence of local authority size and local wealth is much less demonstrable. These results might be seen as important, but both the British and North American studies have been subject to considerable criticism which has undermined the value of their conclusions. Indeed, it can be argued that these criticism are more important than the substantive results of these studies and they are therefore considered in some detail here.

Low R^2 values

One of the most important criticisms has been the fact that the levels of explanation of these studies, defined in statistical terms of R^2 values, have often been extremely small. Admittedly, some of the R^2 values obtained in the regression equations constructed by American economists were initially quite large; Fabricant and Lipsey (1952) for example, obtained values as high as 0.85 (good by any standards in the social sciences). However, over the years there has been a progressive decline in the explanatory power of these studies. Furthermore, the high R^2 values were usually obtained when highly aggregate expenditure measures were the independent variables. When expenditures on particular services were considered separately it was frequently the case that there was a lack of consistency in the array of dependent variables associated with the expenditure variables. Consequently, levels of explanation were frequently small. Brazer was led to conclude that 'with multiple correlation coefficients ranging from 0·756 to 0·242 we know that important forces have been left out of our equations' (Brazer, 1959:31). Similarly, Fisher found an R^2 value of only 0·38 between welfare expenditures and income, urbanisation and population density (Fisher, 1962).

Low levels of explanation are also a feature of British comparative studies. It is important to remember that Boaden (1971) in his analysis of county borough expenditures found that most of the associations were extremely weak. Nicholson and Topham (1972) in their review of Boaden's work note that of 42 correlations relating to 'needs' and dispositions, 25 are less than 0·2 in value, and only 6 are greater than 0·3. No attempt was made to examine the statistical significance of the results or their combined explanatory power in terms of R^2 values. If the latter task had been undertaken in most cases over half of the variation in expenditures would have remained unexplained. Alt's (1971) results also led him to comment upon the poor explanatory power of his variables. Similarly, in their scrutiny of some of the causal factors which have been hypothesised to explain patterns of provision in children's services and local authority health and welfare services for the elderly, Davies and his associates were forced to conclude that the results were more valuable for showing which processes were relatively unimportant than for showing how processes compatible with the results operate (Davies *et al.*, 1971; 1972).

Reactions to these low explanation levels have varied considerably. Dearlove (1973) epitomises one school of thought when he claims:

> These findings point to a close relationship between certain socio-economic conditions and the form of public policies but they provide no clues as to how or why this relationship exists. If we are to deal with these questions (questions which lie at the heart of what most people understand by explanation) we need to move outside the framework offered by these models. (Dearlove, 1973:70.)

A more charitable view is provided by Davies (1975):

> The statistical modelling of the causes in variations in policy is still at an early and unsophisticated state of development. Although it has already yielded much in the area – as much as older techniques of analysis – its future contribution will be far greater. (Davies, 1975:78.)

This latter view argues that quantitative comparative studies are still in their infancy, and that through refinement of measurement and technique better levels of explanation will emerge. It is certainly important to recognise in this context that many of the important variables have hitherto been measured in only a superficial manner, and this is especially true of the concept of needs. Most North American studies have barely treated the issue of needs at all. The early studies of economists used only general environmental variables such as size, density and wealth which made it impossible to determine whether larger amounts of provision resulted from greater needs or larger amounts of resources. Fisher's (1962) study is typical of such work and he was forced to conclude that 'The analysis of course tells us nothing about the desirable levels of expenditures.' Most of the following studies by political scientists used environmental variables similar to those used by economists and similar criticisms apply.

Scant consideration of needs has also been a feature of British studies although in this case the criticism is not as universally applicable. Although in theory needs play an important part in the conceptual frameworks of Alt (1971) and Boaden (1971), in practice their studies are restricted to comparatively simple measures of population size and social composition.

The next step in the developmental sequence of the political complexion of the council has also been typically treated in a superficial manner. Newton and Sharpe (1977) observe that of the 30 or 40 variables typically used in outputs studies only a handful relate to political character. Amongst these variables they are particularly sceptical of the focus upon the proportion of seats held by the Labour Party. They argue that what is probably more important than the size of majority is the length of the Labour Party's tenure in office. This is important because policy changes take time and only when sufficient time has passed can one expect any major change of policy to reveal itself.

There is also a case to be made for focusing explicitly upon policies of Conservative-controlled councils who may be enthusiastic spenders on services necessary to maintain the prosperity of towns, especially seaside resorts and tourist centres. Given the intense competition amongst councils of all political colours to attract industry and employment at the present time, many Conservative-controlled councils may also display favourable attitudes towards expenditure on purely pragmatic grounds to attract and support private industry. The fixation upon the strength of the Labour Party has also led British researchers to ignore the importance of marginality and increased competitiveness upon expenditures.

Given the superficial manner in which needs and political dispositions have been measured, it is not altogether surprising to find that outputs have also often been measured crudely. Most North American 'expenditure determinant' studies have, as the name suggests, concentrated upon *per capita* expenditures rather than examining outputs in terms of the quantity and quality of public services (e.g. Adams, 1967). There are, in fact, sound reasons for this focus upon expenditures, for monetary measures are frequently an indication of the relative priority given to a particular service. Thus, Brazer (1959) points out he is interested in expenditures *per se* rather than the amount or character of the goods and services they procure. The early comparative studies by political scientists in the early 1960s in America and the early 1970s in Britain also focused almost exclusively upon relatively simple measures of output in terms of *per capita* expenditures.

In response to these studies Sharkansky (1967) argued forcefully that there need be no necessary correspondence between spending and physical levels of output. Furthermore, as Newton and Sharpe (1977) point out, even for broad departmental headings such as education or housing, the total budget is in many respects little more than an aggregate accounting device. Most of the operational units of local government operate at smaller levels than a whole department. Most controversial political issues revolve around particular institutions – closing a day nursery, opening a sports centre and the like – rather than broad expenditure decisions. In response to such criticisms the range of variable used by political scientists has increased. Walker (1969), for example, derived non-monetary measures of innovation in local authorities, while Fry and Winters (1970) devised measures of the net redistributive impact of tax burdens and expenditures across income classes.

Statistical deficiencies

Allied to the inadequate measurement of the key concepts has been the somewhat simplistic nature of the statistical techniques employed. Most studies have used multiple partial correlations or multiple regression models, but there is little recognition in these studies of the numerous statistical assumptions which must be satisfied in order to obtain reliable results (Poole and O'Farrell, 1971). Issues such as skewed frequency distributions, non-linear relationships and autocorrelated residuals are seldom, if ever, mentioned. This may reflect the relative inexperience of political scientists in using statistical techniques, and economists with their strong econometric tradition have a better technical 'track record'. It may also reflect the inadequacy of geographers in making clear the problems involved in using cross-sectional geographical data sets with complex spatial autocorrelation properties.

One of the most serious omissions from these studies has been any detailed consideration of the problem of multi-collinearity – the presence of strong inter-correlations between the independent variables. This has been a particular problem in British outputs studies, because high-need areas of poor social conditions tend to produce Labour Party control, relatively small *per capita* rateable values and high rate poundages. Conversely, Conservative-dominated councils tend to be associated with relatively smaller needs, greater wealth and lower rate poundages. When attempting to evaluate if party political control has any independent effect it is vitally important to control for other variables such as needs and wealth. Large correlations between supposedly independent variables can seriously upset this procedure because the least-squares estimation methods will then produce large mean-square errors and extremely unreliable regression and multiple partial correlation coefficients. This means that, at the very least, some of the results from outputs studies should be regarded with extreme caution.

Inherent limitations in quantitative comparative studies

One might conclude from the above comments that with more sophisticated measurements and refined statistical techniques considerable improvements in explanation levels will be obtained from outputs studies. Yet while there is undoubtedly room for improvement, it would also seem important to recognise that much of the variation in these studies will inevitably be difficult to measure because of two factors.

First, there are factors which vary systematically across all the local government areas under consideration but which cannot be measured in any detail (so that highly inaccurate surrogate measures are required) or else cannot be measured at all (and must in consequence be omitted from the analysis). Examples of this category include variations in costs between local authorities, the extent of professionalism in local departments and variations in pressure group activity. A second category comprises unusual local circumstances and factors particular to individual authorities which are further likely to increase deviations from predictable relationships when considering a set of local authorities. Examples of this second category include local staff shortages, financial problems and the influence of powerful local personalities.

A number of writers have recognised this second type of factor. Fisher (1962), when attempting to account for his relatively low levels of explanation, drew attention to the importance of what he termed 'individual type' factors and, similarly, Wood (1961) placed emphasis upon what he termed 'historical caprice' and 'random shocks' as determinants of local authority behaviour in particular areas. Sharkansky and Hofferbert (1969) also argued that a large proportion of the variation in quantitative studies would inevitably be difficult to explain because of the interaction of unique circumstances in particular political jurisdictions.

Additional problems are caused by the fact that, since both of these factors are either difficult or impossible to measure at an aggregate level, they are often confused in empirical studies. Boaden, for example, questioned the conventional wisdom that councillors make policies which administrators execute, instead asserting that permanent officials in the local authority bureaucracy have considerable scope to influence decisions (Boaden, 1971). It is further suggested that this degree of influence will be related to the degree of professionalism amongst the administrators, since this should affect the degree to which they wish their services to expand and develop. However, as Boaden notes, it is impossible to obtain accurate comparative information on the attitudes of local officials for a large set of local authorities. He is therefore forced to use as surrogates the number of committees and subcommittees, and whether or not the authority employs an operations and methods officer. These are at best extremely crude measures of the influence of local officials and have only tenuous links with what can be regarded as professionalism (which in any case would probably vary within separate departments of local authorities). At worst, these measures throw no light upon the validity of an initially promising hypothesis and it is not altogether surprising that these measures reveal consistently negative correlations with variables representing individual services.

The prime lesson to be drawn from such results is that when considering jurisdictional partitioning one should investigate problems relating to the broad structural characteristics of local authorities rather than to those characteristics which relate to individual decision-making. Just as certain phenomena are more amenable to observation at certain scales of analysis, so the factors which cause these phenomena are also amenable to observation at certain scales. Theories relating to the interaction of individuals are more likely to be useful in the study of particular decisions, whereas expenditures and broad patterns of resource allocation are the outcomes of numerous decisions (or non-decisions) and are more likely to reflect the impact of broader factors. This distinction is an important one and is similar to Alford's (1967) distinction between a 'decision' and a 'policy' (which involves numerous decisions). There is, of course, considerable overlap, for particular decisions can dramatically affect overall expenditure outcomes.

Given the above it seems inevitable that a large proportion of the variation in outputs displayed by local policies will be difficult to explain by the comparative approach. The only real solution to this problem would seem to lie in the integration of comparative studies of many local authorities with detailed case studies of individual authorities. As Davies (1977) points out, case studies have difficulties in relating events to their broader context, and the importance of many factors may become exaggerated. This fact is well demonstrated by Dearlove (1973) in his case study of Kensington and Chelsea. After a fierce attack upon the outputs approach he concludes:

> It would be foolish to claim that the borough is somehow typical of other local authorities, but at the same time unless the supposed criteria of typicality are clearly spelled out and comparison made with a specified number of local authorities, then it is not really possible to point to the typical and untypical features. (Dearlove, 1973:6.)

Case studies are therefore limited as a basis for broad generalisations about patterns of resource allocation; but, on the other hand, much of the diversity of local policy is lost in the broad measures. Case studies do, however, have the potential to unearth this diversity and the complex interaction among various institutions, organisations and personalities. Local governments vary enormously in character and style, and these variations cannot be related to crude factors, such as total expenditure or the proportion of seats held by one particular party.

If Boaden had seriously wished to investigate the influence of professionalism in local authorities, a more fruitful approach would have been to undertake a more detailed comparative analysis of a wider range of indices of standards of service provision, and on the basis of these results to have selected a number of detailed case studies for intensive analysis of the attitudes of local officials.

The relationships of outputs studies with theoretical perspectives
Much of the criticism of the outputs approach stems not only from low explanatory power in a purely statistical sense, but also from low levels of explanation in terms of an ability to integrate with major theoretical frameworks in the social sciences. Few of the

authors of outputs studies have cast their results in a broader
context but instead have produced a series of *ad hoc* rationalisations
for their numerous contradictory findings. How, then, do these
results integrate with the major explanatory frameworks outlined in
Chapter 1?

Not surprisingly much of the North American work on the effects
of jurisdictional partitioning has strong links with the dominant
public-choice paradigm on that side of the Atlantic. As Sharpe (1981)
observes, one of the assumptions of Key's model is that what
governments do is a reflection of the popular will. From this
perspective what is crucial to the effective working of the system is
the way in which the popular will is translated into politics and
policies. If this transmission process is defective because voters are
denied a realistic choice in an uncompetitive political environment
then their interests will not be met by the government. In this
context the socio-economic variables are commonly regarded as
surrogate measures of collective demand.

Here we should note a major conceptual inadequacy in practically
all outputs studies. Key's analysis assumes that political mechanisms
are ways of aggregating preferences, and in Dawson and Robinson's
model political variables are portrayed as major elements in the
system translating preferences or demands into policies or outputs.
This again implies the 'public-choice' market view of the public
sector, in which individual demands are one of the basic determinants
of public policy. According to this conceptualisation environmental
conditions are mediated by political variables (see model a in Figure
2.7). However, Key's model does not imply that political variables by
themselves should exercise some independent effect upon expenditures, yet this is the hypothesis which has been tested in practically
all the studies. This implies the rather different model b shown in
Figure 2.7. Since the majority of American studies have found that
political variables do *not* exercise an independent effect this has led
to the hypothesis that socio-economic conditions have some direct
effect upon outputs and expenditures irrespective of political systems
– the third possibility shown in Figure 2.7. This, in turn, has
prompted the near panic and intense effort to prove that politics is
important after all, but in a sense the search is somewhat fruitless
for it is based upon a mis-specification of Key's work (Hansen, 1981).
It thus leads to the somewhat implausible conclusion that environmental characteristics have a direct effect upon policy outputs; but
how can this occur without some form of translation through the
local political and bureaucratic system?

Hansen (1981) has put forward a method for escaping from this
apparent impasse:

> Rather than regarding socio-economic variables as causes of
> the decisions, it seems more reasonable to treat them as

Figure 2.7 Interpretations of the policy-making process in local government

MODEL A.

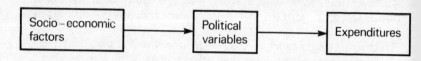

MODEL B.

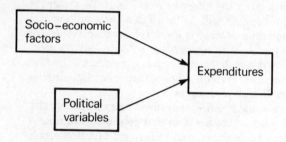

MODEL C.

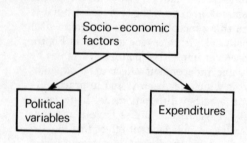

decision-making *criteria* upon which public authorities may act. It is important to notice the difference between a causal factor and a decision-making criteria. While a causal factor is automatically related to the effect variables, the relationship between a decision-making criterion and the decision has to be *established* by the decision-making body. In other words, the decision-makers select the criteria upon which the decision is going to be based, and this selection process will be determined by the political values of the decision-makers. (Hansen, 1981:31; author's emphasis.)

The major limitation of the outputs approach, then, is that by virtue of its method it treats much of this complex process as a 'black box' and produces results which are not ambiguous in terms of the major theoretical perspectives. Thus, it is difficult to evaluate whether a strong association between social conditions and expenditures denotes:

1 the effectiveness of local politicians in responding to local needs (either as a result of a response to local demands or the imposition of policies based on their own political ideology – or some interaction of the two); or
2 the power of local bureaucracies in overriding political ideologies and ensuring uniform patterns of service response; or
3 the ability of central government to impose uniform standards across local governments.

In the British context however the frequent lack of association between social conditions and outputs, and the powerful 'independent' effect of Labour Party control at any given level of need and local resources does enable some positive conclusions of theoretical value. Although the results are now commonly accepted they have served to dispel the long-held view in many quarters that British local governments have become mere agents of central government. They have shown that neither increasing central intervention in local government, nor the growth of professionalism in local authority departments has eradicated local autonomy to the extent of producing uniform expenditure responses to local conditions.

These are, however, conclusions derived from work undertaken in the 1960s and 1970s and may need revision in the light of Thatcherite policies in the early 1980s. The implications of these developments for future studies are discussed in Chapter 6.

3 Externalities, locational efficiency and conflict

Introduction

In this chapter the analysis shifts to the intra-authority scale to examine the distribution of services *within* local government units and administrative boundaries. Although, once again, a wide range of services are considered, they are linked by the common theoretical concept of externalities. Put simply, an externality is an unpriced effect. It may be a benefit received by those who do not pay for it or a loss incurred by someone who is not compensated (Margolis, 1968). If someone gains this is known as a *benefit, utility* or *positive externality*; conversely, if someone loses this is known as a *disbenefit, disutility* or *negative externality*. These external effects are also sometimes termed spillovers or third-party effects. Such unpriced effects can emerge in the spheres of both production and consumption. The positive externalities derived by industries agglommerating in large centres are of course one of the main reasons for the growth of cities during the Industrial Revolution. The classic example of a negative side effect in the sphere of production is the air pollution which may emerge from some industrial processes. Similar effects can emerge in the realm of consumption through the exhaust emissions of automobiles. Much of the political conflict in cities can be interpreted as disputes over the distribution of externality effects.

Since a pure public good is defined as one which, if available to anyone, is available to all others at no extra cost, then clearly, it represents an extreme case of an externality. As stressed in Chapter 1, however, in reality the influence of space means that public sector goods become impure in character. The concept of externalities is therefore largely geographical in character. All activities must take place at a specific location and the side effects of these activities will therefore emanate from these locations to affect the surrounding areas. It is likely that these external effects, whether positive or negative, will be more intensively experienced close to the source of the activity than further away. The most obvious example is that of noise. Figure 3.1 shows the degree of noise generated by a football match which is perceived as a nuisance by residents surrounding

Figure 3.1 A spatial externality field: the perception of match-generated noise surrounding The Dell, Southampton.
(Source: Humphreys, Mason and Pinch, 1983)

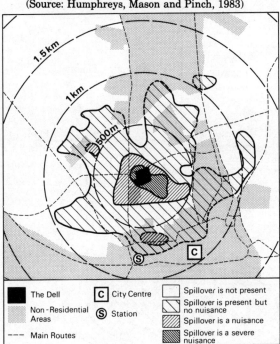

Southampton Football Club's ground. The closer to the ground, the louder the noise and the greater the intensity of nuisance, although the prevailing south-westerly wind appears to affect the intensity of nuisance. Such externalities thus exhibit 'distance decay', and may be envisaged as extending in a 'spatial field' as represented in Figure 3.2.

The bulk of the literature on externalities has focused on those activities which display negative externalities such as noise, smell pollution and traffic congestion. Activities which produce such disbenefits are often termed 'noxious' facilities and include industries, airports, motorways and refuse tips. However, many facilities, especially in the field of collective consumption, have desirable properties which benefit those who are closest to them. Such facilities, which typically include parks, hospitals, schools and sports facilities, are often termed 'salutary' facilities.

The reasons that individuals closest to salutary facilities benefit most were made explicit by Losch (1954). He noted that the total cost of a good to a consumer will depend upon two factors: first, the price of the good at the source of supply; and second, the costs incurred by an individual in travelling to the source of supply. In general

Figure 3.2 A diagrammatic representation of distance-decay effects and spatial externalities

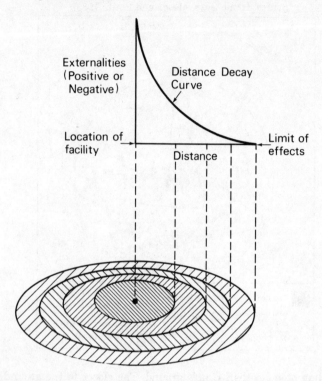

transport costs tend to increase with distance so that those further away will incur greater costs. This leads to the formation of a price funnel as shown in Figure 3.3a. The law of demand suggests that, as the price of an item increases, so its rate of consumption decreases. This means that individuals operating within a fixed budget constraint must either consume less of a good and/or, visit the source of supply less frequently. The spatial expression of this is the demand cone as shown in Figure 3.3b. Ideally, there will be a point at which the individual cannot afford to purchase the item and this defines the range of a good. These increased costs are sometimes termed 'tapering effects', and apply to goods and services supplied by both the private and public sectors. Even if the good is provided at no cost at the point of supply, distant consumers with a limited budget will obviously incur greater costs. Those closest to desirable facilities will therefore gain a benefit for which they have not paid and in these circumstances accessibility produces a form of positive externality.

There is now a substantial body of literature which emphasises the importance of distance-decay effects on human behaviour. For

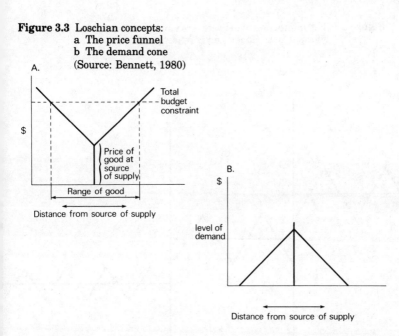

Figure 3.3 Loschian concepts:
  a The price funnel
  b The demand cone
  (Source: Bennett, 1980)

example, those who live furthest from doctors' surgeries are less likely to arrange for a consultation during times of illness or medical emergency (Ingram, Clarke and Murdie, 1978). Similarly, Kirby (1979) discovered that the school in Newcastle which was least accessible to its pupils had the highest rates of non-attendance.

If, as in the case of emergency services, the facility is delivered to the consumer, greater costs are incurred by the provider of the service in reaching more distant locations. Furthermore, the quality of the service is likely to diminish in these distant locations; it would for example take the ambulance, fire engine or police car longer to respond to an emergency call. It may be recalled that one important criterion defining a pure public good is non-rivalness, or joint supply, which means that if a good can be supplied to one person it can be supplied to all others at no extra cost. Irrespective of whether the consumer travels to the service, or the service is delivered to the consumer, the effects of distance serve in both cases to undermine the assumption of non-rivalness.

These *within*-area externality effects will interact with the *between*-area levels of resource allocation which were described in the previous chapter. Figure 3.4 is an attept to represent such interactions graphically with a hypothetical example. The bold horizontal lines show the average level of resource allocation to a particular service within three differing political jurisdictions. The broken lines represent the various gains and losses to households at various distances from these facilities.

Figure 3.4 The interaction of between-area and within-area externality effects. (After Honey and Sorenson, 1984)

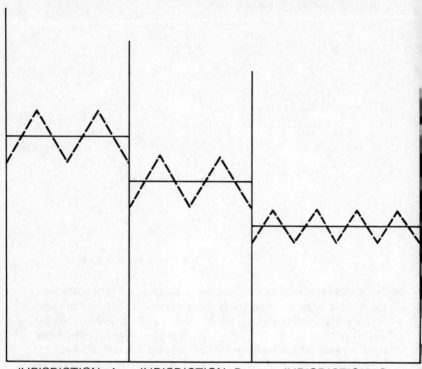

JURISDICTION A.   JURISDICTION B.   JURISDICTION C.

During the early 1970s there were a number of attempts to link both accessibility to desirable facilities and proximity to undesirable facilities within the broad framework of externality theory (Harvey, 1970; Cox, 1973). As stressed in Chapter 1, Harvey's paper was probably the most influential. He argued that the net effect of all the costs and benefits emanating from positive and negative externalities could be aggregated to form a measure of 'real income'. However, work on positive and negative externalities has tended to exist in separate schools of analysis, the former concentrating on locational efficiency and the latter on locational conflict. Each of these types of approach is initially examined separately.

Tapering effects and the locational efficiency approach

The study of accessibility has a relatively long history and involves a basic geographical problem: given a set of individuals or households located at various points across a plane, what is the point at which a facility can be located in order to maximise its accessibility to the surrounding population? This is the problem which appears in various forms in the classical location theories of Von Thünen Christaller (1966) and (Alfred) Weber (1929), since these are, in essence, distance-minimisation models. They are, however, primarily concerned with aspects of production and consumption in the private sector and, as we have seen, it is only comparatively recently that location theorists have directed their attention towards the positioning of public facilities.

The simplest way to measure accessibility is to note the number of areas in a city, the centroid of which lies outside a certain threshold from a facility. This threshold can be measured in terms of physical distance, or else the time or cost involved when travelling by a particular mode of transport. Figure 3.5 demonstrates this approach in the case of playgroups in Southampton. These facilities provide day-care for children below the age of five and are organised on a voluntary basis by committees of parents. Delivering a child to a playgroup is typically the responsibility of the mother, and this is often done on foot since the family car if there is one is usually monopolised by the father in order to travel to work. Mothers with young children are therefore amongst the most immobile sections of society and even small variations in the location of facilities can affect their degree of use. Various threshold distances were considered but eventually half a mile was considered to be the maximum desirable limit. There are, thanks to the activities of the Pre-School Playgroups Association, a wide spread of playgroups in the city and only 49 of the 450 enumeration districts lie outside the threshold distance. Generally the newer peripheral housing estates are less accessible to playgroups than the older inner-city areas. However, given the tendency of playgroups to cluster in the older parts where there happen to be suitable premises such as church halls, the least accessible areas just happen to be in the 'watersheds' between these clusters. Further analysis revealed that these inaccessible areas have relatively little in common in terms of housing and social composition.

A similar approach is to calculate the number of opportunities, or facilities of a particular type within a certain distance, time or cost range (Knox, 1980). Such measures could include: the number of job opportunities (if any), and the number of services available – such as shops, cinemas and the like – together with measures of open space, parks and playing fields. As with the previous approach, this type of analysis can be refined to develop better measures of facility size. Thus, as well as the presence of a facility, one can note the number of places available, hours of opening, number of staff employed, the quality of premises and many of the numerous measures of service quality noted in Table 2.1 of the previous chapter.

Figure 3.5 The distribution of enumeration districts whose centroid lies more than half a mile from a playgroup, in Southampton. (Source: Pinch, 1984)

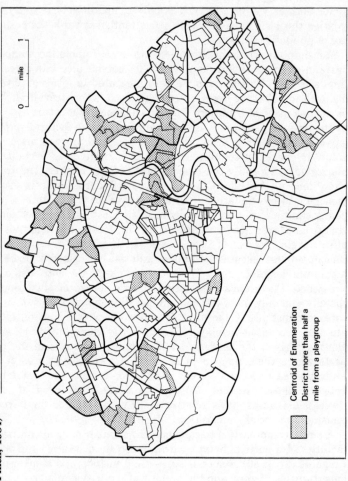

Centroid of Enumeration
District more than half a
mile from a playgroup

However detailed are the measures of facility size, a major limitation of this threshold approach is that it does not take into account the tapering or distance-decay effects noted earlier. Most movement in cities, whether temporary or permanent, does not decline as a simple function of increasing distance but often displays an initial sharp decline with distance, and then a more shallow slope. The technical name for this is a negative exponential function. This friction effect of distance must be balanced against the greater attractiveness of many larger facilities.

The model most commonly used to incorporate the counteracting effects of distance and facility size is, of course, the gravity model. When restated as an accessibility index this model typically looks as follows:

$$Ai = \sum_{j=1}^{N} \left(\frac{Sj}{Dijk} \right)$$

where
A   is a measure of the accessibility of area i
Sj   is the size of the facility in area j
Dij is the distance between areas i and j
k   is the distance decay function

The sophistication of this model will obviously be affected by the way in which each of these elements in the model is constructed. For example, the distance-decay function can incorporate indices of time or cost rather than physical distance. In addition, mode of transport is a critical factor affecting the degree of mobility amongst various social groups. Thus what may only take a few minutes in a car can often take hours by public transport. Indeed, in their study of access to dental facilities Bradley, Kirby and Taylor (1978) found that, on average, travel time by car was 4.75 times the physical distance; while travel time by bus was on average a ratio of 14.5 times the straight-line distance to facilities. The measure of accessibility was therefore weighted according to rates of car ownership, incorporating measures based on travel speeds by car and public transport. This produced an index with the following form:

$$Ai\ (t) = C_1 \left(\frac{Ai}{Tc} \right) + (100 - C_1) \left(\frac{Ai}{Tp} \right)$$

where
Ai (t) is a time-based accessibility index for neighbourhood i.
Ci   is the percentage of car-owning households in the neighbourhood i.

Tc   is the average time taken to travel a given distance
      by car.
Tp   is the average time taken to travel a given distance
      by public transport.

This accessibility index was then weighted to take into account the
varying numbers of persons living in different neighbourhoods.

The amount of variation displayed by the accessibility values can
provide a measure of the degree of equity in the relative levels of
accessibility to service provision. The lower the coefficient of
variation in the accessibility index, the greater will be the equity of
accessibility to services. The overall efficiency of the system can also
be described in terms of aggregate travel distance by consumers of
the service.

$$E = \Sigma \left(\frac{Ai\ (t).Mi}{Mi} \right)$$

The larger the value of E, the less the amount of distance travelled
by consumers and the greater is the overall efficiency of the system.

Accessibility indices can be useful not only in assessing the degree
of equity or efficiency in existing distributions of facilities but also
for evaluating the impact of differing locations for new facilities.
However, realistic evaluations of alternative locational strategies
soon generate conceptual and computational problems of enormous
dimensions. As Teitz (1968) was amongst the first to point out, these
complications are especially acute in the sphere of public services. In
this context one is typically not concerned with the locational
efficiency of an isolated facility such as an office or shop, but with a
set of public facility centres, as in the case of schools, libraries and
fire stations. Given a limited budget constraint, complex decisions
have to be made about the number and size of facilities judged
against the average distance that consumers or service delivery
vehicles must travel. Clearly, there may be a conflict between a
strategy of providing a large number of small decentralised facilities
close to consumers offering a limited range of opportunities,
compared with a policy of concentrating a wide range of resources in
large centres which in aggregate are more distant from the public.

The complexity of these problems has led to the growth of a vast
number of sophisticated mathematical allocation models (see Hodgart,
1978). These models involve various types of optimisation criteria
and, as in the case of territorial justice evaluation described in
Chapter 2, these raise complex ethical as well as technical issues. A
choice may have to be made between choosing the location which
maximises the aggregate travel distances of all individuals in the
area under consideration, balanced against the choice which reduces
the longest journey of any consumer to the minimum. To review

these methods in detail would require a book in itself, but enough has been presented to indicate the tremendous potential of the approach in assisting public decision-making. The crucial point is that the values implicit within the various optimisation criteria be made explicit. As will be shown in the conclusion to this chapter, however, the spatial efficiency approach has been subject to enormous criticism in recent years.

Spatial externalities and the locational conflict approach

Most of the work concerned with spatial externalities has examined the shape and impact of the resulting externality fields. In many respects this work has not proceeded as far as other areas of public policy analysis, but the bulk of literature does permit a number of generalisations.

First, the character and size of the externality field will depend upon the type and size of the facility. All things being equal, the larger the facility the greater the intensity and extent of the external effects should be. To take an obvious example, a major international airport is likely to generate more noise than a small provincial runway. On the positive side, it can be expected that the larger the area of open space or parkland the greater will be the impact upon the property values of surrounding districts.

The character of the facility will also affect the shape of the distance-decay curves of the externality effects. For example, traffic noise is often intense close to a road but falls off rapidly with increasing distance. In a similar manner it may be that only those properties directly overlooking an area of public open space have substantially increased desirability and that the positive externality effects upon house-values fall off rapidly with distance from the park. Such cases would create a steep distance-decay curve as shown in case a in Figure 3.6 (see also Dear, 1976). In other situations it is conceivable that externality effects are a simple function of distance as shown in case b. Probably more common, however, is case c shown in Figure 3.6, in which there is a negative effect in the immediate vicinity of a facility due to traffic congestion, parking difficulties, or noise; but an increase in property values in the surrounding area. Thus, many wish to have a fire station, ambulance service, school or police station in their neighbourhood, but not directly on the street in which they live.

A further complication is that a single facility may emit various types of externality effects. We have already seen the extent to which noise from football games is perceived as a nuisance by residents surrounding Southampton Football Club (Figure 3.1). There are, however, also other side effects from football grounds which have differing levels of intensity and extent. These results in

Figure 3.6 Various types of spatial externality effects

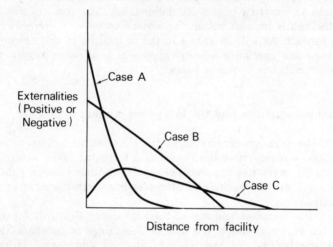

Externalities
(Positive or
Negative)

Distance from facility

various types of externality field are shown in Figure 3.7. Case a shows the nuisance field of parked cars. Like many British football clubs, Southampton is located in the middle of a relatively high-density residential area. The ground was built in 1898, before the widespread growth of the automobile – indeed the original site had extensive parking for bicycles – and there is little provision for parking today. The parked cars nuisance field displays no simple distance-decay pattern, however, because there is a match-day 'no parking' rule close to the ground. This fact, combined with a residents' parking scheme close to the ground which ensures that residents are guaranteed a parking space in their street – means that it is only at some distance from the ground that parked cars belonging to football spectators represent a severe nuisance. These areas are particularly concentrated to the west of the ground, and are largely comprised of terraced houses without garages where residents must park their cars in the street. Since there is no Residents' Parking Permit Scheme (unlike areas at a similar distance to the eastern side of the ground), these western residents have no guaranteed parking space, and frequently find it impossible to park in the street where they live.

The traffic nuisance field is, as might be expected, the most extensive negative externality field (see case b) whereas the pedestrian nuisance field (case c) is much more restricted and declines relatively sharply with increased distance from the ground. The latter has a pronounced north-south pattern which reflects the main routes to and from the railway station. Finally, case d of Figure 3.7 shows the intensity of 'hooliganism' perceived as a nuisance by residents. This includes a range of behaviour ranging

Figure 3.7 Types of spatial externality fields surrounding The Dell, home of
Southampton Football Club, Southampton:
a The parked cars nuisance field
b The traffic nuisance field
c The pedestrian nuisance field
d The 'hooligan' nuisance field
(Source: Humphreys, Mason and Pinch, 1983)

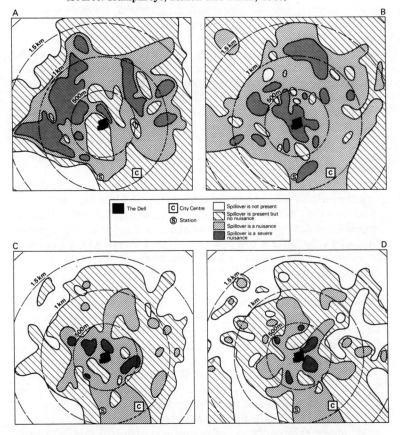

from verbal abuse, damage to property and physical assault. This
nuisance field is closely related to the pedestrian nuisance field, but
is less distinct. The intense policing in the immediate vicinity of the
ground creates a 'shadow effect' protecting local residents, but
'hooliganism' appears to be a significant nuisance along the routes
taken by visiting supporters to their coaches or to the railway
station and is often the result of Southampton supporters 'baiting'
the visiting fans. It should be noted that, despite the considerable
press coverage given to hooligan behaviour, this was not the major
problem in the eyes of most respondents. Overall, traffic congestion

is perceived as the main problem. The major conclusion which can be drawn from this example is that a single externality field can mask a complex set of external effects.

It is also possible for a single facility to have both positive and negative external effects. Airports are an obvious example, for they can generate noise, which is resented by those living in the flight path of aircraft, but can also create employment, which is welcomed by many. Similarly, roads generate social costs in terms of noise and pollution for those living nearby, but often have benefits for other areas in terms of the greater access they promote. Finally, not all the external effects of football grounds are negative. Local traders, shopkeepers and publicans together with transport firms are likely to experience a considerable increase in trade on match days (although many forego this additional business by closing early because of the fear of shoplifting, vandalism or physical assault from football spectators). Football clubs also generate a considerable amount in the local economy through their purchases from catering firms, printers, sports equipment retailers and the like, as well as their contributions to local taxes through rateable values – although this is partially offset by the extra policing required outside football grounds which is paid for by the local authority. Less tangible, but arguably no less important, is the sense of civic pride and prestige that a successful team can generate. Indeed, it has been argued that by enhancing the image of a town a successful football club can be of help to local authority industrial promotion efforts.

It would also appear that a team's success can have a positive psychological effect upon a city's residents. Derrick and McRory (1973) investigated the effect of Sunderland Football Club's surprise Cup Final victory in 1973 on the people of Sunderland, and found that there was reduced absenteeism at work, less problems of crowd control at football matches, and an improvement in the local self-image of the town. Clearly, some of these positive externalities of football grounds will be highly localised near the ground while others will extend over a much wider area.

The above remarks lead to the next point, which is that the extent to which an externality is positive or negative will largely depend upon the perceptions of the individual. People will obviously value things like noise, employment and traffic congestion in different ways, and this heterogeneity of community values will obviously complicate efforts to generalise spatial externality fields. Thus, attitudes towards football-generated activities may depend upon the degree of hostility or enthusiasm felt towards football in general: the cheers of crowds may be noise for some but music to the ears of others!

Attitudes towards externalities would seem to depend in large measure upon whether or not the individual makes use of the facility generating the effects. It may be a considerable saving in transport costs and hence a strong benefit to have a facility nearby for the user, but if the facility conflicts with the lifestyle of surrounding non-users it may be a source of negative externalities for other residents. A common complaint from mothers in many new British housing estates is the lack of areas in which young children can play, yet the location of such areas can be highly controversial. Older residents, or those younger households without children, often dislike the sound of children at play; although again there is frequently a diversity of opinion, since some elderly persons claim to like the sounds emanating from playgrounds.

In an attempt to clarify such conflicts Dear (1976) makes a distinction between 'user-associated' externalities and 'neighbour-hood-associated' externalities. In a series of papers with numerous co-authors he has examined the impact of community-based mental health facilities in North America (for the most comprehensive treatment see Dear and Taylor, 1982). These facilities can be of considerable benefit to the user since modern psychiatric techniques enable mentally-ill persons to live in the community and avoid incarceration in large psychiatric hospitals. These effects may be termed 'personal-user externalities' since they affect the individual. They can, of course, be negative since there is a stigma attached to the use of many welfare institutions. Other externalities may affect the user but their effects lie outside the individual. Whatever the benefits to patients, it is clear that many of the non-users of community local mental health facilities perceive these as noxious facilities. In one of these studies the effects upon property values, traffic congestion, and the aberrant behaviour of users of the facilities were amongst the greatest fears of non-users (Dear, Taylor and Hall, 1980). However, it is important to stress that these negative sentiments were confined to a relatively small area within one block of the facility; beyond six blocks there was a much more tolerant attitude. Furthermore, the majority of residents interviewed were relatively favourably disposed towards the facility, and the hostility was confined to a vocal and somewhat unrepresentative minority. It should also be noted that other work has failed to confirm the negative impact of community-based mental health facilities either upon overall property values or the number of property transactions (Boeckh, Dear and Taylor, 1980).

These complexities raise many issues for further analysis, but one of the most pressing needs is some evaluation of the collective impact of these externality effects upon various social groups. However, as in the case of outputs studies, one of the major problems confronting those who wish to establish generalisations about intra-city patterns of resource allocation is the sheer diversity of the case studies that are available. Once again, many of the studies have been undertaken in apparent isolation from major theoretical developments, or else have some under-developed theoretical structure which is only implicit within the approach. The separation of the locational conflict and locational efficiency schools has only served to intensify these problems.

In broad terms two types of allocation patterns have been suggested. The public-choice theories outlined in Chapter 1 suggest that many different outcomes are possible as a result of conflicts over the location of both desirable and undesirable facilities. Nevertheless, with the state acting as a neutral referee, the net result will *not* be to the overall favour or detriment of any one particular group, and should be more or less random. In sharp contrast, Harvey (1970) suggested that the net outcome of all the costs and benefits emanating from positive and negative externalities – what he termed 'real income' – would be to the overall benefit of the more affluent.

The pluralist approach: an evaluation

Before assessing which of these patterns is most common in Anglo-American cities, we should note at the outset the near impossibility of assessing the pluralist approach within its own terms since it is based on an almost irrefutable set of assumptions. Pluralists have argued that public policies will reflect public preferences because: the stronger are the feelings of a group of individuals about their interests the more likely they are to take action; the stronger are these feelings the stronger the political actions will be; and the stronger these political representations the greater the likelihood that politicians will respond. In the context of the terminology established in previous chapters, this means that the pluralist approach focuses exclusively upon the voice option and individuals 'expressed needs'. This conforms to the old American adage that 'the squeaky wheel gets the grease', or in other words 'those who shout the loudest receive the most'. This is a commonly held and widely approved view of the way in which the American – and to a lesser extent the British – local democratic systems operate.

This approach assumes that within a pluralist society composed of many complex groups, political conflicts will *not* reflect the broad economic divisions between major classes. Society is seen to comprise many shifting and non-overlapping groups who come together to petition over many different and complex issues. Thus, a hypothetical citizen might be a member of a trade union lobbying for more jobs to boost the local economy, a member of a local neighbourhood organisation resisting residential development or a new road, and a member of a local group attempting to keep a school in the local area. The pluralist approach assumes that these complex groupings will not have any overall class bias, and that all such organisations have an equal ability to influence the outcomes of local government.

Much of the appeal of the pluralist approach would seem to stem from the fact that it highlights one of the most important and noticeable developments in Western cities since the Second World War – the proliferation of pressure groups. In Birmingham for example, Newton (1976b) found no less than 4,250 formally organised voluntary associations with interests related to local government activity, and noted that further research would have undoubtedly unearthed more groups. Numerous typologies have been constructed to classify these groups depending upon the range of their interests and their form of organisation. Some groups are continuously active in representing the interest of their members whereas other 'cause' groups may exist for a relatively short period to resist a certain development proposal or petition for a new facility. The groups also vary in the extent to which their interests have some identifiable geographical focus. Nevertheless, these groups share in common a formal structure of office holders, including a chairman and secretary, and – with the exception of certain trade unions and professional organisations – a voluntary membership. The vast majority of these organisations are politically inactive (Newton found that only 30 per cent of the 4,250 formally organised voluntary organisations claimed to have been politically active in the previous twelve months) but those which do exert pressures in a typical city still constitute a large number.

Inequalities in political resources
From the point of view of service provision the most immediately obvious limitations of the pluralist approach is that it ignores the widely differing political 'purchasing power' of these various pressure groups. It would appear that it is often the more affluent and better educated sections of society who are able to organise themselves more effectively to get their demands met. As Kirk (1980) points out, in Britain in the field of planning there are many organisations such as the County Landowners' Association, the National Farmers' Union, the road transport lobby, the construction lobby and the National Association of Property Owners, who although they are small in size, have considerable financial resources to make representations at both local and national level. Generally speaking, such organisations will have more resources than those groups representing the poorer sections of the community.

However, it is not only money which is of use in influencing the political system: knowledge, professional expertise and organisational ability are also crucial to enable a pressure group to get its message across to decision makers. These factors go some way to explaining why small amenity groups, bent on the conservation of older buildings or the environment, and with their articulate middle-class membership (many with professional contacts) – can have such an important effect upon planning policy. These organisations tend to make representations in ways which are regarded as legitimate by local councillors and officials: they typically have a formal committee structure and make their demands through acceptable channels such as petitions and lobbying. In recent years many such groups have also learned how to use the mass media to good effect.

Lowe (1977) notes that such organisational resources are frequently to be found in abundance in what he terms 'local environmental pressure' groups or 'amenity societies' concerned with protecting and enhancing the environment and accessibility of an area. He quotes one survey of Yorkshire amenity societies which revealed that 62 per cent of societies could call upon more than six different skills from the following list: teacher, architect, historian, lawyer, financier, planner, surveyor, estate agent, journalist, archaeologist, youth leader and forester. Furthermore, only 13 of 40 urban-based societies and 3 of 11 village-based societies could call on neither architectural nor planning skills, the majority of societies being able to combine both of these professional talents.

Newton's (1976b) study of voluntary organisations in Birmingham also demolished the pluralist assertion that political resources are equally distributed between groups. The middle- and upper-income professional and trade organisations tended to have more financial resources and better organisation. Furthermore, there was no evidence for the pluralist assertion that each group produces its own opposition thus promoting a system of 'checks and balances'. Newton found that amongst 100 issues of pressure group interest only in 3 cases were groups aware of any opposition. This does not of course mean that there was no opposition but if it was widespread, effective and likely to produce an equality of outcomes, one would have expected local groups to have some knowledge of their opponents.

Saunders (1979) gives a good example of a well-organised, largely middle-class organisation in the London borough of Croydon that mounted a most effective campaign for a day-nursery in an area of low provision. Saunders notes how, despite numerous demonstrations, the organisers managed to achieve a careful balance between conciliation and coercion. In particular, they were careful not to employ any tactic which could have been defined by the local council as irresponsible or illegitimate. Thus, all the protesters sat quietly through the council debates and behaved in a good-humoured manner in all their demonstrations. Newspaper reporters were on hand to record the presentation of a bouquet of flowers and a petition to the new lady mayor by the three-year-old daughter of one of the campaigners. Undaunted by earlier defeats, the protesters maintained their pressure for a nursery with the added support of a survey of local residents which demonstrated the need for day care in the area.

In marked contrast, many deprived groups with limited resources are unable to get their objectives into the political arena for debate.

This is especially true of those community-action groups seeking a redistribution of resources in favour of poorer areas. In Birmingham, for example, Newton found that the interests of the coloured population were under-represented at local political level. Such groups may often have widespread local support, but a lack of organisational structure, finance and professional organisation can prevent effective campaigning. If such groups are forced to resort to 'militant' tactics, such as demonstrations, their actions can easily be labelled as 'subversive' by local councillors and the press.

In Croydon Saunders noted many such campaigns. In 1969 the council reduced its contributions to a variety of voluntary organisations, a policy which prompted an *ad hoc* amalgamation of many left-wing groups in opposition. However, disruptions to council meetings and ejections from the council chamber did not endear the cause of the group to either the council or the press. Similar protests have arisen over the years in response to increases in council rents and the extent of homelessness in the borough, but once again all disruptions were easily labelled as illegitimate and undeserving of serious attention.

The attitudes of local councillors
These examples reveal that it is not only the amount of financial resources, organisational abilities or the nature of political representations which determine the effectiveness of local pressure groups but the attitudes of local councillors to the issue in question. This fact was underlined by Dearlove's (1971) examinations of the relationship between interest groups and local councillors in the inner-London borough of Kensington and Chelsea – a high-need but Conservative-controlled, non-marginal seat. The chairman of the council claimed that his main aim was to cater for the 'needs of the ratepayer' by keeping public expenditure to the minimum possible. Consequently, the council encouraged those voluntary pressure groups which emphasised collective self-help, thereby reducing demands upon the public purse and at the same time ignoring those groups whose demands would imply additional expenditure. Newton (1976b) observed a similar relationship between the city council and certain voluntary pressure groups in Birmingham. He concluded that, in effect, many of the groups were being exploited by the council to the extent that they were undertaking functions such as welfare provision, which would otherwise have been the responsibility of the local authority, at considerable saving to the council budget. Dearlove did not examine the impact of these attitudes on policy decisions but further analysis has shown that, in keeping with many other Conservative-controlled London boroughs, Kensington and Chelsea tend to provide below-average levels of public housing and personal social services, given its level of needs for these services (Pinch, 1978).

It is not only Conservative-controlled councils which can resist pressures from the local populace, as Dunleavy (1977) demonstrated in his study of the Labour stronghold of Newham. Following the collapse of one of the borough's twenty-four-story high-rise blocks at Ronan Point in May 1968, a pressure group from the Beckton area of the borough collected signatures for a petition against being rehoused in the new high-rise flats. Despite 700 signatures, the council refused to discuss the issue with the protest group until after an inquiry had been held. This inquiry eventually proposed substantial alterations to building methods in order to increase safety standards in high-rise blocks; but in spite of this the council went ahead building high-rise blocks, albeit with reduced numbers of storeys. It was only after this decision was taken that the chairman of the Housing Committee agreed to meet the Beckton residents to 'explain the position'. There followed a protracted series of meetings and escalating demonstrations, which were all doomed to failure since the key decisions had already been taken. Public meetings demonstrated the intense hostility of many residents to the high-rise blocks, but since they were faced with little choice the residents reacted to the council's immovable position with attitudes of despair.

Such studies have undermined the pluralist's portrayal of the local state as a passive receiver of demands from the electorate and a neutral arbiter of competing interests. Indeed, the pluralist claim that local governments are weak units without any developed sense of ideology is simply not justified by the evidence. It is clear that many social groups and especially poorer working-class organisations, have relatively little power in relation to the local state. It cannot therefore be assumed that those who make no representations towards the political system are satisfied with their position because of an underlying consensus in favour of existing institutions. What the pluralist framework ignores is the fact that many groups may not participate, either because they lack the resources to do so effectively or else because they feel their views will not be recognised as legitimate. Thus, as revealed by the Dunleavy study, although high-rise blocks seem to have been universally unpopular in Britain in the 1960s, there has been little effective opposition to their construction given the enormous coercive powers of slum clearance in the hands of the local state.

A similar difference between official policy and public attitudes exists in the context of pre-school provision in Britain. Studies have shown widespread support for more extensive day care facilities for children below five (Bone, 1974). However, these views contrast sharply with those of the two main central government departments responsible for pre-school services, the Department of Health and Social Security, and the Department of Education and Science; their view is that children under three should not be separated from their mothers, and then for only a few hours each day (Pinch, 1984). Despite considerable strength of feeling in favour of more pre-school services, mothers lack sufficient purchasing power both of an economic and political kind to attain their objectives. Looking after young children is typically a time-consuming, exhausting and isolated activity which tends to inhibit collective organisation for political ends. In this context it should be noted that, although eventually successful, the day nursery campaign in Croydon made little impact upon the overall low level of service provision in the borough. Indeed, it could be argued that this campaign was successful at the expense of others in more needy but politically disorganised areas.

The pluralist faith in the political accountability engendered by periodic elections is also open to serious question. The percentage of the electorate who bother to vote in British and American local government elections is typically quite low, averaging at about 40 per cent (Newton, 1969). Although local issues and local personalities can have an important impact upon electoral outcomes, there is now overwhelming evidence that local elections in Britain are determined largely by national events. In particular, popular disquiet with the central government of the day is registered in local elections. It is not therefore the activities of local politicians which are primarily being judged.

Following from the discussion in Chapter 1, it might be argued that the pluralist approach is most applicable in the American context, where it originated, since it more accurately typifies the enormously complex and vocal set of interested groups making demands at various levels of government; and where, unlike in Europe, issues are less focused around broad class lines. However, once again recent studies would tend to undermine this view. For example, Jones and his associates (1980) undertook a detailed analysis of a variety of public services in the Detroit area. One of their main observations was the absence of organisational activity concerned with service distributions. There was sporadic activity by community and neighbourhood groups, but sustained pressure of the type that would be necessary to explain service outcomes was not observed. Furthermore, as will be discussed later, there is also evidence that American interest groups exhibit a middle- and upper-income bias.

The major limitation of the pluralist approach then, is that in assuming that political inactivity implies consensus, it focuses only upon those issues which lead to overt political controversy. As Bachrach and Baratz (1970) point out, power can often be exercised by excluding certain issues from the political agenda. This, they argue, is part of the 'mobilisation of bias', the manipulation of public opinion by powerful interest groups to divert demands which would undermine the status quo. Thus, it is not only the actions of governments but those things which they fail to do – the so-called 'non-decisions' – which determine 'who gets what'. Furthermore, it would appear that some powerful interest groups can exert their influence in a covert manner through informal contacts with decision-makers, without resorting to explicit petitioning. Studying what fails to happen does, of course, present numerous methodological problems but the importance of these criticisms is clear in the case of public services. Not only are many of the key decisions taken away from the public view, but it is also the failure to provide services which is as important as their actual distribution.

Yet within its own terms the pluralist approach fails to address these questions, since it is assumed by definition that policies will reflect preferences. What the approach lacks is any theory of ideology to explain why people come to believe what they do. Saunders in fact argues that pluralist approaches are not theories at all:

> It is not therefore surprising to find that representational approaches have no theory of ideology since they are themselves ideological. They provide not an explanation of political processes but a description couched in terms of the system itself – a description which necessarily justifies whatever processes they find. At a theoretical level, therefore, there is no way in which criticism can impinge upon them, for alternative theoretical perspectives will always be dismissed as utopian or metaphysical, as bearing no relation to the 'facts'. (Saunders, 1979:156.)

Despite much previous criticism, we have again examined the pluralist approach at some length because of its enormous influence upon previous work, and because the weaknesses of the approach have important implications for future studies. Ideally, we should look at the net effect of *all* positive and negative externalities upon communities irrespective of the degree of overt political controversy they have engendered. Such a task is of course impossible in any comprehensive manner, but we need to move beyond those issues which have led to overt political conflict. Nevertheless, provided we bear in mind the caveats noted above, we can examine the distribution of conflicts in cities to see which issues have most often come into prominence and which groups have been most powerful in attaining their goals.

The collective impact of tapering effects in cities

Where private markets predominate one can be reasonably certain that the more affluent groups in society will gain maximum advantage from externality effects. In the case of private housing for example, higher income groups will use their greater purchasing power to bid up the cost of housing in areas where there are numerous desirable positive externalities such as open space, low densities, clean air, little traffic congestion and low crime rates. Indeed, Harvey (1970) suggested that the stability of social areas in cities is enhanced by social segregation designed to protect external benefits and to eliminate as far as possible external costs. Shopping facilities will also tend to gravitate towards those areas where purchasing power is greatest. Thus, the decentralisation of the more affluent groups in American cities has been associated with the widespread growth of out-of-town shopping centres. This pattern is also under way in Britain, albeit heavily constrained by the system of land-use planning.

In North America health care is also largely based upon free-market principles, and doctors are mostly influenced in their choice of location by the *per capita* incomes of the areas they serve (Shannon and Dever, 1974). The overall pattern is one of under-supply in the deprived and high-need inner-city areas and concentration around the affluent white suburbs. The pattern is also modified by the availability of certain facilities, including office space and specialist hospital facilities which leads to a focus around major centres of commercial activity in the suburbs. Such patterns have led one British doctor to propound the so-called 'inverse-care law'.

> In areas with most sickness and death, general practitioners have more work, larger lists, less hospital support, and inherit more clinically ineffective traditions of consultation, than in the healthiest areas, and hospital doctors shoulder heavier case-loads with less staff and equipment, more obsolete buildings, and suffer recurrent crisis in the availability of beds and replacement staff. These trends can be summed up as the inverse-care law: that the availabiity of good medical care tends to vary inversely with the need of the population served . . . The force that creates and maintains the inverse-care law is the operation of the market . . . The more health services are removed from the force of the market, the more successful we can be in redistributing care away from its natural distribution in the market economy (Tudor-Hart, 1971:412).

Since these private market allocation mechanisms can be assumed to be generally regressive in terms of their income distribution effects, it is in those cases when the public sector intervenes, either to provide services directly, or else to regulate the distribution of private facilities through land-use controls, that we can, in theory, expect to find distributions favouring the most disadvantaged groups in society.

Doctors, chemists and dentists

The impact of such intervention has been evaluated in the context of health care facilities in Britain (Knox, 1978). Before the inception of the National Health Service the distribution of health care facilities in Britain was not unlike that currently to be found in American cities. However, in 1948 Medical Practices Committees were established with the aim of eliminating the maldistribution of doctors. Areas were classified according to the average number of patients on the doctors' lists, and a system of controls and financial incentives attempted to steer new practices towards the 'under-doctored' areas. This policy brought about a dramatic and rapid redistribution of manpower, but in recent decades there has been something of a reversion back to the pre-1948 pattern. A number of factors have been responsible for this – not the least important of which have been the restrictions on the total numbers of doctors available. Although the absolute levels of GP provision are higher than in the days before the National Health Service, doctors are most attracted to the more affluent 'southern' areas of Britain. Consequently, many of the high-need northern and industrial areas are relatively disadvantaged in terms of medical personnel.

Knox (1978) also examined the distribution of doctors' surgeries at the intra-urban scale. Four Scottish cities were used as the basis for the analysis – Aberdeen, Dundee, Glasgow and Edinburgh. The details of the patterns varied between the different cities but there was no universal evidence for the inverse-care law. In fact, surgeries tend to cluster around the older residential areas of Scottish cities, many of which are adjacent to deprived inner-city areas. One of the major factors accounting for this pattern seems to be a locational inertia of doctors which tends to discriminate unsystematically between various types of housing in the inner city. However, it was also clear that there were relatively few surgeries on the new peripheral housing estates both in the private and public sectors. When models of accessibility took into account the varying rates of car ownership between the working-class and middle-class outer estates, it became clear that the former were relatively disadvantaged in terms of access to doctors' surgeries. Although no statistical evidence was produced by Knox to confirm the issue, it can reasonably be assumed that many of these peripheral working-class estates are some of the areas with the highest rates of mortality and morbidity and in consequence there is a high need for medical care. Given the strong evidence for the effect of increasing distance upon reducing consultation rates there would seem to be a strong case for the redistribution of doctors' surgeries at the intra-city scale.

Another important link in the health care system is the retail pharmacy, which not only dispenses the medicines prescribed by doctors but also serves as a source of first aid and informal professional advice for minor illnesses (Knox, 1981). Once again, it is likely that those who are least accessible to chemists will utilise their services less often in times of need. Although allocated by the private sector and therefore dictated largely by market forces, the location of retail pharmacies is also dependent upon the location of doctors' surgeries. Since the majority of individuals wish to obtain medicines from the nearest available outlet, most chemists in urban areas have attempted to locate in a position which will give them a local monopoly over an area and at the same time be close to a general practitioner who is making prescriptions. Traditionally this has resulted in a highly dispersed pattern of outlets but in recent years there has been a shift towards larger chain stores and cut-price shops which have reduced the numbers of small independent chemists. The tendency for doctors to locate in group practices has also encouraged this trend. The net result of these processes upon the distribution of chemists in Edinburgh is that once again it is the working-class public sector estates on the outskirts of the city who are most disadvantaged in terms of access (Knox, 1981).

Another service which has been studied at the intra-city level is dentistry. Bradley, Kirby and Taylor (1978) examined spatial variations in the need for dental treatment amongst children in a sample of schools in Newcastle, and correlated this variable with the distribution of public sector dental facilities in the city. Studies at the national level have shown that middle-class children tend to have higher levels of dental health than their working-class counterparts – a finding which appears to be related in part to the greater knowledge of middle-class parents concerning issues of dental health and their greater likelihood of ensuring that their children use dental facilities. However, none of the national studies has examined the impact of accessibility upon differential utilisation patterns of dental facilities between various social groups. The Newcastle study revealed wide variations in the need for dental care – as assessed by the School Dental Service – between different school catchment areas, but instead of social class the variable most significantly correlated with need was access to dental facilities. Those areas with on average a higher percentage of children with better teeth were more accessible to dental facilities. In this study the social class variables were mostly unimportant in explaining variations in the need for dental treatment, but the authors note that this finding does not contradict previous studies at the national level. Indeed, this study provides an excellent example of the way in which geographical 'scale' or the level of analysis can influence the results that are obtained and the nature of the processes observed. School catchment areas in Newcastle tend to group together districts with similar levels of accessibility (in technical terms this variable exhibits positive spatial auto-correlation) and by the same token tend to blur social class differences. The nature of the spatial aggregation inevitably emphasises accessibility rather than class.

Aggregate accessibility patterns in North America

Despite the vast number of case studies of different types of service facility location in cities, there are few studies which have examined the collective impact of a wide range of services in a city. One notable exception is Knox's (1982) study of Oklahoma City in which he examined access to ambulance services, banks, community centres, day nurseries, elementary schools, fire stations, general medical practitioners, golf courses, hospitals, libraries, managerial jobs, post offices, public parks, service jobs, unemployment offices and department stores. Various multi-variate techniques were used to relate the spatial variations in accessibility to these services with the social geography of neighbourhoods within the city. The poor inner-city areas were characterised by below-average incomes, poor housing, high levels of unemployment, high proportions of the elderly and single-parent families and low levels of car ownership and educational attainment. One inner-city district had high levels of accessibility to employment and public parks concentrated near the city centre, but very poor accessibility to community centres, libraries, hospitals and ambulance services. Other adjacent areas with similar but less extreme levels of deprivation were also deficient in terms of access to health-care facilities and community centres. The black ghetto area had relatively high levels of accessibility to public parks but poor accessibility to elementary schools, community centres and health-care facilities.

Surrounding these inner-city areas were various types of more affluent suburbs. As might be expected, these areas tended to have higher degrees of accessibility to the decentralised facilities including general practitioners, hospitals, ambulance services and golf courses but were poorly placed in relation to many other types of facility near the city centre such as service jobs, public parks, and shopping opportunities. One suburban area, characterised by average levels of income, did not enjoy accessibility to any of the services examined and was significantly deficient in terms of accessibility levels to elementary schools, post offices, libraries and community centres.

This study serves to emphasise the way in which the differing organisational structure of American health care leads to differing patterns of accessibility within the city compared with Britain. Whereas policies of urban containment combined with locational inertia have led to concentrations of doctors and hospitals in the older parts of British cities, the widespread decentralisation of facilities in America has led to greater access to health care in the suburbs. However, the most remarkable feature of the Oklahoma study is the fact that, despite the widespread decentralisation of people, jobs and shopping facilities, the suburban areas were less accessible to facilities than much speculative writing would lead one to suppose.

The collective impact of negative externalities

Establishing generalisations about the differential impact of negative externalities and noxious facilities upon various social groups in cities is also made difficult by a large number of case studies which have focused upon isolated conflicts. By definition, the locational conflict approach examines those issues which have aroused political controversy and there is an absence of information about the overall distribution of negative externalities in an urban environment. The distribution of these externalities at any point in time will reflect the outcome of many previous conflicts. Thus, some areas will inevitably have larger proportions of those activities, such as industries, roads and commercial activities, which generate negative side effects. The advantages conveyed by agglommeration economies led many industries to concentrate near the centres of cities during the early years of their growth and, despite the recent decentralisation of employment in both British and American cities, many of these inner-city areas still have large amounts of activities which can have a detrimental effect upon surrounding areas. However, the extent to which such negative externalities lead to overt political controversy can be envisaged as the result of two other factors: first, the extent to which areas are undergoing change of an existing or proposed nature; and second, the attitudes of the local inhabitants to these changes. Each of these factors will now be considered in turn.

The impact of environmental change
Changes, either of an existing, proposed or anticipated character, can result from two basic processes. The first pattern is one in which the social structure of an area remains reasonably stable over time but the pattern of land use is undergoing change. It may be that either a completely new type of activity is proposed in an area or else that the scale of an existing activity is modified. This contrasts with a second approach in which the pattern of land use remains reasonably constant over time but the social fabric of an area changes and the new inhabitants object to certain aspects of the environment. This second process can in theory take place either if the area increases in status (a process sometimes termed 'gentrification') and the new middle-class inhabitants object to certain features of the environment, or else if the area declines in status and the new lower-class population again finds some aspects of the neighbourhood which are in conflict with their life styles.

In some cases it may be that it is both a changing population and changing physical environment which leads to conflict, but the bulk of evidence that is available would suggest that land-use changes are most important. Clearly then, it is in those areas of the city which are undergoing the most rapid physical change that, all things being equal, we can expect to find the greatest local conflict.

In this context it is worth drawing attention to the work of Janelle and Millward (1976) for, rather than focusing upon single issues, they examined the spatial distribution of all locational conflicts in the city of London, Ontario in Canada, as reported by the local newspaper in a single year. On the basis of their analysis they produced a tenfold classification of conflict-generating issues: redevelopment; preservation; transportation; housing; noxious encroachments and nuisance necessities; public services and utilities; retailing; schools; recreation; and cultural issues. The authors argued that there were two basic conflict-generating forces which were likely to lead to conflict over these issues in particular neighbourhoods of the city: first, regional growth processes leading to urban expansion; and second, structural ageing leading to environmental deterioration and obsolescence. This suggests that locational conflicts 'characterised by a strong spatial bias to the arguments advanced by conflicting participants' (Janelle and Millward, 1976:102) should predominate on the urban periphery and in the inner-city areas, which are experiencing the most rapid change.

Janelle and Millward examined the intensity of conflict by the number of column inches which the issues generated in the local newspaper and plotted the results against increasing distance from the city centre (see Figure 3.8). The results broadly confirmed their initial hypothesis. In general, conflicts are most intense in the inner-city areas, and reportage declines rapidly to a distance of 2.5 miles from the city centre, only to increase again towards the urban periphery. Conflicts were pronounced in the inner areas being redeveloped or not possessing the full range of modern urban amenities, and in the new suburbs where there was a time lag in the provision of services. Certain types of conflict were most prevalent in certain zones. For example, redevelopment and preservation conflicts occurred almost exclusively within two miles of the city centre, whereas schools and recreation issues were dominant in the two- to three-mile zone. Beyond three miles conflicts over the provision of public services and opposition to noxious and nuisance-generating facilities were much in evidence in the new suburbs. Housing and transportation issues exhibited a bi-modal distribution similar to the overall pattern of conflicts with peaks in the transition-zone areas and towards the urban periphery.

There is no comparable analysis for a British city but it seems highly likely that an examination of newspaper articles would reveal similar patterns. In the Southampton city region for example, the early 1980s have revealed a number of major locational conflicts. In what might be regarded as the 'outer city' – the new commuter settlements surrounding the older part of the city proper – a major concern of existing residents has been to prevent excessive growth of new housing. This has led in many cases to considerable local opposition to the proposals for urban growth incorporated into the

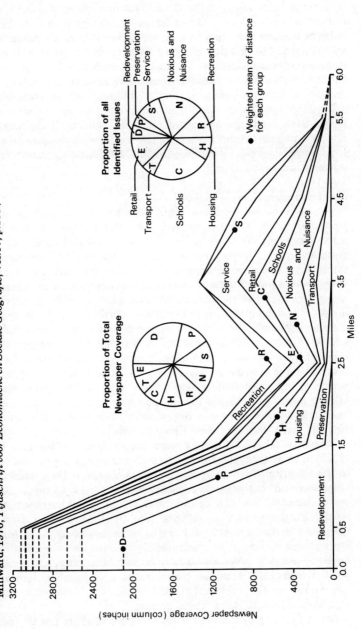

Figure 3.8 Cumulative graph of conflict intensity with distance from city centre, London, Ontario, 1970-72. (Source: D.G. Janelle and H.A. Millward, 1976, *Tijdschrift voor Economische en Sociale Geografie*, vol.67, p.108.)

South Hampshire Structure Plan. This is despite the fact that, in overall terms, the growth proposals are relatively modest, still preserving large areas of the Green Belt and effectively containing the urban environment. Other issues which are dominant in the suburbs include: attempts to increase services on new estates; local opposition to the creation of gypsy sites; traffic congestion; and the nuisance effects of facilities such as local authority incinerators. In the inner-city areas population decline rather than growth is a key feature of the environment, and a different set of issues have dominated newspaper headlines. Amongst the most contentious issues have been: the closure of inner-city schools in the wake of falling numbers of school children; the lack of maintenance on some local authority housing estates; the failure of housing improvement schemes; and vandalism.

Local attitudes to neighbourhood change
The extent to which these physical changes will lead to overt political conflict will also depend upon the attitudes of the local inhabitants to these changes. This was revealed strikingly by Goodman and Clary's (1976) study of community responses to aircraft-generated noise around Los Angeles International Airport. Only about a half of those respondents who expressed some degree of annoyance with jet noise actually took part in political activities aimed at reducing the amount of noise. Furthermore, there was no simple relationship between the degree of exposure to noise and the extent of their political activism: it was not the case that those communities closest to the airport protested most. In effect, a complex set of attitudinal variables were found to influence political activism, but important amongst these was socio-economic status. Higher status individuals were more likely to feel that the airport authorities lacked a sense of responsibility to surrounding communities and were therefore more likely to protest.

Somewhat similar findings were reported by Taylor and Hall (1977) in their analysis of the factors affecting response to road noise in the Hamilton-Toronto area of Southern Ontario. They found that respondents of higher socio-economic status tended to report being more disturbed by both specific and overall neighbourhood noise levels. Furthermore, respondents who had taken some form of complaint action against road traffic noise tended to be of higher socio-economic status as measured by income or education. The authors note that, given this bias in complaint activity, it is doubtful whether complaint activities can be taken as a reliable measure of annoyance as they seriously under-represent disturbance levels, especially amongst lower status groups.

Given that higher income groups are more likely to use the 'noise' option, the representativeness of local residents' organisations is perhaps questionable in areas of diverse social structure. This point was emphasised by the Ferris (1972) study of pressure group activity in the Barnsbury area of Islington. This is an older working-class area of London which has experienced an influx of young professional workers. Ferris documents the way in which these newcomers formed the Barnsbury Association and successfully resisted the local plans for redevelopment, persuading the Council to instead adopt a scheme of general areal improvement and traffic management. Ferris argues that this pressure group represented the interests of the more affluent and vocal minority and pursued policies which ran counter to the interests of the working-class majority, who were primarily concerned with obtaining better housing standards. Indeed, the Barnsbury Action Group was formed in 1970 to represent these working-class interests and it petitioned against both the new traffic management scheme and the policy of improvement which were seen as encouraging the process of 'gentrification'.

It would be unwise to generalise from this case study, for the scale and intensity of gentrification in areas of London such as Barnsbury has been far greater than elsewhere in Britain. Furthermore, in other areas working-class community action groups have also resisted local authority redevelopment schemes in favour of housing improvement schemes. Nevertheless, this study does emphasise the way in which unrepresentative but vocal groups can dominate political decision-making processes, and highlights the fact that social polarisation can produce conflict at the micro-scale as well as between neighbourhoods and larger local government areas.

The stridency of these middle-class communities in defending their areas from unwanted intrusion is related to the concepts of use value and exchange value noted in Chapter 2. Where individuals have some degree of choice they can be expected to reside in areas with facilities which suit their own life styles and will attempt to maintain and preserve those facilities which they find useful, whether they be parks, sports centres, shops or schools. However, it would seem that at the heart of many locational conflicts lies the issue of exchange values – the effects of land-use changes upon the price that properties will command at some future date. Use values and exchange values are of course closely related, but it is the former type of issue which most often dominates political debate – the latter remaining part of what Robson (1982) terms the 'hidden agenda' of local conflict.

Impacts on service facility location
If middle- and upper-income groups are more likely to protest and form neighbourhood associations to counteract changes in their local communities which they find incompatible with their life styles, are more likely to have resources to mount effective political campaigns, and are more likely to meet a favourable response from sympathetic councillors – it can be expected that facilities producing noxious side

effects will tend to be located in low-income areas where they will meet least resistance. There is now a large body of information which would support this hypothesis.

Davidson (1981), for example, examined the distribution of community-based treatment centres for drug addicts, juvenile offenders, mentally-ill persons and homeless adults in the county of Newcastle in the United States, and found that such centres were disproportionately represented in the inner-city 'transition zone' areas. These are the areas characterised by the largest proportions of individuals exhibiting 'deviant' behaviour, and are, of course, the largest source of clients for the centres. Consequently, these inner-city centres had larger proportions of users who were characterised as 'dangerous' compared with the predominantly low-stigma users of suburban centres. Davidson notes that many factors were responsible for the location of such centres, but that the lower level of organised resistance and greater tolerance of such centres in inner-city areas were amongst the most important. Dear (1976) found similar distributions of community-based mental health centres in American cities such as San Francisco, New York and Philadelphia. Faced with considerable opposition to such centres in many neighbour-hoods, mental health facility planners have reacted by seeking those locations where little opposition may be anticipated. Such areas tend to be the 'downtown' or 'transition zone' areas characterised by large numbers of lodging houses and much commercial and industrial activity.

Just as middle- and upper-income neighbourhoods will be more likely to organise to resist what they regard as undesirable facilities, so it can be argued they will also be more likely to petition for those desirable public services, which induce positive externalities. However, upon first reflection this would seem to run counter to much of the evidence presented previously. In many British cities for example, it would seem that as a result of locational inertia it is the suburbs, and more especially the newest ones, that are under-represented in terms of services. However, when accessibility models incorporate the effects of differential car ownership it is predomi-nantly the low-income estates which lack facilities. There is an additional consideration for middle-class suburban residents in this context: since many public facilities may have an undesirable effect upon local property values the facility needs to be outside the immediate locality, but not so far away that it is inaccessible to the car owner.

Education is, however, a much valued resource to the middle class, and this is especially true in America where it is seen as the key to social mobility and personal enhancement. A school which performs well in terms of enabling its students to obtain academic qualification is thus a much valued local asset, and can play an important part in maintaining local property values. However, in recent years a combination of falling numbers of children of school age and increased financial stringency in local government has forced many school boards to close some of their schools. This process has been frequently associated with enormous political conflict (Reynolds, 1984). Honey and Sorenson (1984) examined the distribution of school closure decisions throughout a set of central city school districts in the metropolitan areas of Minnesota, Wisconsin and Iowa. Within these medium-sized midwestern cities there was a greater likelihood of schools closing in the low-income black areas, whereas newer, high-income suburban areas characterised by high levels of education were more likely to retain their schools.

Given such a large number of cases, the authors were unable to examine in any rigorous manner the extent to which these patterns reflected the better organisation of neighbourhood associations in favour of school retention in higher-income neighbourhoods. They do note, however, that in the case of Cedar Rapids, Iowa, inarticulate leadership worked against one group's efforts to save their neighbourhood school, even though by the district administration's own published criteria another school (located in an influential, upper-middle-class area) should have closed. However, once again it would appear that neighbourhood organisation and political power are not the only factors at work; the 'technical' criteria drawn up by many of the school boards – such as the average age of buildings, school costs, and population trends in the local area – inevitably discriminate against the older inner-city neighbourhoods with their rapidly declining populations. Furthermore, although the overall pattern is remarkably clear, many of the variables were not statistically significant, and so there was little evidence of blatant discrimination. Nevertheless, it does appear that the costs of closures tend to impinge most heavily upon those sections of society least able to afford them.

It is not only the greater effectiveness of middle- and upper-income pressure groups but also the structure of Anglo-American local government and land-use planning systems which enable wealthier communities to benefit most from conflict over positive and negative externalities. It is at this point that the study of externalities links with the study of jurisdictional partitioning. The political fragmentation of many American cities, discussed in Chapter 1, enables wealthier suburban communities to practise exclusionary zoning and prevent the intrusion of land uses and social groups which would lower house values. In Britain there is less fragmentation of the local government system, but policies of urban containment and rigid planning controls in Green Belts have had similar, albeit less extreme, results. In both Britain and America the system has features which lead to an inbuilt bias in favour of higher-income groups so that in many cases they need not resort to the 'voice' option. This serves to emphasise even further (if further emphasis were needed) the limitations of the pluralist focus upon overt conflict.

This chapter has focused upon externality effects within single local government jurisdictions but clearly these side effects can extend across local government boundaries. The most obvious example is the air pollution which emerges from an industrial plant in one area and extends over other, surrounding jurisdictions. Industrial waste that is pumped into rivers can have a similar effect upon downstream local authorities. However, it is not only negative side effects which are exported by local authorities: many provide extensive shopping, cultural and recreational facilities which are consumed but not fully paid for by 'free riders' from other local government areas. This has led to the famous suburban–central city exploitation hypothesis – the idea that suburban commuters make additional demands upon central city services. As with many of the issues discussed in this chapter, the aggregate effect of these processes are difficult to quantify and the validity of this hypothesis is still open to question. Nevertheless, what is clear is that many of the inner-city local governments, both in Britain and the United States, are caught in a downward spiral of decline. The decentralisation of people and employment has led to a loss of local income which central funding schemes do not fully compensate, leaving behind a decaying physical environment and a growing concentration of high-need households. This had led to the widespread phenomenon of fiscal stress – the implications of which for service provision are discussed in Chapter 6.

Summary and conclusions

Externality theory would seem to provide an extremely powerful framework for integrating the wide range of conflicts over service provision and land use which emerge in cities. In particular, this framework enables the integration of the locational efficiency and locational conflict approaches which have hitherto tended to remain separate. Furthermore, despite a plethora of case studies, it has been possible to make some generalisations about the collective impact of service distributions. Free-market allocation mechanisms in the private sector tend to produce consumption patterns which favour middle- and upper-income groups, and it is to the public sector that one must look to find distributions that favour the least well-off. In practice, however, public sector intervention produces a wide variety of outcomes favouring upper-, middle- or lower-income groups depending upon the service and the city under investigation. Overall, it would seem that there is little evidence of persistent inverse care, and in many cases locational inertia results in concentrations of public facilities near deprived inner-city areas.

Studies of public services catering for particular client groups such as the elderly, mentally handicapped, and unemployed have revealed concentrations around inner-city areas close to the deprived populations they serve (Dear, 1980). Wolch has argued that the social polarisation resulting from decentralisation in American cities is creating a population of service-dependent non-working households clustered around such service facility centres (Wolch, 1979). Both inner-city and suburban low-income groups can suffer adversely in terms of accessibility to facilities depending upon the degree of centralisation of the facility in the city under study, but there is little evidence of persistent discrimination against the most deprived sections of the community. By the same token, however, there is little evidence of positive discrimination in favour of those on lowest incomes, and since many of these groups have the greatest needs, the net effect of many service distributions is likely to relatively disadvantage those on lowest incomes. As will be discussed below, the methodology of the locational efficiency approach has prevented an explicit consideration of these issues.

In the case of conflict over the location of noxious facilities the evidence is clearer. Middle- and upper-income groups are better organised both to resist the location of facilities which are likely to lower house prices in their neighbourhoods, and to attract and retain those facilities which will lead to an increase in local amenities. Consequently, many noxious facilities such as roads, factories and treatment centres tend to be directed towards the deprived areas of cities which will put up least resistance. However, it cannot be assumed, as in the pluralist approach, that the acquiescence of many deprived groups to the imposition of the facilities in their neighbourhood indicates either a preference for, or indifference towards, these activities being nearby. Although it is impossible to prove the issue in any conclusive quantitative fashion, the bulk of literature on positive and negative externalities in cities would therefore support Harvey's (1970) assertion that the net effect of these side effects works against those on lowest incomes.

The study of spatial externalities raises many unanswered questions, but the approach clearly has considerable potential to aid public decision-making. Provided the values incorporated into the optimisation criteria are made explicit, the locational efficiency approach can assist in finding suitable locations, either for the relocation of existing facilities or else the siting of additional service centres. In the case of 'outreach' services such decisions can literally be a matter of life and death, enabling emergency services such as fire engines and ambulances to get to accidents more quickly. Since there is evidence that supply of services creates demand, in the case of 'point-specific' facilities to which consumers must travel, the location of service centres can affect their rate of utilisation. In the case of old people's homes, for example, it is not uncommon for the location of a new centre in an area to stimulate local applications for the service which in the absence of the facility would have remained hidden as latent demand (or in other words 'felt' needs which were not 'expressed').

The potential of service centre relocation policies was demonstrated by the Bradley, Kirby and Taylor (1978) study of dentistry noted earlier. Most dental policy is based upon the class-based findings from aggregate national level research, and involves education and propaganda, especially amongst the working class, in an attempt to increase the utilisation of dental facilities. However, as demonstrated by the case of smoking, it is extremely difficult to change attitudes, and these may only bring benefits in the long run. Given the importance of distance decay and access to dental facilities upon levels of dental health, a complementary policy aimed at redistributing resources to areas which are underprovided in terms of dentistry might bring rapid improvements in levels of dental health.

Despite the importance of externalities in cities some of the impetus behind the locational efficiency and locational conflict approaches has diminished in recent years. Paradoxically, this decline in the late 1970s took place at a time when many sociologists, economists and political scientists were rediscovering the importance of the spatial dimensions of externalities. There is, however, a growing recognition throughout social science as a whole, of the limitations of the approach. Like jurisdictional partitioning effects, externalities provide a framework for organising certain mechanisms which affect the distribution of collective consumption in cities, but by itself this framework is inadequate in explaining these mechanisms. These deficiencies can be illustrated with some examples.

In the case of point-specific services it has become clear that it is not only distance-decay effects which determine service utilisation levels: many individuals are dissuaded or prevented from using facilities by characteristics of the services themselves, their operating procedures and the attitudes of staff. In the case of doctors' surgeries for example, the defensive attitudes of the receptionist can be as much of a barrier to gaining access to the doctor as the physical constraint of reaching the surgery (Phillips, 1979). It is also clear that the mere receipt of many public services stigmatises the individuals involved, while many public bureaucracies do not treat persons in a manner which enhances their dignity or self-esteem. Furthermore, many persons are prevented from using services by charges levied on their use, or by the operating rules of the service organisations which may serve to discriminate against certain social groups.

It has also become apparent that concepts such as the 'friction of distance', whether measured in terms of time, cost or even psychological barriers, may serve to obscure or at least divert attention from some of the broader social inequalities related to class, sex, age and race which lead to differential mobility rates amongst various groups. Similarly, the behavioural associations which emerge from studies of locational conflict by themselves do not unearth the underlying processes which lead to differentials in political resources and the abilities of communities to resist noxious services and attract salutary facilities. All of these issues suggest a need to place service distributions in their broader social context. It is not sufficient to plot the spatial distribution of services or model optimal distributions of new or existing facilities without consideration of the overall structure of the service: how did it come into existence? what are the functions of the service? whose interests does it serve (the clients, the general public or the service administrators)? – these are the questions that need to be asked.

As with the analysis of jurisdictional partitioning effects, the study of locational efficiency and conflict via the framework of externalities does not explicitly consider the appropriateness of the services under examination for the needs of the populations involved. It is this failure which prevents one from drawing any firm conclusions from this literature about the existence of the inverse-care law in cities. This is not to suggest that the study of externality effects should be abandoned as a mere manifestation of the geographers 'fetish over space', for as we have seen in this chapter, the influence of externality effects is powerful and all-pervasive in Western cities. It does, however, suggest the need to link studies of externality effects with broader social theories which can explain patterns of collective consumption without falling into the trap of public-choice theory. Within urban studies the main inspiration for these broader perspectives has come from two main sources – Max Weber and Karl Marx – whose writings and subsequent reinterpretations are considered in Chapters 4 and 5 respectively.

4 Neo-Weberian approaches

Although Max Weber wrote a great deal about many aspects of evolving industrial societies, and this included his work on the city (Weber, 1958), he is most noted in the sphere of urban studies for his contributions to the study of bureaucracies. Indeed, the term 'Weberian' is often used as a general synonym to denote anyone who refers to the importance of bureaucracies in cities. In effect, as will be described in this chapter, the majority of studies of urban services pay little detailed attention to Weberian concepts or, indeed, the subsequent vast literature within sociology and organisations theory. Consequently, although the majority of the following studies relate to issues raised by Weber, their inclusion in this chapter does not signify any strict adherence to his approach or methodology. Nevertheless, Weber, both directly and indirectly, has exerted a dominating influence upon subsequent writings and since his approach contrasts with the other major influence – Karl Marx – his approach needs elaboration.

Weber's methodology and ideal-type analysis

Weber's approach is based upon individuals, their actions and their consciousness. Put crudely, the role of social inquiry is to explain why individuals acted in the way they did in terms of their own subjective understanding of the circumstances surrounding their action. Thus, his method of '*verstehen*' is concerned with 'interpretative understanding of the subjective basis for social action' (Weber, 1949). Clearly, since we can never be certain of an individual's motives, it follows that only partial or adequate explanations are possible. Our explanations must, however be plausible and account for the degree of rationality, habit or emotion behind an interaction with other individuals and must indicate the probability that an individual will act in the same way under similar circumstances. It is assumed that since individuals have free will there will always be an element of uncertainty behind our explanations, no matter how statistically predictable the events may be. Since all social events are historically unique, there is a need to generalise in order to understand typical motives and general patterns of action. For Weber, this function was performed by the method of 'ideal type' analysis.

'Ideal type' is a method of analysis which reflects the influence of the German ideographic tradition of social science in the nineteenth century. An ideal type is constructed by accentuating the nature of an observed reality to make the characteristic features of that reality clear and understandable (Outhwaite, 1975). It is not a description of reality or an average of many observed events and neither is it an hypothesis (although it may suggest further hypotheses). Instead, ideal types are designed to enable precise definitions and clarity and coherence in concept formation. The fact that not all of the aspects of the ideal type can be found in reality is not a valid objection to further conceptual analysis using the ideal type. Weber argued that reality is so complex that ideal types were essential to impose order, and to sort out those things which are general and important from those which are unique and particular to local circumstances and events.

Weberian concepts of organisations and bureaucracies

Despite his emphasis upon the clarity and coherence of concept formulation, Weber's writings on bureaucracy are scattered in a large set of related themes. But although he never explicitly defined what he meant by the term bureaucracy, Weber used the method of ideal-type analysis to develop notions of bureaucracy in a series of interrelated concepts. Weber was concerned with *Verband* organisations defined by ordered social relationships (Weber, 1947: 145-52). In his analysis of these organisations he developed a distinction between power (*Macht*), the ability of an actor to carry out his will despite opposition, and authority (*Herrschaft*), the exercise of imperative control over others. Although Weber acknowledged that the motivation to obey a command may range from habit through to the rational calculation of advantage, he argued that obedience to commands was primarily dictated by a belief in their legitimacy. Different forms of legitimacy could produce different organisational structures, and Weber recognised three main types: 'charismatic authority' in which obedience was justified because the person giving the order had some sacred or outstanding attribute; 'traditional' authority in which a command might be obeyed because of a reverence for traditional order; and finally, 'legal authority', in which the order was obeyed because of legal regulations. Weber argued that modern organisations were increasingly dominated by legal forms of authority in which interactions were of a rational character (Albrow, 1970).

According to Weber's ideal type, legal rational authority is characterised by the continuous and regulated organisation of official tasks known as 'offices' which are limited by rules (*Ordung*). These offices are organised in a clearly defined hierarchy of authority with clearly defined rights of control and complaint. Like the factory worker, the administrative official is separated from the means of production, but unlike the worker the official has authority. Weber argued that an authority system could take many forms but is found in its most pure expression when associated with an administrative staff or bureaucracy. He refers to patrimonial forms of bureaucracy dependent upon enslaved men as found in ancient societies, but is primarily concerned with rational bureaucracies.

A rational bureaucratic staff is headed by a chief who may be appointed, elected, or otherwise designated as head. The staff consists of officers (*Beamter*) who are free, being in a contractual relationship and subject only to their official obligations. The staff are organised in a hierarchy, each officer having a defined area of competence, and each official being appointed on the basis of his technical qualifications. The officials receive fixed salaries appropriate to their status, promotion being dependent upon assessment by superior officials. For a complete list of these ideal-type characteristics see Table 4.1.

Weber's ideas have been criticised from many perspectives. Probably the most common criticism is that Weber ignored the non-rational aspects of bureaucratic forms of organisations. Weber described how bureaucracies perhaps ought to behave, but officials are social animals as well as administrators and also subject to emotions, fears, prejudices, cliques and interest groups (Albrow, 1970). Much discussion has also centred around whether bureauc-

Table 4.1 Weber's 'ideal type' of rational bureaucracy

Defining characteristics

---

1   The members of staff are personally free, carrying out only the impersonal duties of their offices.
2   There is a clear hierarchy of offices.
3   The function of the offices are clearly specified.
4   Officials are appointed on the basis of a contract.
5   Officials are selected on the basis of professional qualifications.
6   Officials have a money salary, which is graded according to position in the hierarchy, together with pension rights. The official is free to leave the post but, under certain circumstances, may be fired.
7   The official's post is his sole or major occupation.
8   There is a career structure, and promotion is possible either by seniority or merit according to the judgement of superiors.
9   The official may appropriate neither the post nor the resources that go with it.
10 The official is subject to a unified control and a disciplinary system.

Source   Albrow, M. (1970), pp.44-5.

racies do or do not maximise efficiency. However, such criticisms do not ultimately detract from Weber's thesis that 'Bureaucratic administration means fundamentally the exercise of control on the basis of knowledge' (Weber, 1964:339). Although they are complex and at times elusive, Weber's writings on bureaucracy are extraordinarily rich and diverse, and it is hardly surprising that they have come to exert such a powerful influence on following debates.

British studies of urban managerialism

The Weberian perspective was first introduced into the sphere of urban studies in Britain in an explicit manner by Rex and Moore (1967). However, they were not directly concerned with the behaviour of bureaucracies but instead attempted to link the Chicago school's idealised ecological model of urban spatial structure with Weberian notions of social class.

Weber argued that many different types of social class could be defined in any market situation where individuals have different degrees of access to scarce material resources. Thus, classes can be formed other than in terms of rewards obtained from productive activity in the labour market. This enables the construction of many different and complex categories of classes other than the Marxist division between wage-earning labourers and property-owning capitalists. Weber's approach is therefore based on consumption, rather than the Marxist emphasis upon relations to the means of production.

Rex and Moore argued that there is a class struggle over access to housing in British cities. Some groups such as ethnic minorities, are, through discrimination, in an inferior 'housing class' which cannot be explained by their relationship to the means of production. Hence they argued that, although an individual's position in the occupational market has obvious implication for his or her position in the housing market (since it affects income, status in relation to obtaining loans, and security of employment), there was no necessary correspondence between the two.

However, the most important catalyst for the introduction of Weberian ideas into the study of local service provision was Pahl's formulation (Pahl, 1970) as outlined in Chapter 1. As Saunders (1979) observes, like the earlier North American community-power debate, this reflected a dissatisfaction with the ecological theories of cities which had sought to portray patterns as in some senses natural and inevitable. Instead, there was a new focus upon human action and individual decision-making. The ideas were derived by analogy from industrial sociology. Just as factories were regarded as a socio-technical system so cities are regarded as socio-spatial systems.

One important implication of the approach is that spatial factors form an independent constraint upon people's access to scarce resources in an urban community. As Pahl observed in a later paper: 'Within cities there are inevitable inequalities of access which are inherent in the nature of concentration. Not everyone can live close to all the services and facilities they require or sufficiently far from all the disbenefits they abhor' (Pahl, 1979:35). This means that, whatever the mode of production, there is a 'logic of distance' which will inevitably deprive certain groups.

Pahl's emphasis upon spatial access to facilities did much to encourage the locational efficiency school outlined in Chapter 3. However, the most important outcome of his ideas was the so-called 'school of urban managerialism.' Pahl asserted that urban managers or 'social gatekeepers' such as planners, social workers, estate agents and housing managers also had an important independent effect upon access to scarce resources in cities by virtue of the bureaucratic rules and procedures they employed. Clearly, these ideas have strong links with Weberian ideas of increasing bureaucratic domination in industrial societies, and the work has Galbraithian overtones which parallel the focus of industrial sociology upon growing managerial autonomy in industry. The implication of the approach is that all modern industrial societies, both capitalist and communist, are affected by bureaucratic forms.

These ideas spawned a number of studies which examined the activities and attitudes of local managers. Attention has been directed almost exclusively upon housing, and there have been two main fields of focus: one upon local authorities (Bird, 1976; Gray, 1976); and the second upon the various private sector housing agencies (Ford, 1975; Boddy, 1976; Williams, 1976).

Managerialism and British housing policy

One set of studies examined the allocation of improvement grants and the choice of General Improvement Areas (GIA) in British cities. Duncan (1974) for example, considered the distribution of improvement grants in Huddersfield. He compared the actual number of grants received in an area with an expected share for each area, based on the assumption that each enumeration district received a total number of improvement grants in proportion to its number of dwellings without the three basic amenities. Improvement grants made an important contribution in providing amenities in areas where housing was of poor quality. However, the grant allocations tended to avoid the areas with high proportions of rented properties and coloured immigrants – the areas with the highest levels of disadvantage as measured by census indices.

This pattern is interpreted as a reflection of the attitudes of local planners and housing managers who, it is maintained, perpetuate a division between the 'deserving' and 'undeserving' poor. It was also seen as an attempt to concentrate upon areas in which the objectives of improvement policy were most assured, since GIA declarations were made in the areas of slightly better quality housing which had already shown indications of a willingness to take up grants.

Studies of Bristol (Bassett and Hauser, 1975) and Southampton (Pinch, 1981) have revealed similar patterns but these studies suggest a somewhat more mundane explanation than Duncan's 'conspiracy' type of theory. The bulk of information relating to GIA declaration suggests that in the majority of cases these areas were established on purely pragmatic grounds. In some cities, they were the next areas in line for 'treatment' by the local authority, and seldom was their selection based on any comprehensive housing policy or consideration of the overall role of improvement policies. Although the issue is obviously difficult to prove, it does not appear that GIAs have been the centre of extensive political intrigue or connivance. Duncan criticises planners for avoiding the areas of greatest housing stress, but planners would no doubt also have been critical if they had focused the policy of GIAs in areas where it was not likely to have been successful! Although initially local authorities were given little guidance over the selection of GIAs, government circulars soon cautioned against establishing these schemes in the areas of worst housing until more experience of area-based renovation had been gained. In effect, many planners would appear to have displayed much good sense in realising that the provisions of the 1969 Housing Act would do relatively little to attack the severe problems of the worst housing-stress areas. The Housing Action Area (HAAs) created by the 1974 Housing Act were an attempt to deal with these problems and have often been declared in the worst housing areas; but this policy has also been criticised (Monck and Lomas, 1980).

Some of the most vivid descriptions of the powers of planners and public officials have emerged from studies of slum clearance and renovation in the north-east of England. Davies (1972) in his aptly named book *The Evangelistic Bureaucrat* describes the relationships between planners, local councillors and residents of the Rye Hill area of Newcastle. In the mid-1960s, Newcastle planners hoped to introduce a policy of comprehensive improvement in this area – a strategy which proved to be highly unsuitable in what was a 'transition zone', experiencing many complex social problems. The whole of the planning process was characterised by delays and uncertainties and the local residents had enormous difficulties in obtaining information about future plans for Rye Hill. The inevitable result was planning blight and the few, better-off sections of the community who owned their own homes sold these properties to the council at the first opportunity. Delays in the improvement policy meant that these properties were left empty and soon became vandalised, thus intensifying the downward spiral of decline in the area. Most of the remaining inhabitants could not afford to provide their share of the cost of improving their homes, or else thought that the planning department wanted renovation standards which were far in excess of those warranted by the original condition of the dwellings. Eventually, only seven properties were improved, the policy was abandoned and Rye Hill was condemned to clearance.

One of the most significant features of this local drama was the power of the planners over the activities of all the other actors involved. The local councillors, for example, appeared to have little knowledge of the detailed housing and planning issues involved and were therefore forced to delegate communications with local residents to the planners. The planners in turn seemed to be highly insensitive to the needs of local inhabitants, and at times seem to regard the local Residents' Association as an inconvenient obstacle to the implementation of their plans. Dennis (1972) describes similar developments in the Millfield area of Sunderland, demonstrating that the Newcastle experience was no isolated case study; and Gans (1972) has shown that similar developments have taken place in the United States.

Such studies seriously call into question the conventional wisdom that local elected representatives make policy decisions which the local officials implement. Indeed, in recent years, many have questioned the effectiveness of the committee structure (outlined in Chapter 1) as a means of controlling the power of local bureaucrats. Knox (1982) describes a number of methods which local officials can employ to get their own way; these include: 'swamping' councillors with a large number of long reports; 'blinding councillors with science' – obscuring issues with reports full of statistics and technical information; presenting reports which make only one conclusion possible; withholding information or bringing it forward too late to affect decisions; rewriting but not changing a rejected plan, and submitting it after an interval; and, finally, introducing deliberate errors in the first few paragraphs of a report in the hope that councillors will be so pleased in finding them that they let the rest go through.

North American studies of decision rules

By far the largest body of work to highlight the importance of local officials upon service allocations has been the work undertaken by political scientists in the United States. It is important to note that, although these studies have also been concerned with the distribution of services at the intra-city scale, the approach has differed considerably from the locational efficiency and locational conflict approaches of geographers outlined in Chatper 3. First, the political science literature has examined a wider range of local services. These include not only the point-specific facilities such as schools, parks, libraries and fire stations examined by geographers, but also such services such as police patrols, housing and environmental inspections, sanitation services, refuse disposal, street lighting and road repairs. Conversely, political scientists have ignored those aspects of the health care system, hospitals, doctors and ambulance services, which have received such detailed scrutiny from geographers. Second, the methodology employed by political scientists has also differed from that used by geographers. Instead of the accessibility indices, described in Chapter 3, political scientists have used a correlational approach similar to that employed in the analysis of jurisdictional partitioning, albeit at a smaller spatial scale relating to various types of political and administrative district within cities.

The origins of the literature
Much of the impetus for this type of analysis came from the ghetto riots in the major American cities in the 1960s. The Kerner Commission was established to examine these disturbances, and amongst its many conclusions was the fact that inadequate municipal services in fields such as education, recreation and policing were a main reason for the disorders. This prompted a flood of studies which sought to examine if discrimination actually did exist in the distribution of public goods and services to areas of American cities.

Interest in these matters has also been prompted by the Fourteenth Amendment to the Constitution, the so-called 'equal protection clause' which states:

> No state shall make or enforce any law which shall abridge the privileges or immunities of citizens of the United States; nor shall any state deprive any person of life, liberty or property, without due process of law; nor deny to any person within its jurisdiction the equal protection of the laws.

The Fourteenth Amendment has been most controversial in the context of attempts to break down segregation between black and white children in the American educational system (Johnston, 1982). Until the 1950s black and white children were kept in separate schools in many southern states, and a number of court cases proved that this was discriminatory under the equal protection clause. The Supreme Court thus ruled that desegregation should ensue. When many blacks moved to the northern cities, however, their concentration in ghettoes meant that the local schools were predominantly black. Since discrimination was not the result of state policies the Fourteenth Amendment did not apply, but in recent years cases of discriminatory intent have been proved and school districts have been required to produce integration plans through bussing (Johnston, 1982).

The equal protection clause has also been used to contest discrimination in the allocation of other municipal services. The most flagrant violation of the Fourteenth Amendment occurred in the small town of Shaw, Mississippi. Here the black majority received the smallest amounts of local services such that almost all the homes without flood damage protection, paved streets or sanitation were black (Lineberry, 1977). The decision of *Hawkins v The Town of Shaw* (1971) was that equal levels of municipal services should be provided for both blacks and whites, and similar types of discrimination have been contested in other suits. The existence of large inter-jurisdictional variations in school district revenues from property taxes has also prompted litigation, but the outcome of *San Antonio Independent School District v Rodriguez* (1973) was that such situations were not discriminatory.

Another reason for the growth of intra-city studies of service provision was the decline of inter-state comparisons of outputs in the early 1970s. Later studies in the tradition had moved away from concentrating solely upon expenditures, and had sought to obtain measures of policy outputs in physical terms; and this development was represented at the intra-city scale. There was also a reaction against what came to be termed the 'urban crisis literature' – the rather dramatic and pessimistic writings which emerged in the wake of the civil disorders of the 1960s. A feeling emerged that what was important to many citizens were the less dramatic but nonetheless important processes of routine service allocations – what had for long been derided as 'counting manhole covers'. The mood was summed up by Yates who observed that it was 'difficult to see how a government can solve its dramatic problems if it cannot solve its routine ones' (Yates, 1974:213).

The underclass hypothesis

Prior to detailed analysis it was commonly assumed that discrimination *did* exist in the provision of public services and that those who lived on 'the wrong side of the tracks' obtained the smallest amounts of services. This was expressed in Sharrard's (1968) classic words:

> The slum is the catch-all for the losers, and in the competitive struggle for the cities' good and services the slum areas are also the losers in terms of schools, jobs, garbage collection, street lighting, libraries, social services, and whatever else is communally available but always in short supply. (Sharrard, 1968:10.)

In a similar vein, Lowry noted that 'there is a great deal of anecdotal evidence that low-income neighbourhoods within most municipalities are less well-served by municipal governments than high-income neighbourhoods'. Cox (1973) also argued that the patterns of discrimination found in Shaw were 'typical of much larger cities in the US'.

These comments seem to fit in with the obvious manifestations of urban problems in the major cities – the vast differences in residential quality, standards of housing, amounts of litter, age of schools, quality of streets and amounts of recreational space. The ideas also find expression in many traditional aphorisms, such as 'the poor pay more', 'them that has gets', and 'unto him that hath shall be given'. The British expression of these sentiments is of course Tudor-Hart's (1971) 'inverse-care law' described in Chapter 3. In more formal academic terms, these ideas find expression in the so-called 'underclass hypothesis', the idea that all economically disadvantaged groups in cities are discriminated against in the provision of urban services (Lineberry, 1977). In the American context, of course, most interest has focused upon a variant of this – 'the race preference' hypothesis – which suggests that blacks are discriminated against rather than other white poor groups, whether they be Anglos, Chicanos or Puerto Ricans.

Somewhat surprisingly, in the light of all this speculation, the cumulative impact of the now vast American literature on service provision in cities leads to a rejection of any simple 'underclass' or 'race preference' hypothesis. It would appear that the patterns of service distribution are, to say the least, complex; and which group – if any – benefits most depends upon the nature of the service, the type of index used to measure service provision, and the nature of the city under examination. Thus, different services produce different patterns in the same city, while the same service can produce different patterns in different cities.

The evidence from some of the most accessible and therefore most well-known studies will easily demonstrate this point. The general pattern was established in one of the earliest studies by Benson and Lund (1969) in Berkeley, California. They found that while low-income areas used a disproportionate amount of health and 'poverty-related' services, such as nursing, housing inspections and mental health facilities, the higher-income white neighbourhoods consumed more in terms of amenities such as libraries and schools.

However, by far the most influential of the early studies was that undertaken in nearby Oakland by Levy, Meltsner and Wildavsky (1974). They found that library resources and roads tended to favour the upper-income areas. Black areas tended to receive preferential treatment in the field of education with more teachers, but the more skilled and experienced teachers transferred to the richer areas when vacancies became available. None of the three services under examination revealed any bias in favour of the middle-income areas.

The 'sunbelt' cities – hitherto somewhat neglected in American political science – have figured prominently in the urban services debate. This would seem to reflect not only their rapid growth rate but the interaction of a 'south-western' academic network. Lineberry's (1977) study of San Antonio is probably the most well-known. This city, the eleventh largest in the United States, with its small black population, large proportion of Chicanos, and astonishing rate of growth on the urban periphery, contrasts in many respects with the older industrial centres of the north-east. Lineberry summarised the distribution of fire protection, libraries, parks, sewage and police services as one of 'unpatterned inequality'. There were certainly variations in some provision between areas, but none that could be related in any significant way with the underclass or race-preference hypotheses. Indeed, if anything there was a slight tendency for more accessible services near the inner-city minority areas.

A similar pattern was observed in the case of parks by Mladenka and Hill (1977) in Houston; low-income areas were not discriminated against, whether in terms of acreage distribution or the number of park facilities. Overall, there was a slight tendency for residents in lower-income areas to live closer to parks than citizens in wealthier areas. However, as in Oakland, the distribution of library resources was strongly biased in favour of the upper-income areas. Branches located in the wealthier neighbourhoods received more books and periodicals, had larger budgets and better qualified staff. However, in a later study of police services Mladenka and Hill found that police patrol response time was quicker in the low-income areas, and those districts also received higher amounts of police patrol resources (Mladenka and Hill 1978). The city of Houston was also the location for some sophisticated measurement techniques when Antunes and Plumlee (1977) drove a 1972 Chevrolet sedan equipped with a Mays Ride Meter, down a selected number of streets at approximately 20 miles per hour in order to assess the quality of streets. Once again, however, neither race nor income correlated strongly with the quality of street roughness.

In recent years the 'frost belt' centres of the north-east have come to play a more prominent part in the urban services debate. The most detailed and sophisticated analysis has come from Jones and his co-researchers in their study of Detroit (Jones, 1977; Jones *et al.*, 1977; Jones *et al.*, 1979; Jones *et al.*, 1980) – the largest reformed industrial city. Detroit, it should be noted, also has the distinction of having had the worst riots in American history and the highest crime rate of American cities. In the case of complaints to the Environmental Enforcement Division, the middle-income areas generated more complaints and had a greater number of responses from the agency; but these took longer to process, and there was a higher incidence of cases where no action was taken. Overall, the better-off sections of the city had shorter average response times for their complaints and a higher proportion of recorded violations.

In Nivola's (1978) study of housing inspections in Boston, he found that the response time of the housing agency to a complaint and the probability of the agency formally citing the complaint, were better in the middle-income white working-class areas. The low-income black slum areas generally did less well, but surprisingly better than the upper-middle-class areas such as Beacon Hill.

The classic 'machine' city of Chicago formed the basis for Mladenka's (1980) study of a variety of urban services. Once again, parks were more or less equally distributed throughout the city. In the past there was a tendency for black areas to receive fewer facilities, but between 1967 and 1977 policies discriminating in favour of black areas had ensured that this tendency was considerably reduced. The level of fire services was also basically equal between white and black wards of the city, but refuse collection favoured those areas with the highest proportions of home-owners – a pattern not entirely consistent with the number of blacks in a road. Finally, educational resources seem to follow the pattern discovered in Oakland by Levy and his associates. Minority schools ranked high in terms of teacher–pupil ratio, but white schools spent most on staffing and were assigned the most experienced and best-educated teachers.

A final study worthy of note in this context is that by Boyle and Jacobs (1980), in which they examined service distribution across the 62 Community Planning Districts in New York. Although they considered expenditures rather than physical indices of service provision, they did include a wide range of services. Their paper is also unusual in that they used the *per capita* tax contribution of the areas as an explanatory variable, and this was the variable most consistently associated with the expenditure variables. In the case of police, fire and sanitation, the areas which contributed most in resources also received the most in expenditures. However, police expenditures were also strongly associated with the low-income areas. Furthermore, there was also evidence of redistributive or compensatory principles in operation, for the poorer areas received more in terms of welfare and education services. These results are summarised in Table 4.2.

'Ecological' influences
Although these intra-city studies attempted to move away from the 'ecological' lines of the earlier outputs approach, one of the major implications of these studies is the importance of explanations related to the physical structure of cities. In many American cities, and especially the rapidly growing ones such as San Antonio, it is the suburban areas which are deprived of access to many community facilities, largely because the service distribution machine has not been able to catch up with the pace of urban growth on the periphery. There is inevitably inertia in the locational pattern of many expensive fixed-point facilities such as parks, fire stations and

Table 4.2 A summary of the results of decision-rules studies

Study	Location	Services	Results (bias in favour of:)
Levy, Meltsner and Wildavsky, (1974)	Oakland	libraries streets education	higher-income areas higher-income up-land areas lower- and higher-income areas
Lineberry, (1977)	San Antonio	parks fire protection libraries sewage police	slight tendency towards lower-income and ethnic areas little bias
Mladenka and Hill, (1977)	Houston	parks libraries	slight bias towards upper classes strong bias towards upper classes
Mladenka and Hill, (1978)	Houston	police	poor and minority areas
Antunes and Plumlee (1977)	Houston	roads	no bias
Nivola, (1978)	Boston	housing inspections	faster service in low-income areas
Jones *et al.*, (1980)	Detroit	environmental enforcement refuse collection	quicker response in middle-income areas poorer quality in black areas
Mladenka, (1980)	Chicago	parks fire refuse collection education	black areas no bias home-owners upper- and lower-income area
Boyle and Jacobs, (1980)	New York	police fire sanitation welfare and education	high-tax areas low-income areas

libraries, which reflects their initial distribution at a time when cities were more compact and densely populated. Now that the more affluent sections of the population have moved into the suburbs it is the inner-city population of low-income and ethnic minority groups that are closest to the older facilities.

As Mladenka (1980) notes in the case of Chicago, the distribution of parkland is disproportionately affected by a number of particularly large sites located near the lakefront at the turn of the century when the city population was much more geographically concentrated than it is today. In the case of Detroit, much of the inner area was developed by the time it became fashionable to worry about access to parkland. Consequently, the major parks first donated by large landowners were initially located on the outskirts of the city. Some were so far away that streetcars and trains were required to reach them. The parks were, however, closest to the poor who at that time lived on the outskirts of the city. Eventually, the extension of streetcar lines enabled the middle and upper classes to escape the congested city centre. The result is that today the better-off are closest to the major parks.

Another example is provided by the fire service. Until the mid-1960s in Chicago there was a concentration of fire stations near the inner-city areas, reflecting not only the compact city form of an earlier era, but also the horse-drawn fire-fighting technology of an earlier period which dictated that fire stations should be located at relatively short distances from each other. The pattern was also affected by two particularly bad stockyard fires in Chicago in 1910 and 1936, which led to a concentration around now-abandoned stockyards.

In the case of refuse collection, the association with owner-occupied housing in Chicago results from a city code prohibiting collection from multi-family dwellings containing five or more apartments. This rule was adopted because when coal was the major source of fuel in the city, huge heaps of cinders were produced which greatly complicated refuse collection. This was especially the case outside large apartment blocks, where tons of cinders were formed into huge piles which froze solid in winter. Rather than increase manpower to deal with the problem of breaking up the huge piles, the city opted for a policy of excluding large multi-family blocks from garbage collection – a policy which persists until the present, despite the widespread adoption of oil and gas for domestic heating.

However, these service delivery studies did not fall into the same trap as many earlier 'outputs' studies, and assume a simple 'ecological' explanation for these patterns. They recognised that there had to be some process by which the exigencies of the environment were perceived, and translated into policies, facilities and distributional outcomes. Furthermore, they recognised that factors such as 'urban inertia' were the reflection of many previous decisions made by many individuals over a long period of years.

This is the point at which these studies link with the Weberian approach for, without exception, they have pointed to the activities of bureaucracies as the key to explaining these complex patterns of service allocation. Thus Lineberry (1977) argued that they were the 'missing link' between allocative processes and service distributions in cities.

The growth and influence of bureaucracy

It is argued that bureaucracies are able to wield power for a number of reasons. First and foremost, they have grown enormously in the twentieth century in terms of numbers of personnel, the scope of their powers and the size of their budgets. In large part this must be seen as a response to the growing complexity of urban industrial society which demands increased management, regulation and a host of complex services performed by numerous agencies. The Municipal Reform Movement and the city manager systems paved the way for their growth, for in an attempt to eliminate corruption they introduced a professional civil service with security of tenure and systematic promotion by specified criteria of merit. This means that once they are established it is difficult to dismantle bureaucracies.

Antunes and Mladenka (1976) argue that the demise of political parties within the reformed local government systems meant that bureaucrats were subject to only limited control by officials. They claim that individuals, groups and areas are better able to obtain redress for specific grievances in an environment characterised by active local parties, and that their decline has decreased the accountability of public managers. As Greenstone and Peterson observe, 'political actors in fully reformed cities do not have the incentives to control bureaucracies that they have in machine cities ... The expectation in reform cities that administrative practices should be isolated from political influences enables the mayors to hold their supporters' gratitude simply by demonstrating good intentions, even if they fail to exercise effective control' (cited in Lineberry, 1977:149-50).

Even in an active machine environment, however, bureaucracies can remain largely insulated from political pressures, as Mladenka (1980) illustrates in the case of Chicago. The traditional assumption is that the political machines manipulate urban services to win votes; loyal wards are thus rewarded with superior services by machine aldermen. Indeed, Mladenka's interviews with aldermen in Chicago confirmed that this is their own perception of their role, for most expressed confidence in their abilities to win resources from their areas. However, the statistical analysis did not support these assertions. In the case of parks and recreation resources there was a negative association between services received and the degree of support for the political machine. In the late 1960s and early 1970s there was a shift of resources in favour of black areas, but this was seen as a response to urban protest rather than changing patterns of support from the political machine. Similarly, the greater concentration of fire services near black areas was seen as an interaction of changing historical circumstances and the imposition of technical criteria by the bureaucracy, rather than as political factors.

Decision rules
These American studies argue that the key to understanding the behaviour of bureaucracies and their impact upon service delivery in cities lies in the concept of what Levy and his associates call 'decision rules' (Levy *et al.*, 1974) or what Jones and his colleagues call 'service delivery rules' (Jones *et al.*, 1980). Service delivery rules are defined as 'the procedures established by an agency to codify the repetitive decisions it must make in dealing with the recurring situations requiring some effort' (Jones *et al.*, 1980:81). These rules may be based on different sets of criteria such as uniformity, need, demand, efficiency and power. They can be formulated and implemented at various levels in the bureaucratic hierarchy for a number of reasons.

At the higher levels these decision rules may be affected by what Jones terms 'macro-political influences'. This may include the policy of the mayor, council directives, the imposition of central government standards, or the need to accommodate particular pressure groups. They are what Webster (1977) terms 'conscious' policy decisions, in the sense that they are usually formally endorsed by elected decision-making bodies, but the policy may be implicit, in the sense that although decisions of a similar type are consistently made, the basis of these decisions is never stated formally.

The most obvious and controversial example is in the field of education where compensatory principles have been employed. Thus Levy, Meltsner and Wildavsky documented policies designed to introduce more teachers and resources to minority areas in Oakland (Levy *et al.*, 1974). Similarly, in Detroit the city council chose to concentrate playlots in the inner-city areas (Jones *et al.*, 1980). In an attempt to promote an inner city 'renaissance' there has also been a conscious effort in Detroit to acquire additional parkland near the city centre, along the waterfront.

By far the most common policy, however, is one that attempts to achieve a broad uniformity of service outcomes between areas. In Chicago Mladenka found teacher–pupil ratios in the state school system determined by a complex formula designed to achieve identical ratios across all schools. In Detroit, Jones and his research team found that refuse collection was allocated in the principle that each area should receive one collection per week (Jones *et al.*, 1980). The standards imposed by professional organisations are also relevant in this context. Through their various professional associations public officials are part of a broader network, and they receive a continuous flow of technical information and professional gossip from conventions, journals and other publications. Consequently, 'a change in local refuse collection practices is likely to occur because of the diffusion of information via the National Solid Waste Management Association than because of a decision by elected officials' (Antunes and Plumlee, 1977).

There are many examples of such rational technical criteria in operation. For example, the realignment of fire services in Chicago between 1965 and 1978 was the result of detailed technical evaluations of the optimum configurations in terms of access time to vulnerable properties (Mladenka, 1980). In Oakland, the professional decision rules of the streets officials were concerned with technical criteria, which emphasised maximising the speed and volume of traffic flow while minimising accidents. Most of the distributional decisions could be explained by the earmarking of funds for major arterial roads and the rational criteria of traffic engineers. The net result was that local neighbourhood streets that carried small amounts of traffic were regarded as relatively unimportant and received fewest resources. Antunes and Plumlee (1977) found that traffic engineers in Houston were also concerned with traffic volume and safety, like their Oakland counterparts, and with similar distributional consequences. Again, in Oakland, the professional standards of the librarians ensured that the types of books purchased were predominantly white and middle-class in values: books concerned with ethnic history or the practical issues of most relevance to low-income groups were less common, thus serving to reinforce the relatively low readership rates in poorer black areas.

'Street-level' bureaucrats

Despite these observations, one of the most commonly cited features of these urban service bureaucracies is the relatively low level in the organisations at which these decision rules are formulated and implemented. Thus, the allocation of services is frequently dependent upon the discretion of field workers and clerical staff who are in direct contact with the public or their specific client groups. These are classic examples of Pahl's 'social gatekeepers', or, as Lipsky (1976) calls them, 'street-level bureaucrats'.

The degree of discretionary freedom available to street-level bureaucrats varies considerably, and depends largely upon the reasons for their relative autonomy within the local government structure. Considerable discretion may be given to lower-level personnel because the department or agency is uncertain about its overall objectives, and thus avoids the formulation of explicit goals. Nivola's (1978) study of housing inspections in Boston is an excellent example of this strategy. The ultimate objective of the inspections was to arrest blight, but the existence of residential deterioration in American cities is dependent upon many private and public forces amongst which the degree of building-code enforcement must be regarded as highly marginal. Indeed, the service was not always benign in its impact, for excessively rigorous code enforcement could result in increased rents or landlords abandoning property, thus diminishing the overall supply of housing. Consequently:

> Uncertain as to how much code enforcement should transpire, where, when and *with what results* (and in any case unable to manipulate matters fundamentally since the department did not design either the volume or the spatial incidence of its cases), agency chiefs passed down few operational guidelines. (Nivola, 1978:78.)

In this context, the inspectors were forced to devise their own 'hidden code' of practices for dealing with difficult circumstances. Indeed, they would seem to be classic examples of Lipsky's street-level bureaucrats, defined as personnel who work in fraught, often hazardous environments, with inadequate resources, minimal supervision and conflicting role expectations.

The basic problem in Boston was that rigorous code enforcement would have probably entailed citations for most of the houses in the city. Given that the powers of the inspectors were in any case limited, and many landlords did not comply (either because they could not afford to or because they could easily escape conviction), the inspectors ignored minor offences and concentrated upon the most flagrant abuses. Added to this, however, was a relatively lower level of activity in the slums. In these areas of worst housing the inspectors realised that their efforts would be futile: a building which was repaired might soon be vandalised or 'torched', and often the work was of inadequate standard and was not obvious, or overwhelmingly insignificant in the context of the broader environmental dilapidation. Furthermore, work in the slum areas was frequently highly dangerous. Nivola contrasts their work with that of the police in graphic terms:

> Inspectors did not cruise the street in squad cars; their 'beat' so to speak, included the dark hallways and stairwells, hidden passages and yards, rat-infested basements, and the innermost living quarters of sometimes desperate individuals. (Nivola, 1978:75.)

In some areas – notably public housing projects – the inspectors were permitted police escorts, while in others they were informally permitted to curtail their hours in the field ('before the kids get out of school'). These reduced working hours and problems of co-ordinating with the police department inevitably reduced the response time in the worst slum areas.

There was also a tendency for the inspectors to make a distinction between the 'deserving' and the 'undeserving' poor, commonly discriminating along ethnic or class lines. One of the crucial factors was the degree to which the occupants looked after their houses themselves: if internal housekeeping was poor then there seemed to be less likelihood that a complaint would receive a favourable reception. The inspectors appeared to be most favourably disposed towards the independent, self-reliant, working-class areas where complaints were perceived as less trivial than in the middle-class areas, and where the sloth and disorganisation of slum areas was not in evidence.

Nivola argues that Boston's housing inspectors were not a bureaucracy in the classic Weberian sense, characterised by predictable short interactions within a structure of generalised rules and norms. Instead, he claims that the discretionary freedom granted to inspectors meant that much of the work was *ad hoc*, and that administrative reactions varied from case to case. However, Nivola presents no firm evidence to support this conclusion, and to some extent it seems to contradict both his clear evidence of distributional outcomes and his long catalogue of informal procedures. What Nivola's work demonstrates superbly is the way in which the practical difficulties of a job can affect decision rules, even if these rules themselves are not made explicit. Often these problems may seem mundane – for example, since the inspectors worked between 9.00 a.m. and 5.00 p.m. they appeared to have greater difficulty in contacting many middle-class households at home during working hours; but the crucial point is that however trivial or serious these problems may be, important distribution consequences result.

Other writers have questioned the extent of local discretion, and stressed the routine and predictable nature of service delivery which makes the process amenable to control by a set of decision rules. The most detailed evidence about these rules has come from Jones and his research team in Detroit (Jones *et al.*, 1980). Indeed, in their study of housing inspectors they place emphasis upon the factors which encourage conformity amongst the inspectors. First, since the building code is so complex this means that simplifications and rules are required to ensure that it is useful. Second, the building inspectors have similar origins in the building trade, and this provides a powerful socialisation process and similarity of outlook. Third, because of the enormous potential for corruption, the buildings' departments in most large cities have attempted to remove charges of favouritism by enforcing certain norms of behaviour. It follows that just because a set of rules is not explicit it does not imply that the rules do not exist. Indeed, the detailed study undertaken by the Detroit team did not suggest that street-level discretion was an important determinant of the distributional pattern. Despite the absence of formal written guidelines, the seriousness of building-code violations was well understood by the staff and the main feature of the work was its routine character. Similarly, the studies of the police have also suggested the existence of rules to simplify complex decisions. Those officers responsible for the allocation of police patrols in response to calls from the public tend to have a hierarchy of priorities, amongst which 'officer in trouble' demands the most urgent response while 'family disturbance' is generally regarded as a low priority complaint.

The importance of local discretion should not therefore be exaggerated. Clearly, it will depend to a large degree upon the nature of the job. Some occupations such as police protection and building inspection have greater potential for ambiguity of outcome than, for example, refuse collection or fire fighting. Even so, Jones and his colleagues concluded that in Detroit the one service in which systematic street-level discretion was evident and not related to organisational factors was, in fact, refuse collection, which provided a poorer service in black neighbourhoods. The important point is that street-level discretion is not incompatible with regular decision rules with predictable outcomes.

Decision rules are widespread because of the numerous functions they fulfil. First and foremost they enable bureaucracies to perform their routine tasks. As Jones and his colleagues note 'Municipal service organisations do not achieve goals so much as perform tasks' (Jones *et al.*, 1980:239). Organisations rarely consider their ultimate goals, but function towards the immediate tasks in hand. Hence their record-keeping is usually limited to fairly simple indices of performance (what Lineberry terms 'body counts'), rather than more sophisticated measures of the impact on quality of services. This is useful in that it enables the agency to point to its success and divert attention from the more controversial issues of longer-term objectives.

A good example of the use of decision rules is the way in which they help bureaucracies to avoid having excessive workloads. Thus, many departments use consumer demand rather than seeking additional clients who require a service but do not ask for it. If this demand is excessive then of course certain rules help to regulate this by 'syphoning off' those demands which are trivial. There are many examples of departments using demand to allocate services. In Houston it was the case that 'The squeaky wheel gets the grease' – those who complained about the quality of their streets obtained repairs. Although arterial roads received the most attention, side roads were patched up if sufficient complaints were received. Similarly, in Oakland one of the major reasons that the wealthier upland areas received more resurfacing expenditures was because the residents of these areas knew how to register their complaints more effectively. Demand as defined by branch-circulation levels was the primary reason for the greater library acquisition funds in middle-class areas of Oakland, and Mladenka and Hill found an identical set of decision rules in Houston.

The organisational environment

These decision rules interact with other constraints to produce service distributions. We have already noted this in the case of ecological factors, but other interactions occur through the way in which the service is organised in the field. The areas administered by most service agencies are usually subdivided into smaller administrative dimensions, and the nature of this subdivision can lead to uneven levels of service provision. The Environmental Enforcement Division in Detroit, for example, was subdivided on the basis of districts used to allocate refuse collection, and these did not reflect the workload of the environmental inspectors (Jones *et al.*, 1980). The result was that some areas were overloaded with complaints and these received slower and poorer quality contacts with the agency.

Interactions also take place with other agencies. Because it is undesirable to resurface streets and then have them broken up again soon after for work on utilities, traffic engineers in Oakland did not resurface streets in which work on utilities was expected in the next five years (Levy *et al.*, 1974). Since some of the money for street reconstruction came from state petrol-tax revenues earmarked for particular streets, this was another factor which effectively lifted the decision outside the realm of the traffic engineers.

Much depends upon the role of the agency within the wider government structure. It has been hypothesised that agencies follow a life cycle: those that are newly created may be more aggressive in trying to win clients and establish a firm position in the realm of service provision. As the department's position is consolidated it may become less dynamic and simply use consumer demand to allocate services. If an agency is threatened with closure or amalgamation with another department it may engage in a vigorous campaign to win clients and demonstrate its usefulness.

In the United States it has been suggested that the Marijuana Tax of 1937 was the result of an intense campaign by the Bureau of Narcotics rather than a response to moral outrage on the part of the general public, who seemed to have been generally indifferent at the time (Smith, 1984). The agency was faced with a reduction in its budget, and decided to demonstrate its social usefulness in the face of what was portrayed as a serious problem. More recently, the attempt by the National Institute of Alcohol Abuse and Alcoholism to focus upon the problems of teenage drinking has been interpreted as an attempt to increase the relatively low budget of the agency and to resist the threat of incorporation into some more general substance abuse department. Empirical evidence would, in fact, tend to dismiss any simple life-cycle model, but there is little doubt that departments vary enormously in their overall approach to allocating services.

The limitations of the managerialist and decision-rules approaches

In the wake of all this evidence it would seem that few could deny the importance of local officials upon service distributions in cities. Nevertheless, it is important to recognise that these studies have a number of fundamental methodological limitations which at the very least cast some doubt upon many of the findings, and at worst call for a reformulation of the approach.

Some of these limitations should be apparent from the previous discussions in Chapters 2 and 3. The correlational methodology of the decision-rules approach has ignored the complexity of the distance-decay effects analysed by the locational efficiency school (described in Chapter 3). It is likely that re-analysis of the decision-rules literature to take into account 'tapering' effects from point-specific services would lead to some modification of many conclusions regarding the distributions of services.

In this context it is worth drawing attention to a thought-provoking critique of the correlational methodology of service studies provided by McLafferty (1982). Her analysis follows in the vein of Hodge and Gattrell who argued that 'The size, shape and arrangement of residential areas constrain the flexibility of an urban system to achieve equitable public facility locations' (Hodge and Gattrell, 1976:216). McLafferty notes that the spatial structure of cities determines in large part the inequalities observed in the distribution of public services, by limiting the sites for actual service centres, and by affecting the differential accessibility of those cities to various income groups in the city. This proposition is demonstrated by the calculation of correlation coefficients for various service distribution patterns within three types of city. Two of the cities were hypothetical examples – the concentric city model, with low-income areas located in the city centre and progressively higher-income groups at increasing distance from the centre, together with the sector model in which income groups were assigned at random to sectors. The third city was the actual metropolitan area of Cedar Rapids, Iowa. Assuming that no area could have more than one service centre, various possible combinations of service centre locations were simulated and the underlying frequency distributions of correlation coefficients (r values) was calculated.

The results indicated that in all cities the minimum and maximum possible r values differed enormously from the actual limits of r or 1·0 and −1·0. The sectoral city, for example, allowed extreme values of approximately 0·6 and −0·6, with small variations depending upon the number of centres. In such a city the proximity of high- and low-income groups means that neither income group can be strongly favoured over the other in terms of service distribution. In the concentric-ring city the minimum and maximum values of r vary depending upon the number of service centres. With only one centre, the dispersion of high-income groups in the ring implies that no service location can be accessible to all the higher-income groups without at the same time giving access to low-income centres. In the more common example of four or five service centres, however, it is possible to obtain a high negative r if facilities are located exclusively in the wealthy areas on the urban periphery.

The spatial patterning of income groups not only affects the limits of r but the distribution of values between these limits. In the concentric ring city more than 90 per cent of the r values were positive, and low-income groups were relatively accessible to most potential facility sites because of their centrality and high density. In the sectoral city, 70 per cent of all patterns had a positive value, but the bulk of values grouped near 0. Overall, in the sectoral city there is little possible bias in the set of possible locations towards either positive or negative values, since there are few locational patterns which can give clear advantages to either high- or low-income groups.

On the basis of these results, McLafferty argues that the failure of service studies to confirm the underclass hypothesis may simply reflect the effect of spatial constraint. She claims that negative r values indicating territorial injustice and discrimination against the poor are highly unlikely, given the configuration of income classes typically found in many American cities. It follows that the results obtained by American service studies do not necessarily reflect the power, motivations, or resources of the principal actors involved.

Ironically, McLafferty's critique falls into the same trap as the service studies she criticises for, as she admits, her analysis is based upon simple physical measures of distance and thus ignores the time and cost effects analysed by the locational efficiency approaches. As shown in Chapter 3, when such factors are incorporated into studies of service accessibility, they often − although not inevitably − show distributions which discriminate against certain low-income areas. Furthermore, her analysis is based upon the simple absence or presence of facilities, and ignores the issue of service facilities size and quality. One of the advantages of decision-rules approaches is that they have concentrated on a wide range of indices of service provision, rather than focusing like the older inter-city outputs studies upon expenditures.

Nevertheless, McLafferty's analysis does serve to emphasise that ecological factors or spatial constraints such as the availability of land, the capacity constraints of service centres, and the central configuration of income classes in the city can have an important effect upon the distribution of services. However, just as environmental inputs could not be regarded as determinants of local authority expenditures in the 'outputs' debate, so ecological constraints cannot be regarded as the ultimate determinants of service distributions within cities. Once again these constraints must be perceived, interpreted and acted upon by local decision-makers.

This last point has been recognised by the decision-rules and managerialist approaches, but they have often failed to make a conclusive link between the operating procedures of public bureaucracies and the resulting service distributions. This criticism is not universally applicable and the work of Jones and his co-researchers (Jones *et al.*, 1980) is exceptional for the way in which it probes inside the workings of public officialdom. Far more typical, however, has been the tendency to observe a particular pattern of service allocation, and from this make inferences about the underlying decision rules without any rigorous validation of these conclusions. This limitation is very largely a reflection of the enormous difficulties involved in studying complex organisations. Nevertheless, it remains true that most studies in the managerialist tradition have paid only lip-service to the complex ideas of Weber relating to bureaucracies, or the ensuing vast literature in the field of organisation theory. This means that many complex issues such as the meaning of bureaucracy, how this differs from professionalisation, and the nature of professional-bureaucratic conflict have been ignored.

There is another, more powerful explanation for the failure of these researchers to confirm the underclass hypothesis. It relates to the fact that the majority of these studies have continued to use relatively simple socio-economic, demographic, ethnic, and environmental variables, rather than detailed indices of need for public services. Once again the prime concern of these American studies has been to see if there is broad equality of service provision, or discrimination against particular ethnic groups, social classes or geographical areas. However, if needs are initially unequally distributed amongst various individuals or areas, then equal service distributions can have unequal results. Clearly, simple arithmetic equality means that services will be much less effective in dealing with the problems of the high-need areas compared to those areas where problems are less serious.

This points to one of the most important limitations of these service studies: the fact that, like the earlier outputs approach, they have ignored the effects (or 'outcomes') of these service allocations upon the well-being of individuals and neighbourhoods in various parts of the city. It is likely that further information on outcomes would go some way towards explaining the apparent paradox of non-cumulative inequality in service provision, but continuing cumulative inequality in broader aspects of social, economic and environmental deprivation.

Rich (1982) points out that, although North American studies have examined a wide range of public services, they have tended to concentrate upon many basic or relatively pure public services such as police, fire protection, sewers, roads, street lighting and environmental protection, all of which confer roughly equal benefits to a wide section of the public. Such services do little or nothing to counteract the broad dimensions of inequality relating to housing, income and health care. To some extent this may be related to the smaller scope of state-funded welfare services in the United States. But even when services do have redistributive objectives, they often do not begin to cope with the magnitude of the problems posed by the poorest areas or their underlying causes. This is the case despite compensatory schemes designed to overcome the difficulties of the worst areas.

There are many examples of this inadequacy: public housing by itself does not overcome the poverty which prevents many families from adequately caring for their homes; hospitals by themselves cannot deal with many of the underlying causes of ill health; and the provision of additional police resources may not affect the underlying causes of crime. This is not to suggest that public services are irrelevant to the problems – indeed, one of the important consequences of the attack of the 'New Right' upon public services both in Britain and the United States, has been a greater public awareness of the value of many public services; it is merely that, given the scale of many problems, many services by themselves are inadequate. Clearly, the value of public services and public intervention in general – what is sometimes termed 'the social wage' – is an important question for further studies of service provision in cities. (This issue will be taken up in Chapter 6.) What is clear, however, is that future studies of the urban managers should expand the range of services and phenomena under investigation so that they conform more closely with Harvey's original notion of 'real income'. An important part of this concept is the capital accumulation which can result from the ownership of property. In recent years, continuing high levels of inflation have meant that the capital which can be derived from the possession of property can almost equal, and in some cases may exceed, the income derived from the occupational market. Such considerations should lead studies of decision rules to examine in greater detail the operation of the land-use planning system, and the distribution of positive and negative externalities in general. Eventually this should take studies away from the analysis of local services *per se* towards an understanding of the way in which both public and private sector institutions affect welfare outcomes in particular localities. Related to this is the need for more theory about the sources of inequality in general, and a greater understanding of the links between services and local welfare outcomes in particular localities.

This leads to the final, and most important limitation of the managerialist approach: the fact that, by itself, a focus upon decision rules and managerial discretion says little or nothing about the 'external' constraints imposed upon the urban managers. Much of the managerialist writing, and especially the very early work in this tradition, gave the impression that managers are all-powerful, with complete freedom of action to allocate resources as they wish. However, it soon became apparent that the actions of urban managers are constrained by a number of factors and not simply those related to the 'spatial logic' of city organisation. For example, many of the actions of those within the public sector are affected by the activities of the private sector, and local authority officers are involved in much liaison with private companies and private sources of finance. Furthermore, in recent years the activities of British local authorities have become increasingly constrained by central government control (see Chapter 6).

Pahl soon became aware of these problems and summed up his dissatisfaction with the early managerialist approaches in the phrase that they focused exclusively upon the 'middle dogs' in society to the neglect of the 'top dogs' who were ultimately responsible for patterns of resource allocation. This criticism was echoed by many others, and Pahl therefore reformulated his managerialist approach so that it now focuses exclusively upon managers within the public sector (Pahl, 1977). The prime role of these managers is seen as one of mediation between the private and public sectors. However, these bureaucrats are no longer seen as independent variables, but rather as intervening variable allocating resources whose overall magnitude is determined by central government. Pahl's explanation for these patterns of resource allocation is a form of neo-Weberian theory known as 'corporatism'. This theory is considered in Chapter 6 when we examine strategies for further research. Here it should be noted that the extent of local managerial autonomy is a key unresolved issue in urban studies. The major limitation of much of the work reviewed in this chapter is that it does not provide clear and unambiguous methods for evaluating this power. The theories which have been most critical of managerialist approaches, and which have devoted the most attention to the constraints upon urban managers, are the various forms of neo-Marxist theory; and these are considered in the next chapter.

5 Neo-Marxist approaches

Introduction

The most important principle underlying Marxist perspectives is the idea that 'the material world exists prior to our conceptions of it, and that the way in which this world appears to us may conceal or distort its essential character' (Saunders, 1981:15). This means that the material reality of the world – what Marx termed 'essential relations' – are much more complex than our consciousness of the world based on everyday experience of 'phenomenal forms'. The task of science, then, is to probe beneath the level of everyday experience or 'the realm of appearances' and to discover the essential relations which give rise to these appearances. In order to accomplish this task it is necessary to place any given set of phenomenal forms within the context of the broader social relations of which they are a part. For Marx, these essential relations are determined by the dynamics of the capitalist mode of production.

It is important to realise that the essential relations of the capitalist system are not 'things' which can be directly measured according to the norms of conventional science but are, above all, social relationships which produce outcomes. The outcomes can be observed, *but the hidden structures which give rise to these outcomes cannot be directly measured, and cannot be subject to any simple criteria of empirical verification.* As Saunders (1981) notes, it is therefore of little use to criticise the approach on the grounds that it cannot be tested, since the approach involves theorising processes which by definition cannot be amenable to direct observation. This approach has been termed conjectural theory or 'retroduction'. It suggests certain relationships which, if correct, would account for the empirical appearance (Sayer, 1979). These conjectures must bear some relationship to the level of appearances but can never be fully tested. The theories must be plausible explanations both for understanding the world, and for changing the structure of society through political action.

Marx's critique of capitalist relations was based on his version of the labour theory of value. This theory argues that it is the amount of human labour involved in the production of an object which is the true value of what a thing is worth. Marx argued that within a capitalist system the value produced by labour was expropriated by those who owned the means of production. The difference between what capitalists obtained for goods and what they paid labourers (minus the cost of materials and machinery) was the *surplus value*. Payments of interest on money borrowed or rent on the hire of land or machinery are all seen as part of the total surplus value which is produced, since they are not payments for actual work undertaken. This interpretation sees the worker as exploited and deprived of the true value of the fruits of his labour, and contrasts with the numerous other rationales for profit-taking specified in conventional economics, such as that profits are a reward for taking risks or innovating new products. Conventional methods of calculating wages, prices and profits are thus seen as obscuring this exploitative relationship (Smith, 1977).

The labour theory of value serves to illustrate Marx's basic approach, for his analysis is based upon units of socially necessary labour time – beyond which the capitalist extracts surplus value – which cannot be directly measured in the same manner as prices or wages. Prices and wages are the superficial expression of the underlying social relationships.

It was from this basic theory that Marx concluded that capitalist societies were characterised by conflict between two major classes; the capitalist or ruling class (the bourgeoisie) who owned the means of production, and the workers (or proletariat) who owned little but their labour. Capitalism is thus defined as a *mode of production*, characterised by a set of fundamental characteristics which are the basic economic driving forces of the society. These forces include the technical methods through which production is undertaken – the *forces of production* – and the social relationships between classes which permit this productive process – *the relations of production*. Capitalism is thus not simply the ownership of money or machinery but the ability to command labour to produce items and to use capital to accumulate further wealth. Wealth is created by the ability to exploit the proletariat, and is ultimately dependent upon the workers for its existence.

Marx argued that this process of exploitation involved a number of contradictions which manifest themselves in a number of crises for the capitalist system. In particular, he laid stress on the overwhelming desire of the bourgeoisie for increased capital accumulation. This desire could be manifest either in attempts to suppress wages as low as possible or in efforts to invest in machinery in order to increase productivity. However, a population whose living standards are suppressed below subsistence level will have insufficient purchasing power to engage in consumption – the ultimate process whereby the surplus is realised. Furthermore, increases in productivity may produce more goods than a society can absorb. Consequently, there may be a contradiction between the forces of production and the relations of production. In some of Marx's writing the forces of production are seen as developing ahead of the relations of production and are constrained by the latter. In other writings, however, the relations of production play an important part in determining the forces of production.

Differences from neo-Weberian perspectives

It is the Marxist claim to be able to probe beneath the surface of everyday appearances and to relate observations to a wider whole which gives Marxist perspectives such tremendous appeal for many scholars. By the same token, however, it is these very same qualities – suggesting that Marxism is more fundamental than other approaches which remain at the level of 'everyday appearances' – which make Marxism so controversial as a method of intellectual inquiry. It does mean, however, that, despite its numerous variants, Marxism in general represents a very different view of the world from what can be termed conventional social science. It represents a way of criticising and reinterpreting other approaches and, indeed, one could argue that this has been its major contribution to urban studies to date. In particular, Marxist approaches stand in sharp contrast to Weberian approaches.

To begin with, the Marxist claim to be able to collapse the dichotomy between facts and values is contrary to the Weberian approach. Although Weber recognised that completely objective scientific analysis would be impossible, he did place great emphasis upon the need for rigorous testing of hypotheses derived from ideal types. While evidence can be judged, individuals' value systems cannot, and he maintained that conflict between different ethical codes was inevitable.

One of the important implications of the holistic Marxist view is that issues of consumption cannot be seen as separate from issues relating to production. Marxist approaches therefore refuse to equate social welfare with any particular set of needs defined in terms of social indicators, as has been outlined in previous chapters. Marx himself was fierce in his condemnation of 'socialists' who attempted to gain reforms through redistribution of resources without fundamentally altering production relations. It also follows from this perspective that there is nothing inherent in the nature of goods and services which implies that they should be collectively consumed (as is implied by public choice theories). The crucial issue is the extent to which goods and services become commodified as part of capital's search for surplus value. As always, patterns of collective consumption must be seen in the light of processes of capital accumulation and the realisation and circulation of surplus value.

Another consequence of the Marxist approach is to reject as 'ideological' any perspective which focuses exclusively upon individuals such as bureaucrats and politicians. The activities of such persons must be placed first and foremost in the context of class struggle. This of course contrasts with Weber, who rejected attempts to explain events in terms other than the subjectively meaningful actions of individuals.

Marxist approaches also conflict with Weberian approaches over definitions of class. As described in Chapter 4, Weber argued that classes could emerge in various situations in which individuals had differential access to scarce resources. For Marx, however, classes are defined in relation to expended labour power, and whether they are owners or sellers of labour. It follows from this perspective that the struggle between capital and labour is the fundamental struggle in society. Conflict in particular localities over issues such as housing, roads, schools or social services are seen as relatively unimportant because they do not alter the fundamental class relations which emerge in the field of production.

Yet another consequence of the Marxist approach is to attack as 'ideological' any approach which considers space to be an independent variable in the explanation of inequality, since this reveals nothing about the underlying social relations. Conflict is ultimately dependent upon the contradictions inherent within the capitalist mode of production which may have a spatial manifestation but no independent spatial determinant. This contrasts sharply with the Weberian view which regards conflict as inevitable in all societies for a number of reasons other than through the dominant mode of production. In defending this position Saunders thus asked 'Who will live nearest the sewage farm come the socialist millennium?' (Saunders, 1982:187).

Neo-Marxist theories

One of the major difficulties of Marx's work, apart from its inherent complexity, is that despite all his attempts at generalisation it is very firmly grounded in developments in British *laissez-faire* capitalism in the nineteenth century. Obviously, much has changed since then. The interests of capital are now less easily identifiable as a class of factory owners, but have become embodied in a complex set of institutions – banks, pension funds, investment trusts and government agencies. Competitive capitalism has largely given way to monopoly capital dominated by large corporations and oligopolies. Skilled labour and technical knowledge, rather than simple labour power, have become much more important, and social divisions have become much more complex. Added to these developments is, of course, the widespread growth of bureaucracy.

Recent years have thus witnessed the proliferation of various neo-Marxist theories which attempt to reformulate classical Marxism in the light of changes that have taken place in society in the twentieth century. In particular there has been a desire to account for the failure of class-based revolutions in liberal capitalist democracies, and to account for the enormous changes in the scale and character of state intervention in all walks of life. These two issues are seen as closely connected.

One of the main problems facing Marxist scholars is how to explain the functions of the modern state without resorting to some crude and highly implausible theory of economic determinism that portrays the state as a mere instrument of the ruling capitalist class. One approach to this problem has been the so-called 'capital logic' school, which has attempted to show the ways in which the state is necessary to maintain the capitalist mode of production (Jessop, 1977). This has been done in a somewhat abstract manner, reducing the capitalist system to pure forms and then deriving the functions of the state which ensure 'generalised commodity production'.

At one level this task is accomplished by the creation and maintenance of a monetary system necessary for production and exchange of commodities. The legal system guarantees certain political freedoms which are seen as essential for capitalist exploitation to take place. All subjects are in formal terms free to pursue their own ends, purchase certain commodities, and own private property. This enables the capitalist class to hire labour power as a commodity and to accumulate capital. Thus, what appears to be a system based on freedom is in reality based on exploitation. The representative democracies which are a persistent feature of capitalist economies are seen as providing a powerful ideological role in maintaining these myths of equality and self-determination. Other functions of the capitalist state are explained by the 'capital logic' school with reference to the falling rate of profit and the destructive effects of competition.

This approach suggests that the state cannot be regarded merely as a political structure which is established and controlled by capitalists; instead, the capitalist state is an essential element in the social reproduction of capitalism (Jessop, 1977). One of the major problems with this approach, however, is that in reducing the role of state to pure forms, it tends to ignore non-economic influences together with the enormous diversity to be found both within and between capitalist states at various times. Thus, the historical origins of modern state apparatus, together with its evolution over time, and competition between diverse groups over control of state actions, all tend to be ignored. This approach therefore has relatively little to say about collective consumption.

A second and – until recently at least – more influential form of solution to the problems of conceptualising the role of the state within capitalist societies has been a form of Marxism known as structuralism, which is predominantly French in origin. Much of this approach is derived from the complex writings of Althusser and

Poulantzas. This approach recognises the existence of various interrelated levels of social organisation – primarily these are the 'economic', 'political' and 'social'. The economic level is ultimately considered to be the most important level in that it conditions all the other levels, but not in any rigid manner. For this reason the levels are regarded as being relatively autonomous. Fundamental contradictions between the forces of production and the relations of production will find expression at various levels. However, while the state may give in to short-term demands from the working class, it will always work in the long-term interests of the dominant monopoly capital.

Castells and collective consumption

The most influential writer to adopt such a framework has been Castells (1977), in his definition of collective consumption. He argues that the primary function of schools, houses, health care facilities and the like, is to reproduce the labour power necessary for the capitalist system to survive. However, the provision of these facilities is increasingly expensive and they are therefore not amenable to provision by private markets – at least amongst lower-income groups. The state has therefore intervened to provide these facilities on a collective basis, and thereby attempted to overcome the contradictions within the capitalist system. Within this framework, collective consumption is thus defined in terms of its *function* within the capitalist system, rather than in terms of the inherent characteristics of the services themselves. Furthermore, Castells uses the notion of collective consumption to provide a definition of 'urban'. He argues that, whereas the organisation of capitalist production takes place at regional, national and international levels, collective consumption is increasingly organised on a city-wide scale. Cities are thus centres for the reproduction of labour power through collectivised means of consumption.

From this perspective the activities of all the various planners and urban managers considered in Chapter 4 are seen as inherently 'reformist' and limited in scope, since they do not lead to a fundamental transformation of the economic base of society. Managerial initiatives may make the provision of collective consumption more efficient or more equally distributed, but these policies do not challenge the dominant interests of capital; indeed, they serve to reinforce them.

Castells argues that the need to maintain profitability in the private sector will divert investment away from collectivised services. But whereas private consumption can only be attributed to the 'hidden hand' of the market, the state can easily be recognised as responsible for collective consumption, and can be criticised for inadequate provision. Castells therefore maintains that state provision encourages a collective response. With the 'right' organisation, such protests over shortfalls in the provision of collective consumption can attain the stature of 'urban social movements'. These are protest groups who come to see the real 'stakes' at issue behind isolated problems such as shortages of hospital beds, school closures, and homelessness. Such groups will attempt to achieve a fundamental shift in the dominant type of social relations in the interests of the working class; indeed, certain issues may unite both poor- and middle-income groups in the interest of better service provision. The crucial point Castells is making is that the increasingly collectivised nature of consumption, which is necessary for the capital system to survive, leads to the increased likelihood of urban social movements. This is but one of the many contradictions and tensions within the capitalist system.

Although enormously influential, Castell's ideas have a number of fundamental limitations and weaknesses (see Pahl, 1978; Pickvance, 1976; Saunders, 1979). In the context of most British and American cities it is clear that most protests over collective consumption do *not* lead to demands of radical nature or the formation of inter-class alliances. As indicated in Chapter 3, most protests are limited in geographical area and in terms of the scale of demands, typically reacting to an existing proposal rather than suggesting broader changes. Saunders suggests that the numerous neighbourhood organisations in British and American cities, with their limited participatory objectives, are very different from the radical working-class neighbourhood movements that are to be found in France and Italy. In Europe, protest movements are more radical in their demands, disruptive in character and working class in orientation. Furthermore, as Dunleavy (1977) notes, the Castellian approach falls into the same trap as the pluralist approach in focusing upon overt conflict: many of the important – though not necessarily radical – decisions concerning collective consumption are made away from the public gaze through institutional channels and bargaining between agencies.

An important criticism of Castell's approach relates to his interpretation of cities as being spatial units whose primary function is the reproduction of labour power through collective consumption. Indeed, other Marxist writers have given alternative interpretations of the primary functions of cities in a capitalist system. Lojkine (1976), for example, stresses the importance of collective consumption for supporting the rate of profit: some facilities such as roads and public utilities could not be provided solely by private capital without severely undermining capital accumulation.

Harvey and the over-accumulation thesis

Yet another Marxist interpretation of the function of cities is provided by Harvey (1978). His analysis is closely related to the development of North American suburbia after the Second World

War. He notes that after 1945 the United States was confronted with the dilemma of how to utilise the enormous industrial machine that had been developed during the war. Much of this machine continued to produce armaments, but another crucial strategy was the consumption stimulated by the growth of suburbia. Suburbanisation called for the construction of enormous highway networks, stimulated the automobile industry and generally encouraged a home-centred and competitive, consumption-intensive lifestyle. This contrasted with the poverty and communal solidarity of the older high-density working-class districts.

Harvey thus argues that the primary function of cities lies in the management of demand. One of the main problems facing the capitalist system in recent years has been the over-accumulation of capital. This means more capital is produced than can be invested directly in production – what is termed the 'primary circuit' of capital. The result is a flow of capital into the secondary circuit of capital consisting of capital investment and consumption funds. The built environment is an important part of this secondary circuit. Thus, suburbanisation not only provided an area for investment but stimulated demand for the products of industrial capital. The state was, through a variety of fiscal measures – including tax concessions to the building industry and home-owners – a key instigator of this suburbanisation process. From this perspective Harvey, like many other Marxists, sees home-ownership as a means of legitimising the system and maintaining political stability. Thus, debt-encumbered owner-occupiers are seen as unlikely to make radical political demands.

According to Harvey's approach there is no basic difference between struggles at the place of work (or production) and at the place of living (or reproduction): they both represent in different forms the underlying class struggle between capital and labour. The division between work and living is thus an artificial dichotomy imposed upon individuals by the capitalist system.

Cox and turf politics

A similar neo-Marxist interpretation of suburbanisation and associated locality based conflicts is provided by Cox (1984). Cox labels such disputes 'turf politics', and notes that they have only come into prominence, both as a political issue in cities and as a subject for academic scrutiny, since the Second World War. This conclusion is derived from an analysis of controversies over the built environment in Columbus, Ohio, as represented in the local newspaper. Throughout the 1960s and 1970s there was a much greater increase in such conflicts than can be explained by the growth of population in the urban area. Furthermore, the character of the conflicts has changed over time; before 1950 the main concerns were for better services such as roads, sewage, fire stations and street lighting. Since 1950, however, re-zoning issues have been dominant, indicating the exclusionary concerns of current neighbourhood organisations.

Cox argues that the concepts used by conventional (bourgeois) social science, such as externalities, 'consumption cleavages', and 'quality of life' indices, are embedded at the level of phenomenal forms and ignore the underlying generative mechanisms which give rise to these forms. These mechanisms, he maintains, are bound up with the relations of generalised commodity production. Essential for the emergence of turf politics is the commodification of the neighbourhood, which enables people to identify their local area as a 'thing' from which others can be excluded. Given that the relations of generalised commodity production affected the place of production with the Industrial Revolution, it is necessary to explain why commodification of the place of residence did not take place until the late twentieth century. This, Cox argues, can only be understood by an historical analysis of the capitalist mode of production and its separation from the place of reproduction. This separation and the growth of turf politics is seen as enabling the resolution of numerous conflicts within the sphere of production which were initially overcome by mutual aid amongst the working class. This aid, and the close personal relations engendered by the localised extended family, are seen as a response to the chronic material uncertainty which existed in the traditional working-class areas of the major cities. In these environments, it is argued, the individual had no sense of self apart from a specific community; and this accounts for the high degree of attachment the inhabitants of these areas felt towards what were frequently poor social conditions. However, the growth of the Welfare State and the rise of the women's movement are seen as eliminating the need for more informal types of mutual aid, enabling the privatising impulses of the nuclear family to be given free rein in the suburb.

O'Connor and the fiscal crisis of the state

Clearly, Castells, Lojkine and Harvey have all emphasised particular functions of collectivised services in capitalist societies. The work of O'Connor (1973) is especially noteworthy in this context, for he has provided one of the most complex and influential interpretations of the modern state, which integrates many of the functions noted above.

O'Connor stresses the dual functions of state expenditures in enabling the continuation of capital accumulation while at the same time legitimising the existing social order. The accumulation function is undertaken by two aspects of 'social capital', which he terms 'social investment' and 'social consumption'. Social investment consists of expenditures on both human and physical capital – such as roads and education – which are necessary to increase labour productivity. Social consumption consists of both collectively consumed goods and services, and transfer payments such as in social insurance programmes, which serve to reproduce labour power on both a daily and generational basis. If these aspects of social capital were not provided by the state, then capital would have to provide them at enormous expense. Thus, in contemporary capitalist societies both social investment and social consumption serve to increase the rate of profit. In contrast 'social expenses' do not directly affect capital accumulation, but are envisaged as necessary to maintain social cohesion and to legitimise the existing social order by offsetting problems which would threaten its ideological stability. These expenses may involve directly coercive agencies such as the police, welfare services in response to popular agitation, and legitimation activities manifested in school and public participation exercises.

It requires little thought to appreciate that these functions need not be exclusive to particular types of service or expenditure. For example, education can be envisaged as part of social consumption, lowering the costs of class reproduction; but like social expenses it can perform a legitimising role, 'buying off' popular discontent and inculcating values in the young. Furthermore, expenditures on the police, education and welfare services can, through the purchase of buildings and equipment, affect capital accumulation of private companies. Nevertheless, these overlaps of function do not invalidate the core of O'Connor's argument, which is that conflicts and tensions arise in the modern state because of the need to satisfy the differing functions. Indeed, it can be argued that the overlap of functions serves to exacerbate these tensions. In particular, welfare policies designed to create popular support for the system may undermine social investment which is directly necessary to maintain profitability in the private sector. O'Connor goes on to argue that although the state has taken over the provision of many collective services necessary to support the public sector, it has not devised the means of adequately taxing the profits that have ensued. The result has been fiscal stress and in many instances – such as New York in 1975 – a severe fiscal crisis.

O'Connor's theory of fiscal crisis also involves a form of the underconsumption theory. Monopoly capital is seen as increasingly dependent upon state expenditure, but this social capital serves only to expand production beyond the level of demand. The net result is unemployment, welfare expenditure and further pressures upon the state to increase social capital expenditure, with yet further stress upon fiscal resources. As in Harvey's approach, suburbanisation is seen as an important manifestation of the fiscal crisis of the state. The monopoly sector, subsidised by social capital, is increasingly located in the new suburbs while the competitive sector comprising the poorer insecure jobs is confined to the city centre.

The limitations of structuralist approaches

Saunders (1979) has pointed out that one does not have to be a Marxist to accept O'Connor's type of taxonomy, or to recognise the numerous conflicts of interest which emerge in the modern capitalist state – indeed, such problems are also a major concern of liberal and conservative perspectives. The crucial issue is whether one envisages these functions as inevitably tied to the interests of capital, or to some notion of the 'common good' or collective national interest.

In this context, one of the major issues facing the 'needs of capital' type of arguments is the fact that capitalist societies vary so much in the form of their public service provision. The most obvious difference is the variation in the scale of public sector housing between the United States and Western Europe. Less obvious, but no less interesting, are the enormous variations in the extent of pre-school services such as nurseries (Pinch, 1984). Many European societies with their extensive facilities stand in marked contrast to the lack of provision in Britain and the United States. Sweden has especially well-developed facilities, and Adams and Winston (1980) have argued that the system there has more in common with China than North America.

Marxists argue that such variations occur because the class struggle can take various forms in different places at different times. The contradictions between the need for social consumption and social investment necessary for profitable production produce lacunae in diverse areas of consumption. Thus, Duncan (1978) argues that different types of consumption facilities may fall short of social needs in different societies at different points in time, as a result of a wide range of factors which cannot be incorporated into any general theory.

In one sense, however, these structuralist approaches succeed in explaining everything and nothing, for there is no specific indication of why services should vary so enormously amongst different capitalist societies. Furthermore, the framework established by these theories effectively insulates them for any sort of counter-factual evidence which would lead to their rejection. Thus, any policies which would appear to be against the interest of capital can be interpreted as short-term concessions necessary for the long-term preservation of the system. As Kirby and Pinch note, 'like some epistemological game of football, any result – win, draw or lose – can be accommodated into the expectations' (Kirby and Pinch, 1983:241).

Many critics have thus pointed out that these structuralist theories face the same problems as functionalist sociology in attempting to explain causes in terms of effects. Piven and Friedland (1984) note that one of the major flaws of these theories is to assert the effects of public expenditures on the basis of *a priori* categories, rather than subjecting these effects to empirical scrutiny. Thus, concepts like 'social consumption' are used to categorise expenditures without any attempt to ascertain whether such expenditures actually *do* lower the cost of reproducing labour power. They argue that public subsidies for suburban house construction cannot be assumed by *a priori* definition to stimulate life styles conducive to commodity consumption and capitalist growth without empirical verification. Pickvance (1976) has similarly argued that the ability of the state to act independently of particular classes can ultimately be determined only through empirical analysis.

In a similar vein Gough (1975) has stressed the need to separate the origins of state intervention from the subsequent effects of that intervention. It is therefore fallacious to argue that those who currently benefit from policies brought them about in the first place. Many public services were a response to popular pressures, even though such services have subsequently benefited certain capitalist interests.

The example of pre-school services
Pre-school services again demonstrate the above points. In Britain the scale of nursery provision has been related to the need to employ women in the workforce. Widespread female employment has been necessary to ensure survival only during times of war, when extensive nurseries were provided. In times of peace, despite the considerable increase in rates of employment of women with young children, there has been a notable absence of state provision of nurseries. The state has intervened to provide accommodation for those children in most need, and is ostensibly concerned to ensure minimum standards; but in most cases women are forced to use facilities in the private and voluntary sectors. Many persons such as childminders who look after the children of working mothers do so for extremely low rewards, and in this sense businesses are obtaining female labour at a subsidised rate – since few companies provide nurseries directly. Low rates of nursery provision are thus functional for the interests of capitalism, and those few state services that exist are vulnerable to closure since they are not directly responsible or necessary for maintaining profit accumulation in the same manner as roads or public utilities. However, the widespread systems of nursery provision which are to be found in other Western societies would suggest that capitalism need not be associated with any particular level of pre-school provision. Humphries (1977) has argued that it is possible to envisage a system of state child-rearing agencies which would benefit from economies of scale, and which could help provide a workforce with the suitable attitudes and skills necessary for the continuation of the capitalist system. Although it would be expensive, the centralisation involved in the substitution of state for family services would give capital greater control over the administration of resources which could be streamlined in the

interests of capital production. Barrett (1980) has similarly argued that it has yet to be demonstrated that capitalism could not function without the present system of domestic labour and child-rearing, and that explanations based solely around the smooth reproduction of capitalist social relations run the risk of ignoring conflict and political struggle.

Furthermore, although the current low levels of pre-school provision in Britain may be compatible with class interests, there is little evidence that the policy was created with these interests in mind. Concern was expressed at the time of the Boer War about the poor quality of British conscripts, and inadequate nutrition and standards of child-rearing amongst the working-class were blamed for this state of affairs (Lewis, 1980). Eventually a campaign emerged to 'glorify, dignify and purify motherhood', and a set of welfare services were developed, including welfare clinics for mothers, health visitors and hospital facilities for women and infants. These policies were based on an underlying assumption that needs were due to individual moral failure which could be overcome by education, and this diverted attention away from the broader social conditions which contributed to ill health. The focus upon motherhood strengthened the role of women in the home and helped to undermine the need for nursery provision. Nevertheless, as Hall (1979) points out, this ideology of domesticity was strongly advocated by the Evangelical movement and initially adopted by the bourgeoisie during the rapid industrialisation of Britain between 1780 and 1830. The ideology was not developed primarily to subordinate women at home, but was subsequently moulded by economic forces to achieve this end when it spread amongst the working class. Barrett (1980) also notes that although industrial capitalism brought about sweeping changes in the position of women, many developments related to the increased possibilities of divorce, and the rise of notions of romantic love are less plausibly related to specific capitalist modes of production (Barrett, 1980). Other developments, such as protective legislation for working women and the limited growth of pre-school services, are also not strictly explicable within the logic of capitalist development. The early state involvement in education arose from a concern with the health of the working class, but there is little indication that this policy was motivated by the interests of business. Indeed, the early Factory Act legislation threatened the profitability of the private sector by removing a cheap source of labour. Although nursery education may have helped to contribute towards a healthier workforce, the initial impetus came from the zeal of social reformers.

Class struggle and the state
What is missing from Harvey's and many other neo-Marxist interpretations, then, is some notion of the political struggles that lie

behind the creation of policies, state forms, and collective consumption patterns. Within Harvey's approach the capitalist system generates its own crises through its own internal contradictions. The working class are thus seen as a passive and ineffective force manipulated by the forces of capital. The effects of the class struggle, insofar as they are conceptualised at all, are seen as insignificant compared with the forces of the capital accumulation.

It is interesting to note in this context that most of the theories which lay stress upon the internal restructuring of capital and the underconsumption thesis, have emanated from North America. British researchers have tended to be critical of this approach for two main reasons. The first criticism has been based on theoretical grounds, for many have disputed the importance of monopoly capital price-fixing as an important factor in arresting the declining rate of profit. Less complex has been a second type of criticism based on empirical grounds, for in British cities with their tightly-bound structures, the importance of suburbia in demand creation seems less obvious. In the British context at least, public policy would seem to be much more the result of class struggle. Gough (1979) argues that the dominance of the underconsumption thesis in North America may reflect the unique character of American society, in which public expenditure patterns seem to more closely accord with the needs of capital rather than those of a well-organised labour movement.

Gough's own perspective therefore represents a second strand of Marxist thinking, rather different in form from structuralism which gives pre-eminence to the role of class conflict in the formation of policy (Holloway and Picciotto, 1977). He argues that the absence of housing and comprehensive social assistance policies in the United States when compared with Europe, suggests that the introduction of such policies owes much to the existence of a unified labour movement and relatively strong social democratic or communist parties. In contrast, the existence of extensive state education facilities in the United States suggests that working class pressures are less important in this context.

Gough (1979) argues that the threat of a powerful working-class movement can galvanise the ruling class to undertake policies to avert conflict through the operation of the state. The source and form of this state intervention will vary from one country to another. In Germany, for example, Bismarck's welfare policies were very much directed from 'above' to head off the threat posed by the growth of trade unions and the Marxist Social Democratic Party (SDP). In Britain a unitary state and powerful central government facilitated policies to head off social disquiet. In the United States, in the wake of black social unrest in the major cities in the 1960s, it was necessary for the federal government to seize the initiative and bypass state and local levels of government in order to introduce the

Great Society Programme. Gough suggests however, that the absence of a powerful and centralised body to represent the labour movement meant that a thorough restructuring of the state was unnecessary.

Such approaches develop a much greater sense of struggle and domination than is apparent in many neo-Marxist perspectives. Crises are seen as a result of the failure to maintain the domination of capital over labour rather than as a result of some internal weakness in the accumulation process (Jessop, 1977). Furthermore, state intervention is directed towards political crises resulting from the capitalist accumulation process, rather than the need to directly serve the needs of capital. The major limitation of this approach is that when analysing the numerous crises and struggles that are to be found in the modern state, the broad categories of capital and labour become somewhat inadequate in explaining the extraordinary diversity of interest and pressure groups.

Summary
What is needed is some way of escaping from the structuralist impasse. We need to recognise the importance of the dominant capitalist mode of production in affecting and restricting state policies, since the state must attempt to maintain the conditions under which production can take place. However, these relationships need to be analysed in a way which does not resort to economic determinism or become enmeshed in some self-fufilling structuralist framework which is incapable of rejection. It calls for a recognition of the complexity of interaction between many groups and institutions in modern capitalist societies – conflicts which cannot be inevitably reduced to class-based struggles in the realm of production, or dismissed as something epiphenomenal. Essential for such a task are more detailed empirical studies of past struggles between these diverse groups and, perhaps more important, a focus upon the changing character of these struggles in contemporary societies.

Beyond locational analysis and structuralism 6

The preceding chapters have examined the three main reasons for a geographical perspective upon collective consumption – jurisdictional partitioning, tapering effects and negative externalities – together with the three main frameworks for explaining the distribution of collective consumption – pluralism, managerialism and Marxism. Inevitably, many of the controversies have been based upon research undertaken in the 1960s and 1970s. This concluding chapter therefore looks to the future, and examines the implications of these debates for further research. In particular, it examines the most appropriate strategies for study of the geography of collective consumption in the light of changes in the economic and political structure of British and American cities in the early 1980s.

Recent changes in British and American cities

Before examining the relevance of existing theories and the tasks for future research it is important to examine recent developments in British and American cities. There is, of course, always a danger that such considerations will be outmoded in a short period of rapid political or economic change. Nevertheless, as stressed in Chapter 5, current geographical patterns of collective consumption are the outcome of conflict and struggle between various groups. It is important to understand the various strategies employed by these groups and the balance of power between them at any point in time so that appropriate questions can be asked.

Another important implication of the discussion in Chapter 5 is the need to relate developments in the sphere of collective consumption to the broader operation of production. Recent policies both in Britain and North America therefore need to be seen in the light of a recession unprecedented in scale since the Second World War. The inflation of the 1970s has been largely curtailed, but there is now widespread unemployment and declining rates of economic growth.

Deindustrialisation, decentralisation and the growth of the 'sunbelt cities'

Parallel with these developments has been the continuation of two major processes – deindustrialisation and decentralisation. Although the shift from manufacturing and service employment has taken place throughout most of the twentieth century, many commentators have argued that the process has accelerated in recent years. Bacon and Eltis (1976) have argued that this process has taken place at a faster rate in Britain than other advanced economies. Thus, between 1961 and 1974 the numbers employed in manufacturing fell by 13 per cent, whilst the size of the public sector grew by over a third. In the early 1980s manufacturing has virtually collapsed in many areas of Britain, but there has been insufficient expansion of the services, either in the public or private sectors, to curb the dramatic increase in unemployment.

The process of decentralisation out of the major cities into smaller satellite settlements outlined in Chapter 1 shows little signs of diminishing either in Britain or America. It is still the largest cities which are continuing to decline at the fastest rate. Between 1961 and 1971 London and the big conurbations declined by over 10 per cent, whereas medium-sized cities such as Bristol, Southampton and Nottingham fell by just over 5 per cent, and smaller cities by just over 3 per cent. In contrast, seaside resorts, remote country areas and new towns recorded population increases (Office of Population Censuses and Surveys, 1982). These results suggest that the process of 'counter-urbanisation' is taking place at an ever-increasing scale. The principal movements are not simply from older city centres to the suburbs, but from older conurbations in general into smaller settlements in more attractive regions. Hence, the drift to the south-east has slowed down and the regions with the fastest growth rates are the south-west and East Anglia.

Allied to the process of decentralisation has been an inter-regional shift of population often described as the growth of the 'sunbelt cities' (Sternlieb and Hughes, 1975). This has been of particular significance in the United States and has involved massive population and employment increases in cities such as Houston, Dallas, Denver, Phoenix, San Diego and Los Angeles, and a concomitant decline in the older 'frost belt' cities such as Chicago, Detroit, Cleveland and Pittsburgh. Compared with these north-eastern cities, the sunbelt cities of the south-west have many features which have encouraged the growth of new high-technology industries in the spheres of electronics and aerospace. These advantages are often summed up in the phrase 'a climate conducive to business growth', and include: cheap land; a lack of restrictive planning controls; an absence of service infrastructure (and hence low levels of taxation); a less unionised workforce than the north-east (and hence relatively lower wage levels for certain occupations);

an attractive climate (when combined with air conditioning); and the absence of the local government debt problems which beset many older cities. There is certainly poverty in certain areas of the sunbelt cities but it is not on the same scale as in the north east and there is not the same historical legacy of environmental decay. Unlike the immigration which fostered the growth of Chicago and other cities in the late nineteenth century, the immigration into the sunbelt cities has been largely skilled and high-status in character. The net result is a spatial structure rather different to that of the older cities. There is often no single identifiable dominant core as in Chicago, but a vast spread of suburbia interspaced with various high-density central business areas. The sunbelt city, then, is above all designed for the automobile- and home-owner.

Thatcherism, Reaganomics and the 'New Right'
The political response to such developments, both in Britain and America, as in many other Western democratic countries, has been a move to the right. However, this is seen by many commentators as a new form of conservatism from the consensus policies practised by many right-wing governments since the Second World War. Indeed, such has been the magnitude of change that the new policies have been given the labels of 'Reaganomics' and 'Thatcherism'.

Central to Thatcherism has been an attack upon the collective services commonly known as the Welfare State. This is part of a broader assault upon the set of Keynesian interventionist policies which emerged from the Second World War. Thatcherism involves strict control of the money supply, a reduction in the public sector borrowing requirement, a reduction in the level of government expenditure and taxation, and a general shift from direct to indirect forms of taxation. It would, however, be wrong to attribute reductions in the level of social expenditure solely to the Thatcher administration. Between 1975 and 1978, under the previous Labour government, social spending fell by 0.4 per cent in real terms, and there were severe reductions in capital expenditure on housing, health and education. Indeed, it was the Labour government which introduced the system of cash limits which enabled local authority expenditure to be controlled from the centre (Greenwood, 1982). When the Conservatives came to power in June 1979 they made further cuts in housing and education, but the basic plans for the reduction in social spending had already been made.

What the Conservative administration has done in the first half of the 1980s is to make even further cutbacks in the fields of housing, education and personal social services. It is often argued that the Thatcher government has failed to reach many of its objectives, and in particular that it has failed to curb public expenditure. However, the overall increase in public spending conceals very significant changes within the overall structure of spending. Much of the increase in public expenditure has resulted from vastly increased social security payments because of the enormous increase in unemployment, but also from increased spending on the police and armed forces. Thus, in 1975–6 local authority current and capital expenditure accounted for nearly one-third of public expenditure, but by 1980–1 that share was down to one quarter (Wright, 1982).

What is arguably of even greater importance than the actual cuts that have been made is the ideological attack upon the Welfare State that has been mounted by the Thatcher government. This attack is, of course, designed to legitimise those cuts which have already been made in the sphere of collective consumption, and may pave the way for further attack upon public service provision. Thus, whereas the previous Labour administration was largely forced into making expenditure cuts as a result of external pressures from the IMF, the Conservative concern with reductions in the level of social wage results from the motivation of key actors within the political party.

Many have argued that the attack upon the Welfare State represents a reassertion of Victorian values of individualism, self-reliance and family responsibility. These attitudes are reflected in a number of policies: the privatisation of nationalised industries; the sale of council houses, the raising of council rents; controls on direct works departments and the halt in the move towards comprehensive education.

The extent to which these policies do represent a fundamental shift from the past, or are merely manifestations of a government whose actions are severely constrained by a declining economy, is open to debate. As Gough (1982) notes, however, these policies, at least in terms of ideology, amount to a shift from the consensus politics that have characterised British post-war governments. In particular the Thatcher administration is anti-poor, anti-trade union, against the undeserving, anti-deviant, covertly racist, individualist, and, in theory at least, anti-state.

Ideologically, Reaganomics appears to be very similar to Thatcherism; but there are a number of complex differences between the way in which policies have been implemented in practice. The main difference, of course, is that whereas the British economy continues to languish in recession, Reagan has presided over a spectacular increase in economic growth and a reduction in unemployment. To a large extent this reflects the fact that the Reagan administration has managed to cut the level of taxation, whereas the Thatcher government has increased the overall level of taxation in Britain. Furthermore, where the Thatcher government has followed monetarist principles and reduced the public sector borrowing requirement, Reagan has funded his tax cuts and the enormous increase in military expenditure with a huge borrowing deficit.

Fiscal stress and the local state

Despite these differences between Britain and America in terms of national policy there has been a remarkably similar response at the level of local governments responsible for the provision of collective services – namely fiscal stress and in some cases severe financial crisis. In essence, this means that local governments have insufficient resources to meet their obligations. It is relatively easy to isolate the few cases of severe fiscal crisis when cities are on the verge of bankruptcy or unable to meet their operating expenses, but the much more widespread phenomenon of fiscal *strain* is much more difficult to measure. Typical symptoms are rapidly increasing debts, large rises in debts as a proportion of total expenditure, and rapid rates of increase in local taxes, all of which may be associated with widespread reductions in services, reductions in staff and the sale of assets (Newton, 1980). Such fiscal problems are, in fact, widespread in virtually all advanced capitalist economies, although their incidence varies enormously between countries, and between local government within individual nation states.

The most dramatic manifestation of fiscal crisis occurred in New York in 1975. In this year the main New York City banks refused to underwrite or purchase any more New York City notes or bonds, and thus drove the city to the verge of bankruptcy. This action was taken in the face of a cumulative short-term debt of $5.3 billion and a projected deficit which would have been thirty-three times the entire outstanding short-term municipal debt in the United States. One of the concessions extracted by the banks was the creation of an Emergency Financial Control Board with extensive powers. In response to pressure from this board the city introduced a wage freeze and made 56,000 people redundant – no less than 19 per cent of the total workforce (Sheftner, 1980). The city removed workers in reverse order of seniority which meant that many of the blacks who had been recruited in the 1960s were the first to be made redundant. Social programmes were drastically cut, and many of these services in the fields of education, drug addiction, and youth welfare affected blacks more than the rest of the population.

It would be misleading to attribute these financial difficulties exclusively to the growth of the 'New Right', for they reflect the culmination of many processes operating over a number of years. Hence these problems existed before the growth of Thatcherism and Reaganomics, and currently exist in countries with social democratic parties (e.g. France and Scandinavia). Complex though these factors may be, in broad terms local fiscal stress may be envisaged as the consequence of two opposing pressures: on the one hand, local governments in all capitalist economies are faced with pressures from various quarters for increased expenditure; while on the other hand for a variety of reasons these local governments find themselves blocked in their attempts to procure sources of income which would enable them to meet these demands (Newton, 1980). These counteracting forces are each considered in turn.

Increased demands for local public services

Since the Second World War the governments of most advanced capitalist economies have extended their responsibilities on a massive scale, especially in the fields of welfare, health and education. Local governments have been made responsible for the allocation of many of these services, and overall their rate of growth has tended to be more rapid than the increase in total public expenditure. This expansion of local services may be seen as a response to numerous pressures (Newton, 1980).

First, there has been an increase in the size of many of the client groups for local services. Most of the older industrialised nations have increasing numbers and proportions of persons of retirement age, and in particular persons aged seventy-five or over. This has led to a rapid growth in services designed to meet the needs of old people: old people's homes, sheltered accommodation, home helps, home nurses, chiropody, meals-on-wheels, health visitors and many others. It is this growing elderly population, combined with a declining proportion of working population, which has put enormous strains on local services, and which raises one of the greatest challenges for social policy in the future (Pinch, 1980).

Running parallel with the increase in the numbers of old people has been – until very recently – the increasing number of children of school age. This growth, combined with the raising of the school leaving age, has increased the costs of education – already the largest component of most local government budgets. Another important social change has been the dramatic growth in the numbers of one-parent families, which has led to increased pressures for local authority nursery provision (Pinch, 1984).

These demographic pressures have been supplemented by other forces leading to local service expansion. For example, the vast increase in automobile ownership has led to pressures for road construction. In addition, the environmental decay and deteriorating physical fabric of many older cities has led to pressures for urban renewal.

However, it is not only the expansion of existing services but the introduction of new types of service which has led to increased local expenditure. Although responsibilities for local health care were taken away from local authorities with the introduction of the National Health Service, British local governments have been given an enormous range of additional responsibilities over the years. These include: care of the disabled; education of the under-fives; environmental inspections; care of the mentally handicapped; consumer protection; community homes for young children needing care; and community development projects.

Increased costs have also emerged from the increase in standards which is to be found in most of these services, whether new or relatively long established. The issue of standards and the quality of care is enormously complex, as discussed in Chapter 2; and in recent years standards have seriously declined in many services with expenditure cuts. Nevertheless, in a long-term perspective there can be little doubt that many services have improved. This improvement is perhaps best reflected in modern, well-equipped libraries, schools and sports centres. Research by local authority intelligence departments has also provided additional indices of service standards, and has uncovered the specialised needs of particular groups, including the disabled, mentally handicapped, young children and the infirm elderly. It would appear that as living standards rise in general so people demand more public services of higher standards; and this goes some way to explain the proliferation of amenity and environmental groups discussed in Chapter 3. Other pressures upon local authority costs have been discussed elsewhere in this book and need not be elaborated here but they include: central government concern to impose minimum standards of provision; the 'empire-building' of various professional groups in local government; the ideologies of local Labour councillors concerned with public provision; and the costs imposed through creating the infrastructure necessary for economic growth.

No discussion of the increased costs facing local government would be complete without some mention of inflation. The post-war period has seen continual inflation in most Western states which reached considerable levels in some states (especially Britain) following the oil crisis of 1973. It has been suggested that because local authority services are labour-intensive they will incur greater costs during times of inflation since workers will make strong demands for compensatory wage increases. In effect, although local government employs a large number of relatively well-organised professional and trade union groups, wages and salaries have in recent years tended to decrease as a proportion of total revenue expenditure (Newton, 1980). When combined with all the other pressures listed above, however, inflation has been an important factor in contributing to the fiscal crisis of collective consumption, because local governments have generally lacked the means to obtain revenues to meet these pressures.

The inflexibility of local sources of revenue
Directly opposed to this set of pressures working for increases in local public expenditure has been a set of forces serving to restrict local sources of income. It is often asserted that local government expenditure is 'out of control' and that local governments spend 'more than the country can afford', and it is certainly true that in the

post-war period public expenditure has been consuming an ever-increasing proportion of total wealth, and that local government spending has been rising faster than total public expenditure. From this perspective, it is the relatively slow rate of economic growth in many advanced economies relative to the size of the public sector which is blamed for the local fiscal crisis. However, detailed inspection of the available data reveals that the issues are more complex, for there is no simple relationship between economic growth rates, the size of the public sector, and the extent of local financial problems as measured by the size of local debts or rate of local tax increases (Newton, 1980).

Thus, West Germany and the United States with relatively dynamic economies have growing debts and financial shortages amongst their local governments; while Sweden and Denmark have smaller rates of economic growth, larger public sectors, and local governments which are relatively healthy in financial terms.

Another important misconception is that local financial problems are the consequence of local dependence upon central government for financial support. This notion can again easily be dismissed – at least in any simplistic sense – by some international comparisons. Britain, for example, displays considerable financial difficulties at local level and has a system dependent upon central support. This contrasts with most Scandinavian countries, which are heavily dependent upon local sources of revenue but which have so far managed to escape the excesses of debt and fiscal strain prevalent in most other Western nations. In the United States there is also a heavier reliance upon local sources of revenue than in Britain, but in this case the major cities display some of the most severe forms of fiscal stress to be found in any advanced economy.

Rather than economic growth or central intervention, the crucial factor affecting the degree of financial strain at local government level appears to be the type of local tax which governments can draw upon (Sharpe, 1981). In general, central governments take the lion's share of those taxes which are income-elastic and absorb the ravages of inflation well, such as income and sales taxes. In contrast, local governments' access to these taxes is relatively restricted, and they tend to be reliant upon forms of property tax which are relatively inelastic with regard to inflation. It is therefore no mere coincidence that Scandinavian countries with access to a local income tax have the least financial problems at the local level.

In this respect British local governments are unique amongst Western nations in having no access to any form of income-elastic tax. Instead, they are dependent upon a single, property tax – the rates – which seems to be unsatisfactory in many respects. First, although levied on both domestic and commercial properties, it does not raise sufficient revenue for British governments to provide all their services (hence the dependence upon central funding). Second, the tax, although failing in real terms to keep pace with inflation, is extremely unpopular with local ratepayers. Much of the problem stems from the fact that it is a highly visible tax. Although rates can be paid by regular monthly instalments, rate demands are often given to households at six-monthly intervals and payment of this lump sum often breeds considerable resentment. This contrasts with income tax and taxes on commodities which are extracted in a relatively inconspicuous manner. In addition, revaluation of properties takes place at irregular and infrequent intervals. The only other source of internal revenue – fees and charges on services – is also highly visible. The net effect of this system is that the level of the rate is the source of intense debate and political sensitivity, and the inflexibility of the system has done much to contribute to the resource squeeze on British local government. Central government does of course, attempt to compensate for inequalities in levels of local wealth but, as stressed in Chapter 2, these central payments are insufficient to compensate the local authorities which face the most serious problems. Indeed, in recent years government manipulation of central funding has intensified these problems.

Until 1975 British local authorities had enjoyed more than twenty years of unbroken growth (Stewart, 1980), but in that year they were asked by the Labour government to show restraint. These pleas were not effective and in 1976–7 the Rate Support Grant was used as an instrument of control: the grant was cut in volume terms by 2.5 per cent, and this set the pattern for future years such that by 1980–1 the Aggregate Exchequer Grant was worth 14 per cent less in real terms. In 1979-80 the new Conservative administration did not find the degree of expenditure restraint sufficient, especially since many of the Labour-controlled metropolitan districts publicly opposed central policy.

To combat these problems the then Secretary of State for the Environment, Michael Heseltine, introduced a new block grant system to replace the needs and resources element of the old Rate Support Grant. This block grant was designed to reduce the proportion of local expenditure supported by central grant in each authority by the extent to which the authority planned to spend beyond some centrally determined target, or Grant-Related Expenditure Assessment (GREA). The intention was to penalise the 'overspenders' and reward the relatively frugal. Those authorities spending over their centrally assessed need receive a declining rate of grant, and must rely upon the rates. Given the sensitivity of rate increases it was hoped that the system would generate pressures for financial stringency.

An important feature of the system was known as 'clawback'. If the total claims on the resources element of the grant exceeded the grant made available by the government, the 'clawback' arrangement reduced the grant paid to all authorities in receipt of the resources element by a proportionate amount. What this means is that all authorities had their grant reduced, even if the claims upon the resources element of the grant were exceeded by a minority of the high-spending authorities. Furthermore, since grants were related to existing spending levels, increases in expenditures brought increases in grant aid.

The history of this legislation and its subsequent modification is enormously complex (Greenwood, 1982). It appears that the policy suffered from hasty preparation, and the initial effect was to increase spending; but the crucial point is that, in total, the new system amounted to an unprecedented intrusion into local affairs by central government. This control has increased with subsequent legislation designed to reduce the discretion of local authorities to set their own rate levels – the so called 'rate-capping' legislation.

Within the federal system of the United States, the national government makes no formal prescriptions about the functions of local government, and neither does it prescribe a set of services or service levels which local governments must provide. However, local government activities are largely circumscribed by the states, and these specify the types of taxes municipalities may levy. All states permit local governments to levy a property tax, 29 states permit a local sales tax and 13 permit a local income tax (Greenwood, 1982). American local governments would therefore seem to occupy an intermediate position between the dependence of British local government upon a single property tax and the ability of Scandinavian governments to gain access to local income taxes. However, Greenwood argues that there are strict limitations upon the revenue-raising abilities of most local governments in the United States. Most of the states have imposed a maximum property rate limit, although in many areas this can be exceeded if approved by a local referendum. More effective still are absolute ceilings on property tax levies which limit the total amount of revenue a local government can derive from its local property tax. Those states which permit income and sales taxes also impose limits on sales taxes. In recent years, even further restrictions on the issue of long-term obligation debt and tax increases have been imposed by the states, and these can only be overcome by local referenda.

Further pressures upon local government finance have come from the general public. This pressure takes the form of persistent refusals to permit increases in local tax rates in referenda. In New Jersey between 1977 and 1980 there were no less than 117 local referenda, 57 per cent of which failed to sanction annual local spending increases above 5 per cent (Wolman, 1982). In Cleveland, the persistent failure to approve increases in local income tax brought the city to the brink of bankruptcy and caused the temporary closure of the city's schools.

The most extreme example of an anti-tax movement which has

been dubbed the 'New Fiscal Populism' – is the famous Proposition 13 approved by Californian voters in 1978 (Danziger, 1980). This proposition limited the annual tax on properties to 1 per cent of their market value, and limited the increase on assessed market values to 2 per cent per annum. There were also restrictions on the introduction of new taxes which subsequently require a two-thirds vote of the state legislation.

In many respects the Californian case is unique, for the area was characterised by particularly rapid increases in house prices followed by frequent reassessments and increases in property taxes. The state government also possessed a very large reserve fund (Miller, 1979). Furthermore, there is evidence that the effects of the cuts have not been as extensive as many predicted. There have certainly been reductions in a wide range of services, especially the less-essential services such as parks and libraries, but most local government units received about 4 per cent less than in previous years (Kirwan, 1979). There were no massive reductions in the numbers of public employees, and the serious reductions in welfare and social programmes that were feared by many were avoided. To some extent there has been a backlash against those cuts which have been made, especially in the realm of police, fire and hospital services. A subsequent tax-cutting bill, Proposition 9, was defeated in June 1980. Nevertheless, the tax-cutting movement has affected the general climate of local government activity in a symbolic way, and has served to moderate tax increases.

It is clear that the fiscal problems of many American governments are also bound up with a financial system largely dependent upon property taxes, which restricts access to revenues. The problem is exaggerated in the United States, however, by the fragmentation of the local government system, and the enormous variations between cities and suburbs in the ratio of needs to resources. Thus, it is the major cities of the north-east, which are losing both population and employment to the suburbs and sunbelt, and which have the largest concentration of poor groups, that have exhibited the major symptoms of fiscal stress.

Clearly, the degree of control which central governments exercise over local authorities is dependent upon many factors other than the proportion of local authority revenues which come from the central government. Much depends upon the nature and buoyancy of the local tax system, and the nature of the relationships between central and local government. Thus, central provision can be both a cause and effect of fiscal stress.

In Britain a combination of an unsatisfactory property tax and central concern with aggregate public expenditure targets has intensified fiscal stress. In North America, however, aggregate local authority spending is not seen as a major feature of the federal government's macro-economic policy. Nevertheless, although the proportion of federal funding is much less, a much higher proportion of grants are for specific services and functions, thus restricting local autonomy. Although the Reagan administration has reduced the number of specific grants into a smaller number of block grants and has decentralised administration to the state level, there has been a substantial reduction in funding for the new block grants.

The role of space in the study of collective consumption

This is the context in which future research hypotheses must be specified. Before considering these questions and their implications, it is necessary to re-examine the perennial issue of the role of geographical factors in the study of collective consumption.

We saw in Chapter 1 that it was only in the late 1960s that geographers started devoting much attention to spatial variations in the distribution of public goods and services. Nevertheless, before long, much of this analysis was criticised for what was described as 'spatial fetishism' – naive and simplistic explanations based exclusively upon spatial variables. Such criticisms reflect the growth of neo-Marxist explanations in geography in the early 1970s. As described in Chapter 5, Marxist explanations argue that spatial forms are socially produced and cannot be seen as independent of society. This contrasts with Weberian approaches, such as those of Pahl, which envisage spatial factors as an independent constraint whatever the mode of production. The issue is in fact more complex than a simple Marxist-Weberian conflict, however, for Saunders, one of the main advocates of Weberian approaches within sociology, has recently argued that space is relatively unimportant in the study of collective consumption.

Viewed from a distance, much of this debate over the role of space appears similar to the debate over the role of politics in local government resource allocation, as outlined in Chapter 2. Both controversies have had powerful disciplinary interests at stake and both are in some senses 'silly' debates. It is certainly true that factors such as distance decay, jurisdictional partitioning and externalities cannot be studied independently of social processes. Thus, distance-decay effects reflect the differential ability of various groups to overcome the friction of distance. Similarly, the division of nations into separate local government units reflects political processes, while the distribution of externality effects will reflect the differing abilities of neighbourhoods to resist or attract certain activities. As Urry (1981) notes, we should avoid a concept of absolute space which envisages the geography of an area as simply an environment within which social processes 'happen' to take place, since this perspective ignores the way in which most aspects of 'the spatial environment' are humanly produced.

Despite this above it is, however, difficult to disagree with Pahl's assertion that space will always constitute an independent constraint upon the allocation of resources. All societies have facilities which some individuals will generally regard as noxious, and the fact that they have to be located somewhere means that some groups will lose and some will gain. It may be that certain so-called scarce resources are only scarce because of allocative mechanisms in capitalist society, but even the most enlightened and egalitarian society would be faced with the problem of allocating fixed-point facilities, such as hospitals, which will inevitably discriminate in favour of some locations rather than others. In the light of all the evidence presented in previous chapters this might seem obvious, but such comments need to be restated in view of many recent criticisms of spatial approaches.

Where 'spatial fetishism' does arise, however, is when the analysis of geographical influences leads to the neglect of social processes. Thus, as we have seen in previous chapters, jurisdictional partitioning, tapering and externality effects do not by themselves constitute adequate explanations of patterns of collective consumption. There is, however, an equivalent 'social fetish' amongst many researchers which ascribes all issues to social processes. It is important to remember that society is not merely an abstract concept, but the outcome of many complex processes and struggles taking place in different locations. These struggles may be largely socially determined, but they have a clear spatial manifestation in terms of territorial divisions, residential segregation, zoning, and facility location. Furthermore, these spatial manifestations have an important effect, and serve to either reinforce or counteract other social processes. Thus, Newton (1975) observed that the proliferation of politically autonomous suburbs in the United States during the first half of this century probably played as important a part in the social and political life of the country as did the growth of the joint-stock company in the economic sphere. In the final analysis, of course, the division between 'spatial process' and 'social process' is arbitrary: they are both different sides of the reality we seek to understand. Nevertheless, given the complexity of the world some division of labour and simplification of concepts is required. This is not to lose sight of structural determinants, or to argue for some narrow disciplinary chauvinism; for what is needed is both a socially and spatially aware analysis of collective consumption. It does suggest, however, that there are a set of distinct issues relating to collective consumption which do require a spatial perspective.

In this context it is important to note that Saunders's critique of spatial approaches to collective consumption is based upon consideration of the work of Castells. This is dismissed largely for epistemological grounds, because of its structuralist approach. Saunders's other main reason for dismissing spatial perspectives stems from the fact that many aspects of collective consumption – such as social security payments, family allowances and pensions – do not have any explicit spatial reference. He argues that a concern with social provision with a spatial reference is unnecessarily restrictive; and then proceeds to argue that as a result, studies of collective consumption need have no theoretical concern with space. One can certainly agree with the first point, but the second conclusion does not follow.

This debate does, however, point the way towards one of the important issues which requires further analysis, namely: what is the relative importance of spatial and 'non-spatial' aspects of resource allocation in the sphere of collective consumption? This issue was raised in Chapter 2 in the context of territorial justice evaluation. It was suggested that an individual's well-being is dependent upon many other factors than spatial variations in public services. For example, increased pensions are likely to have a more important impact upon the welfare of the elderly than spatial redistributions of fixed-point welfare facilities. This does not mean, of course, that services such as home helps, home nurses or daycare centres are unimportant: the elderly will require such services irrespective of the size of pensions. But studying welfare services should not divert attention from alternative ways of improving welfare. Important though non-spatial income sources are, there are many facilities and services which have been located at specific points and which generate both positive and negative externalities. The relative importance of 'spatial' and non-spatial income sources is a matter for further study.

Given the need for a geographical perspective on collective consumption, and given the rapidly changing character of service provision in capitalist economies, what then are the key questions for future research?

Jurisdictional partitioning

Although some of the momentum behind quantitative comparative studies has declined in recent years, there is still much to be done in this field. First and foremost, there is a need to extend the range of services and facilities which are examined. This will involve studies which cut across the conventional departmental boundaries which are used to classify services, such as housing, education and social services. In particular, there is a need to identify sets of services which satisfy particular client groups or meet particular needs. A good example is the complex set of services which care for children below five, commonly known as 'pre-school' services, which are the responsibility of social services departments, education departments and a wide range of private and voluntary agencies (Pinch, 1984). Sports and leisure facilities are another complex set of services which require detailed subdivision. Allied to this is a need to examine resource allocations by administrative bodies *other* than local governments, such as district health authorities, police constabularies, police divisions and water boards.

Other issues requiring attention in the field of jurisdictional partitioning are:

1 The derivation of more complex needs indices, tailored to particular services and subsections of the population. In this context the complex cross-tabulations which are now possible from the British Census may permit the delineation of detailed 'problem' groups such as single-parent families or elderly persons living alone in poor housing conditions.

2 Analysis of the relationships between financial and physical indices of service provision.

3 Analysis of the 'outcomes' of service provision.

4 More sophisticated analysis of political variables.

5 Improved statistical techniques to take account of problems of multi-collinearity, heteroscedasticity and autocorrelation.

The most urgent task however, is to examine the impact of recent political, economic and geographical trends upon inter-jurisdictional variations in service provision. The impact of fiscal stress varies enormously between different local authorities, depending on a wide range of complex factors. These include: the interest rates prevailing when the local authority borrowed money; the legacy of previous spending decisions; the buoyancy of the local economy; the demographic pressures on the local authority; the impact of central funding decisions; and the nature of local politics. There is clearly an important task to be undertaken in assessing the impact of the new block grant system upon local variations in service provision. Has the increase in central control in Britain increased or decreased variations between authorities in spending and provision levels? Similar questions arise in the context of 'Fiscal Populism' in the United States.

Despite the potential for increasing the sophistication of comparative studies, the inherent limitations of this approach means that the most useful insights from future research will emerge by linking aggregate studies with more intensive case studies. These case studies need to be carefully selected in a form of controlled experimentation. Those authorities with similar economic and social structures but differing policy responses could be examined to evaluate the impact of political initiatives in the face of environmental pressures.

Positive and negative externalities
There is also much work to be done analysing the geographical

distribution of collective consumption within local government areas. A crucial question is the extent to which the drive for financial stringency has affected the distribution of positive and negative externalities in cities. What sorts of facilities are most likely to be closed? Where are they most likely to be located? Which groups will be most disadvantaged in terms of access? The evidence discussed in Chapter 3 suggested that in the United States it was the older schools in the poorer areas which are most likely to be closed under retrenchment programmes, but this type of analysis needs to be extended to other services in various types of locality.

Another issue requiring attention is the character and distribution of spatial externality effects. To what extent are these effects determined by the size and location of the facility, or the nature of the surrounding areas? To what extent is the distinction between 'User-associated' and 'neighbourhood-associated' externalities useful in understanding conflicts other than those in the field of mental health? The motives and strategies of local community and action groups also require more detailed study, especially in the British context.

The role of the state in the study of collective consumption

No less contentious than the role of space in the study of collective consumption has been the issue of how to conceptualise the role of the state. In particular, there is a need to avoid two extreme solutions: at one extreme, pluralist interpretations envisage the state as a neutral arbiter with regard to competing interest groups; while at the other, various neo-Marxist approaches envisage the state as always working in the long-term interests of capital. As discussed earlier, both of these approaches are based upon epistemological assumptions which preclude any refutation of their basic ideas. Both of these approaches do, however, point to the paradox of the state acting in contradictory ways, especially with regard to collective consumption. How then can we conceptualise the role of the state and the provision of collective consumption in a way that is neither completely autonomous from nor completely determined by the capitalist mode of production?

Corporatism
Pahl's most recent contribution towards understanding the role of the state has been the theory of corporatism (Pahl, 1977). This theory has strong Weberian underpinnings, for political power manifest in the actions of the state is seen as autonomous from economic power manifest in commodity markets (Leonard, 1982). It will be recalled from Chapter 4 that Weber defined power in terms of the ability of an actor to carry out his will in the face of opposition

from others. True to Weberian principles, the corporate approach portrays the state as an apparatus which is controlled by individuals who are motivated by specific beliefs and aspirations, and who exert power through state policies. It is argued that although economic and political power may overlap at certain times, there is no inevitable correspondence between these two sources of power.

Following from this, Pahl and Winkler have argued that in Britain the state has assumed a level of autonomy such that it has become independent of the needs of capital (Pahl and Winkler, 1974; Winkler 1975; 1977). It is argued that the state has to intervene to maintain profitability in the private sector, but that because of the concentration of capital in a few large companies, increasing competition, and the enormous costs of investment in many industries, the state has assumed an increasingly directive role. This role is seen largely as a desire for order and stability in economic transactions and is seen as the outcome of bargaining between institutions and agents. This perspective clearly reflects Weber's fears about the growing dominance of bureaucracies in advanced capitalist economies.

The corporatist thesis has been subject to considerable crticism for two main reasons. The first is theoretical: just as the early managerialist approaches gave little insight into the constraints upon local managers, so the corporatist thesis gives little help as to how one might conceptualise the role of constraints upon the 'supermanagers' in central government. Once again, as with the first managerialist thesis, such issues are regarded as matters for empirical analysis. This leads to the second type of criticism, for many have argued that the corporatist thesis does not stand up to empirical testing, at least in Britain. The corporatist concept emerged in the mid-1970s during the era of the Wilson/Callaghan administration, when there was a degree of collusion between organised labour, industry and government in the form of the 'social contract'. However, Panitch (1980) argues that the Planning Agreements system was 'severely emasculated' shortly after Labour took over power – and that it merely subsidised Chrysler – while the selective profit and price controls in exchange for wage restraint were largely symbolic and did not amount to a radical change in the nature of the economic system. Certainly under the Thatcher administration the widespread phenomenon of unemployment has weakened trade union bargaining power, and government-orchestrated industrial bargaining with unions has not materialised.

Although Winkler (1975) claimed that his approach was a mechanism for generating predictions about future development, clearly these predictions have been somewhat inaccurate. As Panitch (1980) observes, there has been a tendency to see a few partial elements of corporatism within existing structures as evidence of new economic and political systems in their own right. Nevertheless, elements of corporatism still exist in Britain. Indeed, Booth (1982) argues that such influences have been prevalent in varying degrees in Britain throughout the twentieth century. He argues that they first emerged under methods devised by Lloyd George in the period 1906 to 1920 to bring together business and labour interests to curb growing social unrest. Booth also suggests that during times of economic recession there has been a move away from such negotiations and a reversion to economic liberalism and 'sound money', as government spending and high wages are blamed for economic problems. This pattern happened in the early 1930s and more recently under the Thatcher administration.

Central to corporatism is bargaining between specific interest groups and government which takes place outside conventional democratic channels. Thus, certain groups have privileged access to government such that issues are taken outside electoral politics. Some groups, including trade union organisations and those petitioning on behalf of the poor, have recently been denied access to central favour; but organisations related to the construction industry, pension funds, financial institutions and business have considerable influence. Harrison (1984) argues that a form of 'welfare corporatism' is emerging, in which powerful interest groups have the ability to reap vast tax and occupational concessions from central government while much of the conventional Welfare State is either cut or restricted in size. Such concessions cannot be explained by any straightforward 'logic of capital' argument, but involve political manipulation by powerful interest groups. However, the problem of conceptualising these influences and the apparently contradictory nature of state actions remains.

Structural segregation: The politics of revenue and vote-generation
Saunders (1981) argues that the apparent contradictory posture of the modern state in capitalist societies, both supporting the interests of monopoly capital and supporting non-capitalist interests, can best be understood by adopting a dualistic perspective of the state. On the one hand there are 'social investment' policies usually developed at the national level between bodies representing capitalist interest and various corporate state agencies. At this level, which is effectively insulated from popular demands, maintaining capital accumulation through investment and fiscal policies is seen as a major priority.

In contrast, social consumption policies in the realm of housing and public services are developed at the local level by elected political bodies which can be affected by 'pluralist' demands. Saunders's pluralism, however, accepts that certain groups may be excluded from effective participation in local affairs, and that as a result of non-decisions certain interests may be neglected.

Nevertheless, he argues that local consumption policies will tend to reflect competitive political struggles between different groups, whereas national investment policies will reflect the demands and requirements of particular factions of capital. Furthermore, the interests of capital will dominate in the long run, because social investment must take precedence over social consumption due to the state's dependence on private sector profitability, and because local government is ultimately subordinate to central government control. The argument does not imply that capitalist interests have no effect upon social consumption or that popular pressures do not affect social investment, but that the way in which these two areas of state involvement will evolve will tend to reflect differing strategies by differing groups.

Saunders's approach echoes that put forward by Piven and Friedland (1984). They argue that the main weakness of pluralist, managerialist and structuralist theories is that they all focus upon particular elements in society to the exclusion of others. In American cities the relationships between public pressures, bureaucracies, and external economic constraints have evolved over many years. These arrangements did not emerge as the result of some inevitable historical process, but developed from the efforts of various classes and groups to change their power in relation to the state, and also from a reciprocal effort by the state to exert its power and influence over these groups. They argue that policies promoting either private profitability or political legitimacy are the result of political conflict; and that by thus specifying the causes of public policy and separating them from their consequences, their approach avoids the type of circular functionalism outlined in Chapter 5.

Piven and Friedland note that Western democracies are legally constrained to guarantee public political rights such as freedom of speech and organisation, together with private property ownership rights. The state is dependent upon public support to sanction its activities through electoral majorities and the use of institutionalised demand-making; but it is also dependent upon private investors to produce taxable revenues from profitable investment. This dual dependence results in 'two realms of public expenditure'. The first realm is concerned with policies which improve mass consumption – the traditional concern of public choice theorists – while the second realm is concerned with policies which improve the profitability of production.

Piven and Friedland use this perspective to analyse the growth of fiscal stress in American cities (see also Friedland, Piven and Alford, 1977). They note that during times of economic growth there need be no necessary conflict between these two main types of local policy. Thus, profitable investments will generate local income which can fund potentially redistributive public services, and which in turn may generate electoral support. Under conditions of economic recession, however, this alliance breaks down. On the one hand, local electorates begin to make intense demands for public services to compensate for the hardships imposed by the workings of the private market; while on the other hand private investors make demands for public expenditures and tax subsidies to restore the profitability of private investment. Rapid structural changes within local economies may intensify these conflicts. Thus, private investors make demands for new public expenditures to facilitate new types of investment, but the local workforce may not be well-suited to the new type of employment opportunities which are being generated.

Such developments are likely to intensify the competition between jurisdictions for the limited investment that is available, and this is likely to force down the amount of local revenues which a local government will be able to derive from private industry. At the same time, however, voters are likely to be struggling to minimise the incidence of taxation on their incomes. The net effect is a conflict between capitalist property rights – the unfettered rights to buy and sell land, property and labour and to trade at a profit – and political rights – free and fair elections at regular intervals.

However, Piven and Friedland argue that these tensions do not often result in direct conflicts between the urban voters and the local investors. The reason for this suppression of conflict is that the politics of vote-generation and revenue-generation are acted out on different stages. When local governments attempt to produce electoral majorities they deal with many diverse and fragmented local groups, but when they attempt to generate local revenues they deal with highly rationalised firms. The multiplicity of groups in the local electorate thus generates a proliferation of many local government agencies to deal with the numerous demands. Furthermore, in order to maintain electoral support it is essential that policies within the public sphere are highly visible so that credit can accrue to local governments for particular actions. In marked contrast dealings with private investors involve a small number of clients. These dealings are capable of centralisation and do not need to be visible; indeed, in the interests of maintaining private profitability it is frequently essential that such negotiations are covert. In the long run it is in the interest of the local state to maintain this segregation so that political demands are not made which would threaten property rights.

Piven and Friedland suggest that the evidence for such structural segregation and differentiation is 'striking'. Thus policies concerned with public services such as schools, fire, police, health care and social services tend to be located in agencies which are relatively accessible to the electorate. They are frequently controlled by elected officials, and their budgets may be the subject of intense public scrutiny. In contrast, policies aimed at sustaining investment and fiscal capacity are located in agencies such as ports, highways, sewage disposal and industrial promotion agencies – to which popular access is difficult, whilst access by private investors is unhampered. Such agencies develop strong client relationships with private investors and since their success is dependent upon efficient service provision they develop a strong technocratic ethos. Piven and Friedland argue that this technocratic ideology further serves to legitimise the insulation of such agencies from electoral control.

These structural arrangements thus separate those public agencies with the power to deal with some of the causes of poverty from those agencies that must absorb some of the consequences of this impoverishment. Thus, local protests are generated against welfare agencies because they are exposed and accessible, rather than against the enclosed and inaccessible development agencies.

Production, consumption and the local state
The differences of emphasis between the approaches of Saunders, and Piven and Friedland can be related to differences in the local government structures of Britain and America. In the United States there is a much stronger link between local sources of revenue and expenditure patterns, such that conflicts between the politics of revenue-generation and vote-generation are more likely. In Britain the high proportion of centralised taxes and central funding of local governments means that corporate bargaining at the centre takes on greater importance at certain times. The important point is that irrespective of the degree of local fiscal autonomy, social investment issues tend to be insulated from electoral considerations and separated – at least in the public eye – from matters of social consumption. Saunders argues that such a dualistic perspective provides a way of analysing the capitalist state while avoiding the extreme assumptions of pluralism and functionalist-Marxism:

> Thus a dualistic perspective that holds that local consump-
> tion policies will reflect competitive political struggles
> between different groups while national investment policies
> will reflect particular demands and general requirements of
> different sectors of capital implicitly contains two counter-
> factual statements which can be assessed in empirical
> research; that non-capitalist interest will not generally
> assert any significant influence over the determination of
> social investment, and that capitalist interest will not
> generally exert any significant influences over the determi-
> nation of social consumption. (Saunders, 1981:272.)

Duncan and Goodwin (1982), however, have taken issue with this approach. They argue that a separation between production and consumption is unhelpful, especially between central and local levels. Thus, the central government is concerned with legislation in the field of consumption, while production issues arise at the local level.

Housing is a good example of the links between production and consumption at the local level. As Ball (1983) demonstrates, the geographical distribution and organisational structure of housing cannot be seen simply as a manifestation of consumer preferences; instead it also reflects the changing character of the building industry. As a response to the problems of maintaining adequate profit levels there has been a shift towards larger companies using industrialised production techniques – including timber-framed buildings – with increasing proportions of relatively unskilled labour on large building sites. The resulting decentralised settlement patterns are not so much the reflection of free-market preferences for 'suburban' life styles, as the result of a powerful rural image promoted by a skilful publicity machine and allied to a system of powerful financial inducements which make it relatively easier to obtain a mortgage for these new properties. The much-vaunted ability of existing residents to resist such develoment can also easily be overstated. In the Southampton area for example, the reduction in the size of the new growth areas would seem to be less a product of public response to the elaborate public participation exercises, than the result of reductions in population projections and local housing demand estimates.

These settlements also generate conflicts between the needs of production and consumption. The new, decentralised city structure demands enormous investment in infrastructure systems such as roads, water supply and sewage disposal before private building can take place, and subsequent investment in community facilities as the population becomes established. The Southampton city region is one of the fastest growing parts of Britain's 'sunbelt', but the central government makes no special financial allowance for the costs of the investment needed for new building. This, in turn, has posed problems for the Conservative-controlled Hampshire County Council, which has always been concerned to keep public spending to minimum levels. The net result has been a complex process of bargaining between the local government and builders to ensure that the latter meet the costs of infrastructure provision. Builders have agreed to do this in return for planning permission to build at higher densities so that they can recoup the costs involved. Shortages of resources for social investment mean that once they are completed many of these new estates lack facilities such as shops, schools and community centres, and this has led to new local campaigns to improve accessibility to these services. These new residential groups have a clear geographical expression related to the age and character of the developments, and their campaigns in an era of privatisation and fiscal retrenchment contrast with the struggles of residents on earlier peripheral estates. They also illustrate the way in which capitalist interests within the building industry have an impact upon the distribution of collective as well as private consumption.

Another link between production and consumption arises in the context of what Duncan and Goodwin call 'the politics of factories'. Although much of the bargaining between business interests and local governments over social investment issues is covert, there are numerous examples of such issues assuming electoral importance and interacting with consumption issues. Ley and Mercer's (1980) study of Vancouver documents the growth of a white-collar political organisation – The Electors' Action Movement – which opposed the business and property interests that had dominated city politics until the early 1970s. The new political movement was motivated by a liberal ideology, and reflected the interests of lawyers, teachers, architects and other liberal-minded professionals who were concerned to create a 'liveable city'. The movement therefore attempted to put environmental and aesthetic considerations above those of outright profit and growth. The study reveals that these attitudes raised some complex political problems when faced with the operations of private markets.

There is also evidence from local politics in Britain which would tend to refute the idea that non-capitalist interests will not exert any great influence over social investment. In the current recession local governments are engaged in a desperate struggle to attract employment to their areas, as witnessed by the proliferation of economic development and industrial promotion agencies. It would seem that increasingly local governments are being judged by their abilities to attract or create jobs. Many would argue that much of this activity is fairly fruitless, since the resources available are inadequate to promote industrial regeneration in economies dominated by large national and multinational enterprises. Furthermore, many see the current faith in the ability of the small-firm sector to generate jobs as misplaced. The net effect is that many local governments are competing with one another to attract some of a relatively small number of footloose firms. Nevertheless, the important point in this context is that social investment issues are matters of public concern and electoral consequence. Many industrial promotion exercises are an attempt at least to be seen to be doing something about a problem, on the principle that if everyone else is doing this why shouldn't we?

Much of the new type of industrial development consist of high-productivity, high-technology industries in metropolitan ring areas outside the older declining cities. This decentralisation of manufacturing activity into suburban areas also means that issues at the place of work increasingly intrude into the place of residence. Again in the Southampton city region it would seem that while builders have been relatively successful in obtaining land for residential development, industrial interests and retailers have had much more difficulty in decentralising their activities in the face of considerable community opposition. The ability of residents to resist the large residential growth areas is limited although the size of the sites may be reduced; but a single industrial enterprise is a more isolated, and in many senses more threatening activity, which can generate a more hostile and focused response. It would seem that many suburban residents want sources of employment to be reasonably accessible to their place of residence but not in the immediate vicinity, and similar attitudes seem to apply to large retailing developments. In the current recession, business interests are, of course, using their claimed abilities to create jobs as a bargaining ploy to resist those who may oppose them.

As an alternative to the dual state hypothesis, Duncan and Goodwin envisage the local state as a reflection of the relationhip between dominant and subordinate classes (capital and labour) mediated by local consciousness and unique local histories. Following from the type of argument outlined in Chapter 5, they place emphasis upon the role of the local state in fragmenting working-class consciousness through the paraphernalia of local elections and legal rights. 'The "problem" of local government can be seen as the problem of imposing "the state form" – bureaucratic citizenship – onto local consciousness of class relations, local government can be one way of reducing local class relations and class-based action to the legal relations of individual, abstract citizens' (Duncan and Goodwin, 1982:92).

Duncan and Goodwin are correct to point to the links between production and consumption, but their attempt to reduce the operation of local government to class relations in the field of production seems inadequate compared with the enormous complexity of local conflicts over the distribution of local services. This mismatch between the categories of capital and labour and the diversity of local distributional struggles mediated by political groupings and geographical areas, is an issue which has challenged many social scientists in recent years, and is commonly referred to as the 'boundary problem'. Dunleavy (1982) expresses the issue as that of explaining the comparatively low degree of inter-class conflict in capitalist societies compared with the high degree of intra-class conflict. In this context there would seem to be a great deal of truth in the dual-state hypothesis, for despite the links between production and consumption noted above, it would seem that the structural segregation of state administrative agencies does prevent people becoming aware of the links between social investment and social consumption.

Structural constraints and 'human agency'

Underlying these ideas about the role of the local state is a conflict between two alternative conceptions of society: one which places an emphasis upon the conscious actions of individuals – sometimes termed 'voluntarism'; and one which places emphasis upon the constraints upon human behaviour – sometimes termed 'structuralism'. Clearly, the former approach is embodied in the ideas of Weber (outlined in Chapter 4), which focus upon the subjective actions of individuals; while the latter approach is incorporated into many of the neo-Marxist theories (outlined in Chapter 5), which portray individuals as relatively powerless in the face of the underlying mechanisms of capital accumulation. The basic issue in question is the degree to which individuals acting separately or in groups can affect their own destiny in relation to what in academic terms is often referred to as the role of human 'agency'.

It should be clear that the two solutions to the problem of human agency outlined in Chapters 4 and 5 are, by themselves, both inadequate. If Weber's emphasis upon the subjective actions of individuals is pushed to its logical conclusion, it seems to deny the existence of constraints upon human behaviour; while many of the neo-Marxist theories outlined in Chapter 5 seem to deny the possibility of change through human struggle. In this context it should be noted that Duncan and Goodwin's (1982) critique is an important advance upon many of the structuralist ideas. They stress two issues which are of particular importance. First, there is a need to trace the historical evolution of state structures and policies. This is a feature which is missing from Saunders's dualistic model although it is stressed by Piven and Friedland. Second, it cannot be assumed that everything that happens within capitalist society is functional for capitalism. As Duncan and Goodwin observe, there is no guarantee that monetarism is – or was – functional for various capitalist interests. There is a need to examine which interests are served by what types of state practice, and how capitalist interests can be both supported and thwarted.

One of the most widely cited solutions to the problem of human agency in the face of structural constraints is the concept of 'structuration' which has been advocated by the prolific social scientist Anthony Giddens (1981). His ideas are complex and difficult to describe without recourse to a highly elaborate set of terminology. However, reduced to basics his approach seems to envisage a structure not as a 'thing', such as a business organisation or a university, but as a set of rules and resources. The structure is maintained by the day-to-day practices of human beings applying the rules and distributing rewards. 'Structuration' refers to the way in which these practices lead to the simultaneous maintenance and transformation of the structure. The appeal of this perspective lies in the fact that there is no dichotomy between the individual and society, but a mutual interdependence of structure and actions.

These abstract ideas might seem far removed from the geography of collective consumption, but Giddens's work does suggest some links. Giddens notes that while Weber's approach to social class avoids some of the rigidities of Marxist thinking, it raises the prospect of an endless plurality of various classes based upon numerous distributive criteria (Giddens, 1973). There is, in other words, the problem of making the transition from the diversity of material reward-based relationships (many of which are created within the sphere of collective consumption), to the identification of classes as structured forms. Giddens distinguishes between two types of structuration to perform this task: first, *mediate* form, that is, factors which intervene between the existence of certain market capacities and the formation of classes as identifiable social units; and second *proximate* forms, which refer to localised factors which shape class formation. The elements of jurisdictional partioning and externality effects would seem to be related to this second type of structuration, and suggest an interactive framework which is of some relevance to geographers.

Ultimately the issue of human agency would seem to be a matter for resolution by empirical analysis rather than by theoretical debate. The activities of local politicians and professionals operating within the realm of collective consumption therefore need to be conceptualised as operating within, and at the same time creating, numerous constraints. The most important of these are:

1 *The urban structure*: this includes demographic pressures such as the number of schoolchildren or elderly persons, the buoyancy of the local economy and 'ecological' pressures such as the availability of land, or the position of the area in the urban hierarchy.

2 *The activities of local pressure groups*: this includes both formal and informal channels and all the numerous organisations considered in Chapter 3.

3 *Pressures from the central government*: again these are diverse and will vary between different departments and services.

The extent of these pressures will vary over time and between different local government areas. As stressed in Chapter 2, however, while some developments have inevitable 'knock-on' effects – such as a sudden growth in the birth-rate leading to increased needs for schooling – there is no automatic translation process into public policy; these pressures must be perceived and formed into a local governmental response. In some cases there may be little or no room for manoeuvre (as is suggested by current legislation (1984) over 'rate-capping'); but it is essential to retain a perspective which puts the attitudes, motivations and aspirations of key actors to the fore. The final sections examine some concepts which might assist in this task.

Consumption cleavages
The domination of British local government by the Conservative and

Labour parties means that class divisions are an important element of city politics. As stressed in Chapter 2, however, many of these differences reflect political rhetoric rather than differences in policy. Furthermore, there is considerable evidence of a declining relationship between occupational class and political affiliation. Many of the pressures and representations upon local government cut across conventional class divisions.

To some extent these changes reflect the changing nature of the class structure – the decline of manual workers, and the growth of professional and managerial occupations together with various forms of white-collar service employment. Dunleavy (1980) attempts to further explain the declining relationship between class and voting patterns with the concept of 'consumption cleavages'. He notes that an individual's dependence upon the public or private sectors for housing and transport has an effect upon voting behaviour which can override social class. Thus, manual workers who are owner-occupiers and who own cars are more likely to vote Conservative. These consumption differences are often regarded as relatively unimportant compared with social class, but there is evidence from the February 1974 General Election that, whereas intermediate managerial workers were 4.12 times likely to vote Conservative than unskilled manual workers, home owners with two cars were 4.38 times more likely to vote Conservative than council tenants without a car (Dunleavy, 1979).

Dunleavy notes that differences between the national political parties cannot explain the increasing political salience of these issues. Instead, one must take cognisance of the fact that these housing and transport issues have an important geographical dimension. The decentralisation of home-owners from inner-city areas has strengthened the links between public provision and Labour Party strength in the major cities. Labour-controlled councils have heavily subsidised losses in public transport systems, and have provided extensive concessionary fares schemes. These councils also have a higher rate of council house building and have resisted the attempts of the central Conservative government to encourage the sale of council housing.

In suburban areas, links have also been forged between Conservative councils and owner-occupiers, again based on consumption cleavages. In this case reduced subsidies for public transport together with policies excluding public-sector housing provide benefits for house-owners in terms of lower rate demands and the maintenance of positive externalities. These links between consumption cleavages and political affiliations clearly cut across occupational divisions related to production; furthermore, they cannot simply be dismissed as 'ideological', since positive material benefits ensue from these policies. In addition, these cleavages have a very important geographical manifestation. The links between these sectoral consumption cleavages and jurisdictional partitioning and externality effects clearly constitute an issue requiring further analysis. These cleavages and differences between Labour- and Conservative-controlled authorities may become even more important in the light of future attempts to 'privatise' local services.

Bureaucracies and professionals
No future analysis of collective consumption will be adequate without due regard to the powers of local authority bureaucracies in the formation of policy and the allocation or closure of public facilities. In this context, one of the major limitations of previous managerialist and 'decision-rules' studies is their neglect of the influence of professionalism, and the way in which this phenomenon interacts with bureaucracy.

It will be recalled from Chapter 3 that Weber was concerned with the legitimacy of the rules and roles of officials in an organisation, and suggested that technical competence and control by knowledge were the basis of legitimation. Parsons (1960), however, suggests that such criteria are the basis of *professional* authority; and the neglect by Weber of professions has been one of the major criticisms directed against this approach.

Although there is widespread agreement that professions are an important feature of modern industrial societies, there is little consensus over what constitutes a profession and how this form of organisation differs from bureaucratic forms of organisation. One approach is to define professions by a series of attributes (Johnson, 1972). A profession is generally seen to possess knowledge based on a consistent body of theory of abstract propositions. A long formal period of training in an academic institution is therefore usually necessary to acquire professional knowledge, expertise and judgement. The professional is seen to be concerned with the interests of the community and has a commitment to an ideal of service. Professional knowledge is supposed to be given for the benefit of the client, and used within an ethical code of conduct to prevent abuse of the client. The long period of training also fosters strong norms of behaviour and the rewards of the professional act are said to be symbolic and not ends in themselves.

Professional knowledge and expertise based on that knowledge, together with the ethical code of conduct form the legitimate base of professional authority and the right to determine action for others. Deriving from professional authority is professional autonomy, the right to self-determination. Professionals are able to determine their own definition of their role, the standards of its performance, the right to be judged only by professional peers – since others lack the necessary knowledge and expertise – and control over the selection and admission of new entrants.

Some writers have stressed the process by which an occupational group achieves professional status. Caplow (1954) established several characteristics of occupational professionalisation. The occupation establishes a qualifying association (to control standards of knowledge), controls and limits recruitment, changes its name to establish and identify its new status, implements a training programme and expects a life-time commitment to a 'career', rather than a short-term commitment to a 'job'.

Other writers have stressed the links between professionals and social class and status (Marshall, 1963). It is the status differential between the client and the professional which is seen as the basis of his authority. The power resources of a single occupational group alone are seldom sufficient to impose its own definitions upon others, but when occupational power is allied with membership of a dominant class the occupational group achieves legitimate autonomy. Professional autonomy can thus be linked to social stratification as well as to occupational status.

Despite their diversity, a common theme running through these studies of professionalism is the ability of the professional to act autonomously in his relationship with his client. This contrasts with the employee in a formal organisation who occupies a subordinate position and is bound by the rules of his 'office'. Since professionals are increasingly salaried employees of large organisations rather than independent practitioners, and this is especially true within the sphere of collective consumption, this raises the possibility of professional-bureaucratic conflict. This issue has generated a vast literature, which shows that the nature of this conflict and the way it is ameliorated depends upon the type of profession and the nature of the organisational environment (Etzioni, 1964; Friedson, 1970).

It would seem that an explicit consideration of the effect of professionalism upon service provision has the potential to provide deeper insights than the rather superficial references to bureaucratic forms of organisation that has hitherto characterised much of the managerialist literature. For example, the study of health services, both in Britain and America, cannot be understood without consideration of the dominance of the medical profession in the structure of the service. Perhaps more interesting are the 'semi-professions' – those groups which do not possess the full set of attributes noted above. There has been much concern in planning circles about the status of town planning as a profession, and many of the actions of planners since the Second World War can be interpreted as an attempt to increase their professional status in relation to other workers in local government including architects, engineers and surveyors.

Amongst the numerous issues raised by this perspective the following would seem to be especially important:

1 What is the relative power of the true professions and the
  semi-professions to influence and determine the formation

and implementation of policies at both central and local government levels?

2 What is the relative importance of chief officers and street-level bureaucrats upon public service provision?

3 How important are the professions compared with other local government employee organisations and the trade unions?

These issues would seem to be especially important both in the light of central pressures to 'rationalise' and consolidate certain activities in larger centres, such as in the case of schools; and in the light of attempts by some Labour-controlled councils to decentralise services, such as social work, to a 'neighbourhood' level.

Feminist perspectives
One of the most important developments in the social sciences in the last decade has been the emergence of various types of radical and liberal feminist perspectives. To date such perspectives have had relatively little impact upon studies of collective consumption. This is despite the fact that many of the services considered in this book primarily affect the lives of women. As Cockburn notes, 'who answers the door when the social worker calls? who talks to the head teacher about the truant child? who runs down to the rent office? the woman, wife and mother.' (Cockburn, 1977:58.)

It is therefore essential that future studies of service provision in cities explicitly consider the role of women in society. This will again lead studies of collective consumption to consider a wide range of issues, for apart from inadequate services, women's opportunities are limited by a generally unequal division of labour in the home, socialisation into conventional gender roles, and discrimination against women by employers and trade unions (Allen and Barker, 1976). An important issue for future research is how to conceptualise the role of women in society in a way that is completely autonomous from, or totally constrained by, the capitalist mode of production (Barrett, 1980). A radical feminist perspective suggests that the system of patriarchy is at the root of women's oppression. Patriarchy is a system of male supremacy which pre-dates capitalism, having existed in many forms for thousands of years. There is, however, a growing recognition that patriarchal systems cannot be divorced in the modern world from a study of the economic base and capitalist modes of production. This does not mean that the position of women can simply be attributed to 'the needs of capitalism': the capital accumulation process has accommodated itself to patriarchal power structures, but at the same time helps to perpetuate them.

Study of the role of women in society becomes all the more urgent in the wake of recent, and hitherto little understood social changes. There is some evidence that women have suffered higher rates of unemployment as a result of cuts in public services and occupations such as social workers, school cleaners, nursery staff and teachers. On the other hand, the expansion of the service sector has created a wide range of relatively low-paid semi-skilled jobs, which in many areas have replaced male employment in traditional manufacturing industries. These changes are likely to increase the immobility of labour since there is often a reluctance for households to work in separate areas, and mean that it is difficult to allocate 'families' to a particular class on the basis of the occupation of the male (Urry, 1980). The implications of these changes for struggles over the realm of collective consumption have yet to be evaluated.

Study of the role of women has strong links with the study of professions. By and large the fully-fledged professions such as law and medicine are dominated by men, whereas the so-called semi-professions – nursing, social work and teaching – are dominated by women. Since the latter dominate the provision of collective consumption, it is essential that future studies play greater attention to the links between patriarchy and professionalism (Hearn, 1980).

Spatial scale
The ideas of Saunders, Piven and Friedland that were noted previously regarding the structural segregation of the politics of social investment and social consumption, are but one of a set of ideas attempting to integrate various perspectives. Johnston (1980), for example, has suggested that the value of theories depends upon the time-scale under investigation; structural theories, he argues, may be most suitable in analysing general patterns over many years, whereas other theories may explain short-run manoeuvres and policy shifts. It is clear, however, that his perspective is one that attributes human actions with relatively little room for change, as is summed up by his comment that: 'the details of the performance are contingent upon the actors, who can change the script but not the plot' (Johnston, 1983:262).

In addition to the type of public facility and the time scale under examination, the value of various theories may be related to the spatial scale of the analysis. For example, it would seem that the influence of bargaining by pressure groups is most important in explaining the distribution of collective consumption facilities *within* local government areas. So-called 'pluralist-' type influences will be most applicable in examining isolated issues such as school closures, road widening and the location of particular noxious facilities. Such pressures can, therefore, be linked to the concepts of externalities, tapering effects and consumption cleavages.

In contrast, what can be termed 'managerial', bureaucratic or professional influences, together with their interactions with political factors, will be more useful in understanding the overall level of resource allocation by the authority, and the political and administrative milieu in which the various organisations have to operate. Such perspectives may therefore be more applicable for the study of inter-authority variations, which represent numerous decisions made over many years.

Finally, aggregate social theories relating to the economic mode of production and the political manoeuvres of central government can help to account for the overall level of resources allocated at the national level, and the constraints upon the managers in local government. At this level there is a need for comparative studies of different nations to reveal the impact of different scales and forms of collective consumption. One important question in this context concerns the limits of public intervention in capitalist economies: at what stage is the size of collective services either too large or too small to ensure adequate profitability of capital accumulation in the private sector, and political legitimacy for the central state? Closely allied to this are the limits of deviations from central government policy in local government areas: at what point do these deviations begin to threaten the economic and political domination of the central government?

These concepts of consumption cleavages, professional-bureaucratic conflict, patriarchal power relations and spatial scale are just a few of the wide range of perspectives that will be necessary to occupy the 'middle ground' of social theory, and to explain struggles over the distribution of public goods and services. At a time of rapid social and economic change they have the potential to integrate with notions of jurisdictional partitioning, tapering effects and externalities to illuminate the ever-changing geography of collective consumption.

A guide to further reading

Although it is fairly extensive, the bibliography associated with this book is less than the proverbial 'tip of the iceberg' in relation to the total literature dealing with collective consumption. The scale of the literature is daunting for the researcher, and certainly beyond the wit of one individual to comprehend as a whole. Fortunately, it would appear that much of the work can be ignored since it presents few new insights or illuminating evidence. Some of the books and articles listed in the bibliography might be seen as crucial, but for the vast majority of issues there are a great many other references which would have made the points equally well. The following 'guide to further reading' is therefore a personal selection of some work that I have found interesting and intelligible, which may serve as a springboard for those wishing to explore various fields within the sphere of collective consumption. To assist in this task I have restated some of the crucial questions that I have posed and attempted to answer in this book.

Chapter 1
An introduction to the geography of collective consumption

The concepts of production and consumption are outlined in Smith (1977). Introductions to the geography of public goods and services can also be found in Bennett (1980), Cox (1979), Kirby (1982), and Kirby and Pinch (1983). Harvey (1970) and Teitz (1968) are still worth examining, together with the wide-ranging reviews of Burnett (1981) and Dear (1980). Good introductions to the British local government system are provided by Byrne (1981) and Stanyer (1976). The American political system is outlined in Johnston (1982), while Judd (1979) is a fascinating introduction to the evolution of city politics in America.

Questions arising
How useful is the pure theory of public goods in understanding collective consumption?
What types of public goods and services are most affected by 'factors of geography'?
What are the main differences between the British and American local government systems?

What is the most appropriate definition of 'urban' in the context of collective consumption?

Chapter 2
Jurisdictional partitioning and the 'outputs' approach

Useful recent reviews of the 'outputs' literature are contained in Alt (1971), Danziger (1978), Johnston, (1979), Newton (1984), and Newton and Sharpe (1977). The papers by Sharpe (1981) and Hansen (1981) are especially illuminating. Detailed reviews of the problems of analysing urban service distributions may be found in Rich (1982).

Questions arising
What are the main criteria used to justify decentralised administrative systems, and in what ways do these criteria conflict?
What are the main difficulties in measuring needs for local services?
What are the main differences between territorial justice and positive discrimination?
What are the main differences between resource 'inputs', 'outputs' and 'outcomes' in the context of local government service provisions?
Which services are most affected by political factors?
In what ways does the urban structure affect local service provision?

Chapter 3
Externalities, locational efficiency and conflict

The set of papers by Dear and his associates is probably the best introduction to spatial externality effects (Dear, 1976; Dear, 1977; Boeckh, Dear and Taylor, 1980; Dear and Taylor, 1982; Dear, Taylor and Hall, 1980). Hodgart (1978), Knox (1980) and Massam (1984) provide some overviews of accessibility models. The pluralist position is put forward in Dahl (1956) and Polsby (1963), and is reviewed in Dunleavy (1979), Saunders (1979) and Kirk (1980). An excellent study of pressure group activity in a British city may be found in Newton (1976b). The extensive literature on neighbourhood organisations and their contacts with public bureaucracies is discussed in Burnett (1984).

Questions arising
To what extent is there a conflict between the principles of equity and efficiency in the location of public facilities?
What are the main factors affecting the shape and character of spatial externality effects?
Which groups gain, and which groups lose, as a result of the collective impact of positive and negative externality effects in cities?
What are the merits of the pluralist approach as an aid to understanding the distribution of public services in cities?
Why are conflicts at the place of residence such a widespread and increasing feature of British and American cities?

Chapter 4
Neo-Weberian approaches

Weber's writings are often extremely difficult, but his basic methodology can be gleaned from Weber (1949), in conjunction with Outhwaite (1975) and Saunders (1981). His writings on bureaucracy are widely scattered, but Albrow (1970) provides a clear guide and excellent commentary on this diverse literature. Recent pleas for a 'Weberian' perspective in urban studies have come from Elliott and McCrone (1982), Simie (1981) and Saunders (1981). The managerialist debate is outlined in Pahl (1975; 1979), Williams (1978; 1982), Leonard (1982), and Saunders (1979; 1981). Lineberry (1977) provides an accessible introduction to the American 'decision-rules' literature. Jones *et al.*, (1980) provide one of the more sophisticated studies of this type.

Questions arising
What are the distinctive features of Weber's approach to the social sciences?
In what respects is urban managerialism a Weberian approach to the city?
What are the main differences between the early and late managerialist approaches?
How do decision rules affect the distribution of public services?
What are the major limitations of the decision-rules literature and their findings about service distributions?
What are the best strategies for analysing the extent of local mangerial discretion?

Chapter 5
Neo-Marxist approaches

Marx's ideas, like Weber's, are often impenetrable and this field is made even more difficult by the extraordinary diversity of later neo-Marxist theories. Fortunately, Harvey (1982) has provided a detailed but clear exposition of the basic ideas in *Grundrisse* and *Capital*, although much of this concerns the 'inner logic' of capitalism and does not address the issues of collective consumption in advanced capitalist economies. More useful in this context, therefore, is the work of Gough (1979) which also contains a lucid outline of Marxist approaches and theories of the capitalist state. Excellent discussions of the latter issue can also be found in Jessop (1977) and Dear and Clark (1981), which should be read in conjunction with Holloway and Picciotto (1977).

No student of collective consumption can ignore the early writings of Castells (1977) which should be contrasted with Pahl (1978). Pickvance (1976) provides a clear exposition and critique of the theory of urban social movements (see also Saunders, 1979, Ch. 3). O'Connor (1973) is essential reading, while Dearlove (1979) provides an interesting Marxist interpretation of the reorganisation of British local government. Although flawed in many respects, Cockburn (1977) is a lively and readable interpretation of local state activity. For a broad perspective on Marxist approaches see Sayer (1979), which should be read in conjunction with Giddens (1981).

Questions arising

In what ways does a materialist approach differ from 'conventional' social
    science?
What are the main differences between Weberian and Marxist approaches?
In what ways does the organisation of private production affect the
    distribution of collective consumption?
What are the main differences between the French structuralist school of
    Marxism and the German 'capital logic' approach.
What are the merits and limitations of Castells's notion of collective
    consumption?
Is it possible to reconcile notions of class struggle and conflict with ideas of
    class domination and manipulation?

Chapter 6
Beyond locational analysis and structuralism

Good discussions of the fiscal crisis in European cities can be found in Newton
(1980) and Sharpe (1981), together with Rose and Page (1982). An interesting
collection of largely Marxist interpretations of fiscal stress in American cities
may be found in Alcaly and Mermelstein (1977). As usual, the American
literature is enormous in scale, but O'Connor (1973) and Levine (1980) are
particularly useful. The notion of consumption cleavages together with the
structural constraints upon local governments is discussed by Dunleavy
(1980), while Barrett (1980) provides a particularly thought-provoking
discussion of the role of women in society.

Questions arising

To what extent are the policies of 'Reaganomics' and 'Thatcherism' the
    results of party ideologies and to what extent the dictates of economic
    circumstances?
What are the principal determinants of fiscal stress in major cities?
How relevant are corporatist theories in the 1980s?
Is it possible and desirable to link struggles in the realm of collective
    consumption with struggles in the realm of production?
To what extent do consumption cleavages cut across class divisions in
    society?
How can we best conceptualise the role of women in the context of collective
    services?

Bibliography

Adams, C.T. and Winston, K.T. (1980), *Mothers at Work: Public Policies in the United States, Sweden and China*, New York, Longman.

Adams, R.F. (1967), 'On the variation in consumption of public services', in H.E. Brazer (ed.), *Essays on State and Local Finance*, Ann Arbor, University of Michigan Press, pp.9-45.

Albrow, M. (1970), *Bureaucracy*, London, Macmillan.

Alcaly, R.E. and Mermelstein, D. (1977), *The Fiscal Crisis of American Cities*, New York, Vintage Books.

Alford, R. (1967), 'The comparative study of urban politics', in L.F. Schnore and H. Fagin (eds), *Urban Research and Policy Planning*, Beverly Hills, Sage Publications, pp.263-302.

Allen, S. and Barker, D.L. (1976), *Sexual Divisions and Society*, London, Tavistock.

Alt, J.E. (1971), 'Some social and political correlates of county borough expenditures', *British Journal of Political Science* vol.1, pp.49-62.

Antunes, G.E. and Mladenka, K. (1976), 'The politics of local services and service distribution', in L.H. Masotti and R.L. Lineberry (eds), *The New Urban Politics*, Cambridge, Mass., Ballinger, pp.147-69.

Antunes, G.E. and Plumlee, J.P. (1977), 'The distribution of an urban public service: Ethnicity, socioeconomic status and bureaucracy as determinants of the quality of neighbourhood streets', *Urban Affairs Quarterly*, vol.12, no.3, pp.313-31.

Aronson, J.R. (1974), 'Voting with your feet', *New Society*, vol.29, no.621, pp.545-7.

Ashford, E.D., Berne, R. and Schramm, R. (1976), 'The expenditure financing decision in British local government', *Policy and Politics*, vol.5, pp.5-24.

Bachrach, P. and Baratz, M. (1970), *Power and Poverty*, Oxford University Press.

Bacon, R. and Eltis, W. (1976), *Britain's Economic Problem: Too Few Producers*, London, Macmillan.

Ball, M. (1983), *Housing and Economic Power*, London, Methuen.

Banfield, E. and Wilson, J.Q. (1963), *City Politics*, Cambridge, Mass., Harvard University Press.

Barrett, M. (1980), *Women's Oppression Today*, London, Verso Press.

Bassett, K. and Hauser, D. (1975), 'Public policy and spatial structure: Housing improvement in Bristol', in R. Peel, M. Chisholm and P. Haggett (eds), *Processes in Physical and Human Geography*, London, Heinemann.

Bennett, R.J. (1980), *The Geography of Public Finance*, London, Methuen.

Benson, C. and Lund, P. (1969), *Neighbourhood Distribution of Local Public Services*, Berkeley, Institute of Governmental Studies.

Bird, H. (1976), 'Residential mobility and preference patterns in the public sector of the housing market', *Transactions of the Institute of British Geographers* (New Series), vol.1, pp.20-33.

Boaden, N.T. (1971), *Urban Policy-Making*, Cambridge University Press.

Boddy, M. (1976), 'The structure of mortgage finance: Building societies and the British social formation', *Transactions of the Institute of British Geographers* (New Series), vol.1, pp.58-71.

Boeckh, J., Dear, M. and Taylor, S.M. (1980), 'Property values and mental health facilites in metropolitan Toronto', *The Canadian Geographer*, vol.24, no.3, pp.270-85.

Bone, M. (1974), *Preschool Children and the Need for Day Care*, London, Office of Population Censuses and Surveys.

Booms, B.H. and Halldorson, J.R. (1973), 'The politics of redistribution: A reformulation', *American Political Science Review*, vol.67, pp.924-31.

Booth, A. (1982), 'Corporatism, capitalism and depression in twentieth-century Britain', *The British Journal of Sociology*, vol.33, pp.200-23.

Boyle, J. and Jacobs, D. (1980), 'The intra-city distribution of services: A multi-variate analysis', *The American Political Science Review*, vol.76, pp.371-9.

Bradley, J.E., Kirby, A.M. and Taylor, P.J. (1978), 'Distance-decay and dental decay: A study of dental health among primary school children in Newcastle-upon-Tyne', *Regional Studies*, vol.12, pp.529-40.

Bradshaw, J. (1972), 'The concept of social need', *New Society*, vol.496, pp.640-3.

Brazer, H.E. (1959), *City Expenditures in the United States*, Washington DC, National Bureau of Economic Research, Occasional Paper 66.

Buchanan, J. and Tullock, G. (1962), *The Calculus of Consent*, Ann Arbor, University of Michigan Press.

Burnett, A. (1981), 'The distribution of local political outputs and outcomes in British and American cities: A research review and agenda', in A.D. Burnett and P.J. Taylor (eds), *Political Studies from Spatial Perspectives*, Chichester, John Wiley, pp.201-35.

Burnett, A. (1984), 'Neighbourhood participation, political demand-making and local outputs in British and North American cities', in A. Kirby, P. Knox and S. Pinch (eds), *Public Service Provision and Urban Development*, Beckenham, Croom Helm, pp.316-62.

Byrne, T. (1981), *Local Government in Britain*, Harmondsworth, Penguin.

Caplow, T. (1954), *The Sociology of Work*, New York, McGraw Hill.

Castells, M. (1977), *The Urban Question*, Arnold, London.

Christaller, W. (1966), *Central Places in Southern Germany*, translated by C.W. Baskin, New Jersey, Prentice-Hall.

Cockburn, C. (1977), *The Local State*, London, Pluto Press.

Colm, G. (1936), 'Public expenditures and economic structures in the United States', *Social Research*, vol.3, pp.57-77.

Cox, K.R. (1973), *Conflict, Power and Politics in the City*, New York, McGraw Hill.

Cox, K.R. (1979), *Location and Public Problems*, Oxford, Basil Blackwell.

Cox, K.R. (1984), 'Social change, turf politics, and concepts of turf politics', in A. Kirby, P. Knox and S. Pinch (eds), *Public Service Provision and Urban Development*, Beckenham, Croom Helm, pp.283-315.

Culyer, A.J. (1976), *Need and the National Health Service*, London, Martin Robertson.

Dahl, R.A. (1956), *A Preface to Democratic Theory*, University of Chicago Press.

Danziger, J.N. (1978), *Making Budgets: Public Resource Allocation*, Beverly Hills, Sage Publications.

Danziger, J.N. (1980), 'California's Proposition 13 and the fiscal limitations movement in the United States', *Political Studies*, vol.29, pp.559-612.

Davidson, J.L. (1981), 'Location of community-based treatment centres', *Social Service Review*, June, pp.221-41.

Davies, B.P. (1968), *Social Needs and Resources in Local Services*, London, Michael Joseph.

Davies, B.P. (1969), 'Local authority size: Some associations with standards of performance of services for deprived children and old people', *Public Administration*, vol.47, pp.225-48.

Davies, B.P. (1975), 'Causal processes and techniques in the modelling of policy outcomes', in K. Young (ed.), *Essays on the Study of Urban Politics*, London, Macmillan, pp.78-105.

Davies. B.P. (1977), 'Social service studies and the explanation of policy outcomes', *Policy and Politics*, vol.5, pp.41-59.

Davies, B.P. and Barton, A.J. (1968), 'Child care services', in *Royal Commission on Local Government in England, Research Study 1*, London, HMSO.

Davies, B.P., Barton, A., McMillan, I. and Williamson, V. (1971), *Variations in Services for the Aged: A Causal Analysis*, London, Bell and Sons.

Davies, B.P., Barton, A. and McMillan, I. (1972), *Variations in Children's Services Among British Urban Authorities*, London, Bell and Sons.

Davies, J.G. (1972), *The Evangelistic Bureaucrat*, London, Tavistock.

Dawson, R.E. (1967), 'Social development, party competition and policy', in W.N. Chambers and W.D. Burnham (eds), *The American Party System: Stages of Political Development*, New York, Oxford University Press.

Dawson, R.E. and Gray, V. (1971), 'State welfare policies', in H. Jacob and K.N. Vines (eds), *Politics in the American States: A Comparative Analysis*, Boston, Little, Brown and Co., pp.433-76.

Dawson, R.E. and Robinson, J.A. (1963), 'Inter-party competition, economic variables and welfare policies in the American states', *The Journal of Politics*, vol.25, no.2, pp.265-89.

Dear, M.J. (1976), 'Spatial externalities and locational conflict', in D. Massey and P. Batey (eds), *London Papers in Regional Science: Alternative Frameworks for Analysis*, London, Pion, pp.152-67.

Dear, M.J. (1977), 'Psychiatric patients and the inner city', *Annals of the Association of American Geographers*, vol.67, pp.588-94.

Dear, M.J. (1980), 'The public city', in W.A.V. Clark and E.G. Moore (eds), *Residential Mobility and Public Policy*, Beverly Hills, Sage Publications.

Dear, M.J. and Clark, G. (1981), 'The state in capitalism and the capitalist state', in M.J. Dear and A.J. Scott (eds), *Urbanization and Urban Planning in Capitalist Society*, London, Methuen, pp.45-62.

Dear, M.J. and Long, J. (1978), 'Community strategies in locational conflict', in K.R. Cox (ed.), *Urbanization and Conflict in Market Societies*, Chicago, Methuen, pp.113-28.

Dear, M.J. and Taylor, S.M. (1982), *Not on Our Street,*. London, Pion.

Dear, M., Taylor, S. and Hall, G. (1980), 'External effects of mental health facilities', *Annals of the Association of American Geographers*, vol.70, pp.342-52.

Dearlove, J. (1971), 'Councillors and interest groups in Kensington and Chelsea', *British Journal of Political Science*, vol.1, pp.125-53.

Dearlove, J. (1973), *The Politics of Policy in Local Government*, Cambridge University Press.

Dearlove, J. (1979), *The Reorganisation of Local Government*, Cambridge University Press.

Dennis, N. (1972), *Public Participation and Planning Blight*, London, Faber and Faber.

Derrick, E. and McRory, J. (1973), 'Cup in hand: Sunderland's self-image after the cup', *University of Birmingham Centre for Urban and Regional Studies, Working Paper No. 8.*

Downs, A. (1957), *An Economic Theory of Democracy*, New York, Harper and Row.

Duncan, S.S. (1974), 'Cosmetic planning or social engineering? Improvement grants and improvement areas in Huddersfield', *Area*, vol.6, pp.259-71.

Duncan, S.S. (1978), 'Housing reform, the capitalist state and social democracy', *Urban and Regional Studies, Working Paper No. 9* University of Sussex.

Duncan, S.S. and Goodwin, M. (1982), 'The local state: Functionalism, autonomy and class relations in Cockburn and Saunders', *Political Geography Quarterly*, vol.1, pp.77-96.

Dunleavy, P. (1977), 'Protest and quiescence in urban politics: A critique of pluralist and structuralist Marxist views', *International Journal of Urban and Regional Research*, vol.1, pp.193-218.

Dunleavy, P. (1979), 'The urban bases of political alignment: "Social class", domestic property ownership or state intervention in consumption processes?', *British Journal of Political Science*, vol.9, pp.409-43.

Dunleavy, P. (1980), *Urban Political Analysis*, London, Macmillan.

Dunleavy, P. (1982), 'Class, consumption and radical explanations in urban politics: A rejoinder to Hooper', *Political Geography Quarterly*, vol.1, pp.187-92.

Easton, D. (1957), 'An approach to the analysis of political systems', *World Politics*, vol.9, pp.383-400.

Eliott, B. and McCrone, D. (1982), *The City*, London, Macmillan.

Etzioni, A. (1964), *Modern Organisations*, Englewood Cliffs, Prentice-Hall.

Fabricant, S. and Lipsey, R.E. (1952), *The Trend of Government Activity in the United States since 1900*, New York, National Bureau of Economic Research.

Ferris, J. (1972), *Participation in Urban Planning: The Barnsbury Case*, London, Bell and Sons.

Fisher, G.W. (1962). 'Determinants of state and local government expenditures: A preliminary analysis', *National Tax Journal*, vol.15, pp.84-73.

Fisher, G.W. (1964), 'Interstate variations in state and local government expenditure', *National Tax Journal*, vol.17, pp.64-73.

Ford, J. (1975), 'The role of the building society manager in the urban stratification system', *Urban Studies*, vol.12, pp.295-302.

Friedland, R., Piven, F. and Alford, R. (1977), 'Political conflict, urban structure and the fiscal crisis', *International Journal of Urban and Regional Research*, vol.1, pp.447-71.

Friedson, E. (1970), *Professional Dominance: The Social Structure of Medical Care*, New York, Atherton Press.

Froman, L.A. (1967), 'An analysis of public policies in cities', *The Journal of Politics*, vol.29, pp.94-108.

Fry, B.R. and Winters, R.F. (1970), 'The politics of redistribution', *The American Political Science Review*, vol.64, pp.508-22.

Gans, H. (1972), *People and Plans*, Harmondsworth, Penguin.

Giddens, A. (1973), *The Class Structure of the Advanced Societies*, London, Hutchinson University Library.

Giddens, A. (1981), *A Contemporary Critique of Historical Materialism*, London, Macmillan.

Giggs, J.A. (1970), 'Socially disorganised areas in Barry: A multivariate analysis', in H. Carter and W.K.D. Davies (eds), *Urban Essays: Studies in the Geography of Wales*, London, Longman, pp.101-43.

Goldsmith, M. (1980), *Politics, Planning and the City*, London, Hutchinson.

Goodman, R.F. and Clary, B.B. (1976), 'Community attitudes and action in response to airport noise', *Environment and Behaviour*, vol.4, pp.441-70.

Gough, I. (1975), 'State expenditure in advanced capitalism', *New Left Review*, no.92, pp.53-92.

Gough, I. (1979), *The Political Economy of the Welfare State*, London, Macmillan.

Gough, I. (1982), 'The crisis of the British Welfare State', in N.I. Fainstein and S.S. Fainstein (eds), *Urban Policy Under Capitalism*, Beverly Hills, Sage Publications, pp.43-64.

Gray, F. (1976), 'Selection and allocation of council housing', *Transactions of the Institute of British Geographers* (New Series), vol.10, pp.34-46.

Green, L.P. (1959), *Provincial Metropolis*, London, Allen and Unwin.

Greenwood, R. (1982), 'Pressures from Whitehall', in R. Rose and E. Page (eds), *Fiscal Stress in Cities*, Cambridge University Press.

Griffiths, J.A.G. (1966), *Central Departments and Local Authorities*, London, Allen and Unwin.

Gupta, S.P. and Hutton, J.P. (1968), 'Economies of scale in local government services', *Royal Commission on Local Government in England Research Study No. 3*, London, HMSO.

Hall, C. (1979), 'The early formation of Victorian domestic ideology', in S. Burman (ed.), *Fit Work for Women*, London, Croom Helm, pp.15-32.

Hall, P. (ed.) (1966), *Von Thunen's Isolated State*, Oxford, Pergamon Press.

Hall, P., Gracey, H., Drewett, R. and Thomas, R. (1973), *The Containment of Urban England*, London, PEP and Allen and Unwin.

Hansen, T. (1981), 'Transforming needs into expenditure decisions', in K. Newton (ed.), *Urban Political Economy*, London, Frances Pinter, pp.27-46.

Harrison, M. (1984), 'The coming welfare corporatism', *New Society*, vol.67, pp.321-23.

Harvey, D.W. (1970), 'Spatial process, spatial form and the redistribution of real income in an urban system', in M. Chisholm, A.E. Fray and P. Haggett (eds), *Regional Forecasting, Colston Papers, vol.22*, London, Butterworth, pp.270-300.

Harvey, D.W. (1978), 'Labour, capital and class struggle around the built environment in advanced capitalist societies', in K.R. Cox (ed.), *Urbanization and Conflict in Market Societies*, London, Methuen, pp.9-37.

Harvey, D.W. (1982), *The Limits to Capital*, Oxford, Blackwell.

Hearn, J. (1980), 'Notes on patriarchy, professionalization and the semi-professions', *British Journal of Sociology*, vol.31, pp.184-202.

Hirsch, W.Z. (1968), 'The supply of urban public services', in H.S. Perloff and L. Wingo (eds), *Issues in Urban Economics*, Washington, Johns Hopkins Press, pp.477-525.

Hirschmann, A.O. (1970), *Exit, Voice and Loyalty*, Cambridge, Mass., Harvard University Press.

Hodgart, R.L. (1978), 'Optimising access to public services', *Progress in Human Geography*, vol.2, pp.17-48.

Hodge, D. and Gatrell, A. (1976), 'Spatial constraint and the location of urban public facilities', *Environment and Planning, A*, vol.8, pp.215-30.

Hofferbert, R.I. (1966), 'The relation between public policy and some structural and environmental variables in the American states', *American Political Science Review*, vol.60, pp.73-82.

Holden, M. (1964), 'The governance of the metropolis as a problem in diplomacy', *Journal of Politics*, vol.26, pp.627-48.

Holloway, J. and Picciotto, S. (1977), 'Capital, crisis and the state', *Capital and Class*, vol.2, pp.76-101.

Honey, R. and Sorenson, D.R. (1984), 'Jurisdictional benefits and local costs: The politics of school closings', in A. Kirby, P. Knox and S. Pinch (eds), *Public Service Provision and Urban Development*, Beckenham, Croom Helm, pp.114-30.

Hottelling, H. (1929), 'Stability in competition', *Economic Journal*, vol.39, pp.41-57.

Humphries, J. (1977), 'The class struggle and the persistence of the working-class family', *Cambridge Journal of Economics*, vol.1, pp.241-58.

Hunter, F. (1953), *Community Power Structure*, North Carolina, Chapel Hill.

Ingram, D.R., Clarke, D.R. and Murdie, R.A. (1978), 'Distance and the decision to visit an emergency department', *Social Science and Medicine*, vol.12, pp.55-62.

Jacob, H. and Lipsky, M. (1968), 'Outputs, structure and power: An assessment of changes in the study of state and local politics', *Journal of Politics*, vol.30, pp.510-39.

James, E. (1966), 'Frontiers in the Welfare State', *Public Administration*, vol.44, pp.447-71.

Janelle, D.G. and Millward, H.A. (1976), 'Locational conflict patterns and urban ecological structure', *Tijdschrift voor Economische en Sociale Geografie*, vol.47, pp.102-13.

Jessop, B. (1977), 'Recent theories of the capitalist state', *Cambridge Journal of Economics*, vol.1. pp.353-74.

Johnson, T.J. (1972), *Professions and Power*, London, Macmillan.

Johnston, R.J. (1979), *Political, Electoral and Spatial Systems: An Essay in Political Geography*, Oxford, Clarendon Press.

Johnston, R.J. (1980), 'On the nature of explanation in human geography', *Transactions, Institute of British Geographers* (New Series), vol.5, pp.402-12.

Johnston, R.J. (1982), *The American Urban System*, London, Longman.

Johnston, R.J. (1983), *Geography and the State*, London, Macmillan.

Jones, B.D. (1977), 'Distributional considerations in models of urban government service provision', *Urban Affairs Quarterly*, vol.12, pp.291-312.

Judd, D.R. (1979), *The Politics of American Cities*, Boston, Little, Braun and Co.

Key, V.O. (1949), *Southern Politics in State and Nation*, New York, Knopf.

King, D.N. (1973), 'Why do local authority rate poundages differ?' *Public Administration*, vol.51, pp.165-73.

Kirby, A.M. (1979), *Education, Health and Housing: An Empirical Investigation of Resources Accessibility*, Farnborough, Saxon House.

Kirby, A.M. (1982), *The Politics of Location*, London, Methuen.

Kirby, A.M. and Pinch, S.P. (1983), 'Territorial justice and service allocation', in M. Pacione (ed.), *Progress in Urban Geography*, London, Croom Helm, pp.223-46.

Kirk, G. (1980), *Urban Planning in a Capitalist Society*, London, Croom Helm.

Kirwan, M. (1979), 'How has Proposition 13 worked out?' *New Society*, 2nd August, vol.49, pp.239-40.

Knox, P.L. (1978), 'The intraurban ecology of primary care: Patterns of accessibility and their policy implications', *Environment and Planning A*, vol.10, pp.415-35.

Knox, P.L. (1980), 'Measures of accessibility as social indicators', *Social Indicators Research*, vol.7, pp.367-77.

Knox, P.L. (1981), 'Retail geography and social well-being: A note on the changing distribution of pharmacies in Scotland', *Geoforum*, vol.12, pp.255-64.

Knox, P.L. (1982), 'Residential structure, facility location and patterns of accessibility', in K.R. Cox and R.J. Johnston (eds), *Conflict, Politics and the Urban Scene*, London, Longman, pp.62-87.

Knox, P.L. (1982), *Urban Social Geography*, London, Longman.

Kurrow, E. (1963), 'Determinants of state and local expenditures re-examined', *National Tax Journal*, vol.16, pp.252-5.

Lasswell. H.D. (1958), *Politics: Who gets What, When and How?* Cleveland, World Publishing Co.

Leonard, S. (1982), 'Urban managerialism: A period of transition', *Progress in Human Geography*, vol.6, pp.190-215.

Levine, C. (1980), *Managing Fiscal Stress*, Chatham, NV, Chatham House.

Levy, F.S., Meltsner, A.J. and Wildavsky, A. (1974), *Urban Outcomes: Schools, Streets, Libraries*, Berkeley, University of California Press.

Lewis, J. (1980), *The Politics of Motherhood*, London, Croom Helm.

Ley, D. and Mercer, J. (1980), 'Locational conflict and the politics of consumption', *Economic Geography*, vol.56, pp.89-109.

Lineberry, R.L. (1977), *Equality and Public Policy: The Distribution of Municipal Public Services*, Beverly Hills, Sage Publications.

Lipsky, M. (1976), 'Towards a theory of street-level bureaucracy', in W.D. Hawley (ed.), *Theoretical Perspectives on Urban Politics*, Englewood Cliffs, Prentice-Hall.

Lojkine, J. (1976), 'A Marxist theory of capitalist urbanization', in C.G. Pickvance (ed.), *Urban Sociology: Critical Essay*, London, Tavistock, pp.119-41.

Losch, A. (1954), *The Economics of Location*, Yale University Press.

Lowe, P.D. (1977), 'Amenity and equity: A review of local environmental pressure groups in Britain', *Environment and Planning, A*, vol.9, pp.35-58.

Madgwick, P. (1970), *American City Politics*, London, Routledge and Kegan Paul.

Margolis, J. (1968), 'The demand for urban public services', in H.S. Perloff and L. Wingo (eds), *Issues in Urban Economics*, Baltimore, Johns Hopkins Press, pp.536-6.

Marshall, T.H. (1963), *Sociology at the Crossroads and other Essays*, London, Heinemann.

Marshall, T.H. (1970), *Social Policy*, London, Hutchinson.

Massam, B.H. (1984), 'Policy evaluation and selection: Can formal methods help?', in A. Kirby, P. Knox, and S. Pinch (eds), *Public Service Provision and Urban Development*, Beckenham, Croom Helm, pp.131-51.

McLafferty, S. (1982), 'Urban structure and geographical access to public services', *Annals of the Association of American Geographers*, vol.72, pp.347-54.

Miller, S.M. (1979), 'Social policy on the defensive in Carter's America', *New Society*, 1st November, vol.49, pp.244-7.

Mladenka, K.R. (1980), 'The urban bureaucracy and the Chicago political machine: Who gets what and the limits of political control', *American Political Science Review*, vol.74, pp.991-8.

Mladenka, K.R. and Hill, K.Q. (1977), 'The distribution of benefits in an urban environment: Parks and libraries in Houston', *Urban Affairs Quarterly*, vol.13, pp.73-94.

Mladenka, K.R. and Hill, K.Q. (1978), 'The distribution of urban police services', *Journal of Politics*, vol.40, pp.112-33.

Monck, E. and Lomas, G. (1980), *Housing Action Areas: Success and Failure*, London, Centre for Environmental Studies.

Musgrave, R.A. (1958), *The Theory of Public Finance*, New York, McGraw Hill.

Newton, K. (1969), 'City politics in Britain and the United States', *Political Studies*, vol.17, 208-18.

Newton, K. (1974), 'Community decision-makers and community decision-making in England and the United States', in T.N. Clarke (ed.), *Comparative Community Politics*, New York, Wiley, pp.55-85.

Newton, K. (1975), 'American urban politics, social class, political structure and public goods', *Urban Affairs Quarterly*, vol.11, pp.241-64.

Newton, K. (1976a), 'Community research in Britain', *Current Sociology*, vol.22, pp.49-86.

Newton, K. (1976b), *Second City Politics*, Oxford, Clarendon Press.

Newton, K. (1978), 'Conflict avoidance and conflict suppression: The case of urban politics in the United States', in Cox, K.R. (ed.), *Urbanization and Conflict in Market Societies*, London, Methuen, pp.76-93.

Newton, K. (1980), *Balancing the Books*, Beverly Hills, Sage Publications.

Newton, K. (1984), 'Public services in cities and counties', in A. Kirby, P. Knox, and S. Pinch (eds), *Public Service Provision and Urban Development*, Beckenham, Croom Helm, pp.19-43.

Newton, K. and Sharpe, L.J. (1977), 'Local outputs research: Some proposals and reflections', *Policy and Politics*, vol.5, pp.61-82.

Nicholson, R.J. and Topham, N. (1971), 'The determinants of investment in housing by local authorities: An econometric approach', *Journal of the Royal Statistical Society, Series A*, vol.134, pp.273-320.

Nicholson, R.J. and Topham, N. (1972), 'Review of urban policy-making', *Public Administration*, vol.50, pp.222-4.

Nicholson, R.J. and Topham, N. (1975), 'Urban road provision in England and Wales, 1962-68', *Policy and Politics*, vol.5, pp.3-29.

Nivola, P.S. (1978), 'Distributing a municipal service: A case study of housing inspection', *Journal of Politics*, vol.40, 59-81.

O'Connor, J. (1973), *The Fiscal Crisis of the State*, London, St James Press.

Office of Population Censuses and Surveys (1982), *Census 1981: Preliminary Report*, London, HMSO.

Oliver, F.R. and Stanyer, J. (1969), 'Some aspects of the financial behaviour of county boroughs', *Public Administration*, vol.47, pp.169-84.

Ostrom, V., Tiebout, C.M. and Warren, R. (1961), 'The organisation of government in metropolitan areas', *American Political Science Review*, vol.55, pp.831-42.

Outhwaite, W. (1975), *Understanding Social Life: The Method called Verstehen*, London, Allen and Unwin.

Pahl, R.E. (1970), *Whose City?*, London, Longman.

Pahl, R.E. (1975), *Whose City?* (Second Edition) Harmondsworth, Penguin.

Pahl, R.E. (1977), 'Managers, technical experts and the state', in M. Harloe (ed.), *Captive Cities*, London, John Wiley, pp.50-60.

Pahl, R.E. (1978), 'Castells and collective consumption', *Sociology*, vol.12, pp.309-15.

Pahl, R.E. (1979), 'Socio-political factors in resource allocation', in D. Herbert and D. Smith (eds), *Social Problems and the City*, Oxford University Press, pp.33-46.

Pahl, R.E. and Winkler (1974), 'The coming corporatism', *New Society* vol.30, pp.72-6.

Panitch, L. (1980), 'Recent theorizations of corporatism: Reflections on a growth industry', *British Journal of Sociology*, vol.31, pp.159-87.

Parsons, T. (1960), *Structure and Process in Modern Societies*, New York, Free Press.

Phillips, D.R. (1979), 'Public attitudes to general practitioner services: A reflection of the inverse-care law in intraurban primary medical care?', *Environment and Planning A*, vol.11, pp.815-24.

Pickvance, C. (1976), 'On the study of urban social movements', in C. Pickvance (ed.), *Urban Sociology: Critical Essays*, London, Tavistock, pp.198-218.

Pinch, S.P. (1978), 'Patterns of local authority housing allocation in Greater London between 1966 and 1973: An inter-borough analysis', *Transactions of the Institute of British Geographers* (New Series), vol.3, pp.35-54.

Pinch, S.P. (1979), 'Territorial justice in the city: A case study of the social services for the elderly in Greater London', in D.T. Herbert and D.M. Smith (eds), *Social Problems in the City*, Oxford University Press, pp.201-23.

Pinch, S.P. (1980), 'Local authority provision for the elderly: An overview and case study of London', in D.T. Herbert and R.J. Johnston (eds), *Geography and the Urban Environment, vol.3*, Chichester, John Wiley, pp.295-343.

Pinch, S.P. (1981), 'Area-based housing improvement', in C.M. Mason and M.E. Witherick (eds), *Dimensions of Change in a Growth Area: Southampton since 1960*, Aldershot, Gower, pp.145-69.

Pinch, S.P. (1984), 'Inequality in pre-school provision: A geographical perspective', in A. Kirby, P. Knox and S. Pinch (eds), *Public Service Provision and Urban Development*, Beckenham, Croom, Helm, pp.231-82.

Piven, F. and Friedland, R. (1984), 'Public Choice and private power: A theory of fiscal crisis', in A. Kirby, P. Knox and S. Pinch (eds), *Public Service Provision and Urban Development*, Beckenham, Croom Helm, pp.390-420.

Polsby, N. (1963), *Community Power and Political Theory*, New Haven, Yale University Press.

Poole, M.A. and O'Farrell, P.N. (1971), 'The assumptions of the linear regression model', *Transactions of the Institute of British Geographers*, vol.52, pp.145-58.

Rex, J. and Moore, R. (1967), *Race, Community and Conflict*, Oxford University Press.

Reynolds, D.R. (1984), 'School budget retrenchment and locational conflict: Crisis in local democracy?', in A. Kirby, P. Knox and S. Pinch (eds), *Public Service Provision and Urban Development*, Beckenham, Croom Helm, pp.94-113.

Rich, R.C. (1979). 'Neglected issues in the study of urban service distributions', *Urban Studies*, vol.16, 143-56.

Rich, R. (1982), *Analysing Urban Service Distributions*, Lexington, Lexington Books.

Richards, P. (1970), *The New Local Government System*, London, Allen and Unwin.

Robson, B.T. (1982), 'The Bodley barricade: Social space and social conflict', in K.R. Cox, and R.J. Johnston (eds), *Conflict Politics and the Urban Scene*, London, Longman, pp.45-61.

Robson, W.D. (1966), *Local Government in Crisis*, London, Allen and Unwin.

Robson, W.A. and Regan, D.E. (eds) (1972), *Great Cities of the World*, vol.I, 3rd edn, London, Allen and Unwin.

Rose, R. and Page, E. (eds), (1982), *Fiscal Stress in Cities*, Cambridge University Press.

Sacks, S. and Harris, R. (1964), 'The determinants of state and local government expenditures, and inter-government flows of funds', *National Tax Journal*, vol.17, pp.75-85.

Samuelson, P.A. (1954), 'The pure theory of public expenditures', *The Review of Economics and Statistics*, vol.36, pp.387-9.

Samuelson, P.A. (1955), 'Diagrammatic exposition of a theory of public expenditure', *The Review of Economics and Statistics*, vol.37, pp.350-56.

Saunders, P. (1979), *Urban Politics: A Sociological Interpretation*, London, Hutchinson.

Saunders, P. (1981), *Social Theory and the Urban Question*, London, Hutchinson.

Saunders, P. (1982), 'Urban politics: A rejoinder to Hooper and Duncan/ Goodwin', *Political Geography Quarterly*, vol.1, pp.172-187.

Sayer, D. (1979), *Marx's Method*, Hassocks, Harvester Press.

Shannon, G.W. and Dever, D.E.A. (1974), *Health Care Delivery: Spatial Perspectives*, New York, McGraw Hill.

Sharkansky, I. (1967), 'Government expenditures and public services in the American states', *The American Political Science Review*, vol.61, pp.1066-77.

Sharkansky and Hofferbert, R.I. (1969), 'Dimensions of state politics: Economics and public policy', *The American Political Science Review*, vol.63, pp.867-89.

Sharpe, L.J. (1973), 'American democracy reconsidered', *British Journal of Political Science*, vol.3, pp.1-28 and pp.129-67.

Sharpe, L.J. (1981), 'Is there a fiscal crisis in Western European local government? A first appraisal', in L.J. Sharpe (ed.), *The Local Fiscal Crisis in Western Europe*, London, Sage Publications, pp.5-28.

Sharrard, T.D. (1968), *Social Welfare and Urban Problems*, New York, Columbia University Press.

Sheftner, M. (1980), 'New York fiscal crisis: The politics of inflation and retrenchment', in C. Levine (ed.), *Managing Fiscal Stress*, Chatham, NJ, Chatham House, pp.251-72.

Simie, J.M. (1981), *Power, Property and Corporatism*, London, Macmillan.

Smith, C.J. (1984), 'Economic determinism and the provision of human services', in A. Kirby, P. Knox and S. Pinch (eds), *Public Service Provision and Urban Development*, Beckenham, Croom Helm, pp.176-212.

Smith, D.M. (1968), 'Identifying the grey areas – a multivariate approach', *Regional Studies*, vol.2, pp.183-93.

Smith, D.M. (1979), 'Conclusion', in D.T. Herbert and D.M. Smith (eds), *Social Problems and the City*, Oxford University Press, pp.261-6.

Smith, D.M. (1977), *Human Geography: A Welfare Approach*, London, Arnold.

Smith, D.W. (1970), 'Substandard housing in Welsh towns', in H. Carter and W.K.D. Davies (eds), *Urban Essays: Studies in the Geography of Wales*, London, Longman, pp.49-56.

Stanyer, J. (1976), *Understanding Local Government*, London, Fontana.

Sternlieb, G. and Hughes, J. (1975), *Post Industrial America: Metropolitan Decline and Inter-Regional Job Shifts*, Rutgers University, New Brunswick, Centre for Urban Policy Research.

Stewart, J.D. (1980), 'From growth to standstill', in M. Wright (ed.), *Public Spending Decisions*, London, Allen and Unwin.

Taylor, S.M. and Hall, F.L. (1977), 'Factors affecting response to road noise', *Environment and Planning, A*, vol.13, pp.150-57.

Teitz, M.B. (1968), 'Towards a theory of urban public facility location', *Papers and Proceedings of the Regional Science Association*, vol.31, pp.35-44.

Thompson, J.H. (1964), 'What about a geography of poverty?', *Economic Geography*, vol.40, pp.238.

Thompson, W.R. (1965), *A Preface to Urban Economics*, Baltimore, Johns Hopkins Press.

Tiebout, C.M. (1956), 'A pure theory of local expenditures', *Journal of Political Economy*, vol.64, pp.416-24.

Tudor-Hart, J. (1971), 'The inverse-care law', *The Lancet*, February, pp.405,12.

Urry, J. (1981), 'Localities, regions and social class', *International Journal of Urban and Regional Research*, vol.5, pp.455-74.

Uslander, E.M. and Weber, R.E. (1975), 'The politics of redistribution: Towards a model of the policy-making process in the American States', *American Politics Quarterly*, vol.3, pp.130-70.

Walker, J.L. (1969), 'The diffusion of innovation among the American states', *The American Political Science Review*, vol.13, pp.880-98.

Warren, R.O. (1964), 'A municipal services market model of metropolitan organisation', *Journal of the American Institute of Planning*, vol.30, pp.194-204.

Weber, A.J. (1929), *Uber den Standort der Industrien*, translated by C.J. Frederichs, Chicago, University of Chicago Press.

Weber, M. (1947), *The Theory of Social and Economic Organisation*, New York, Free Press.

Weber, M. (1949), *The Methodology of the Social Sciences*, New York, Free Press.

Weber, M. (1958), *The City*, Chicago, Free Press.

Weber, M. (1964), *Economy and Society*, New York, Free Press.

Webster, B. (1977), 'Distributional impacts of local government policy'. Paper presented to IBG Urban Geography Study Group, at the University of Leicester.

Wildavsky, A. (1964), *The Politics of the Budgetary Process*, Boston, Little, Brown and Co.

Williams, P. (1976), 'The role of institutions in the inner-London housing market: The case of Islington', *Transactions of the Institute of British Geographers* (New Series) vol.1, pp.72-82.

Williams, P. (1978), 'Urban managerialism: a concept of relevance?', *Area*, 10, 236-40.

Williams, P. (1982), 'Restructuring urban managerialism: Towards a political economy of urban allocation', *Environment and Planning, A*, vol.14, pp.95-105.

Willmott, P. and Young, M. (1960), *Family and Kinship in a London Suburb*, London, Routledge and Kegan Paul.

Winkler, J.T. (1975), 'Corporatism', *The European Journal of Sociology*, vol.17, pp.100-36.

Winkler, J.T. (1977), 'The corporatist economy: Theory and administration', in R. Scase (ed.), *Industrial Society, Class Cleavage and Control*, London, Allen and Unwin.

Wolch, J.R. (1979), 'Residential location and the provision of human services: some directions for geographic research', *Professional Geographer*, vol.31, pp.271-7.

Wolman, (1982), 'Local autonomy and intergovernmental finance in Britain and the United States', in R. Rose and E. Page (eds), *Fiscal Stress in Cities*, Cambridge University Press.

Wood, R.C. (1961), '*1400 Governments*', Cambridge, Mass., Harvard University Press.

Wright, M. (1982), 'Pressures in Whitehall', in R. Rose and E. Page (eds), *Fiscal Stress in Cities*, Cambridge University Press, pp.17-43.

Yates, D. (1974), 'Service delivery and the urban political order', in W.D. Hawley and D. Rogers (eds), *Improving the Quality of Urban Management*, Beverly Hills, Sage Publications, pp.213-40.

Young, M. and Wilmott, P. (1957), *Family and Kinship in East London*, London, Routledge and Kegan Paul.

Index